SHAKESPEARE:
THE LAST PHASE

By Derek Traversi

STANFORD UNIVERSITY PRESS
STANFORD, CALIFORNIA

Stanford University Press
Stanford, California
All rights reserved
Library of Congress Catalog Card No.
65-18304
Printed in Great Britain

*First published in the United States in 1955
by Harcourt, Brace & Company
Reissued in 1965 by Stanford University Press*

SHAKESPEARE: THE LAST PHASE

CONTENTS

AUTHOR'S NOTE

THE series of comedies with which Shakespeare rounded off his career as a dramatist are still too often considered as a somewhat irrelevant appendix to his work. It is hoped that the present study will contribute to correcting this impression through a close examination of the texts. As a result of this examination, the plays here studied are seen to be closely related to the great tragedies which preceded them, and the apparent conventionality of their conception is revealed as the vehicle for a profoundly personal reading of life.

The question of critical indebtedness in a book of this kind is not easy to define. I should stress, perhaps, that I have considered the findings of purely textual criticism to be irrelevant to my purpose; this is a field which calls for authoritative treatment or none at all, and I have formed the view that my argument is not directly affected by any conclusions which are likely to be established through it. The fact that this book has been written away from complete libraries confirms me in this belief, but is not, I think, the cause of it. Where writers who have dealt with the plays on the lines here followed are concerned, I am less aware of particular obligations than of a general debt to those who, in the last twenty-five years, have considered Shakespeare as a poet who found in a personal development of the dramatic form the complete expression of his artistic needs.

Certain parts of this book have already appeared elsewhere. Some of my argument concerning *The Winter's Tale*, and a few paragraphs in the introductory chapter, were published in my book *Approach to Shakespeare* (Sands and Co., 1938), and a rather more considerable part of the study of *The Tempest* appeared in *Scrutiny* in 1949. Permission to use this material is gratefully acknowledged.

Santiago de Chile,
January 1953.   DEREK TRAVERSI

vii

AUTHOR'S NOTE TO THE SECOND IMPRESSION

THE first edition of this book appeared as long as twelve years ago. Under the circumstances, it contains a number of statements that I should now wish to modify, more particularly in the introductory chapter, which I feel would benefit from some re-writing. Unfortunately, the conditions of reprinting make this impossible; but I should at least like to say that I am now less inclined than in 1953 to think of *Hamlet* as being in any way a dramatic failure.

A number of critics have suggested that I have laid too much stress on the symbolic and religious elements in the final plays at the expense of those of romance and fantasy. The tendency to read explicit statements of Christian belief into Shakespeare seems to me indeed to have been carried considerably too far in certain places. I do not myself believe that much can usefully be said concerning Shakespeare's personal beliefs, and I am certain that none of his plays were written to illustrate religious dogmas or to point preconceived moral judgements; but—I must add—it seems to me no more than natural that a writer of his time and place should be aware of Christian tradition as an influence moulding his thought and that he should even seek, in his latest plays, to present in terms of a highly personal reading of that tradition some of his final conclusions about life. For taking the plays seriously, for reading them as something more than poetic fantasies in dramatic form, I offer no apology; their seriousness and originality seem to me to be clearly written on practically every page.

Madrid
February 1965

D. A. TRAVERSI

I

INTRODUCTION

AMONG the most fruitful aspects of recent Shake-spearean criticism has been the realization that there exists, behind the long and varied sequence of the plays, a continuous development of theme and treatment which makes it impossible to regard any of them, even the greatest, as mere isolated masterpieces. The last comedies, in particular, have gained enormously in stature from being read in the light of this understanding. It is no longer possible to think of them merely as exercises in decorative fancy, the work of a tiring or even 'bored' genius (the last epithet, singularly inappropriate, is Lytton Strachey's) relaxing from his great tragic effort or simply responding, as a practical dramatist, to the public demand for plays in the sentimental style of John Fletcher. The parallels with Fletcher, indeed, in so far as they exist, make themselves felt most strongly at the moment in which Shakespeare (as in certain scenes of *Cymbeline*) is least himself; and the possi-bility of 'boredom' is effectively denied by the undoubted mastery, at once supremely free and charged with intense feeling, of the greater part of the verse. Shakespeare, in fact, neither relaxed nor repeated himself in these plays. Far from falling back on convention, or lapsing from the tremendous achievement of the great tragedies, they show him reaching out in conscious experiment towards new dramatic forms, a natural response to fresh needs and emotions. The outcome of this development is a series of plays—*Pericles*, *Cymbeline*, *The Winter's Tale* and *The Tempest*—as closely related in conception as any previously written by Shakespeare, and scarcely paralleled in English literature.

That these comedies, apparently produced in the space of some two years, between 1609 and 1611, form a close artistic unity is revealed clearly in the pattern discernible in their respective plots. At the heart of each, present in various forms and clearly responding to a definite continuity of purpose, lies the conception of an organic relationship between breakdown and reconciliation, between the divisions created in the most intimate human bonds (and more especially in the unity of the family) by the action of time and passion and the final healing of these divisions. Near the opening of each play—even in *Cymbeline*, where the central theme is partially obscured—a father loses his offspring through the effect of his own passion-driven folly; the main action is devoted, though again with less than complete clarity in *Cymbeline*, to the suffering and remorse which follow from their mutual estrangement, and—at the end of each play—the lost child (invariably a daughter whose name has clear symbolic associations: Marina, Perdita, Miranda) is restored to her father's blessing and becomes an instrument of reconciliation. In these plots, the harmonizing theme first attempted in *King Lear* and there broken, after the brief restoration of the aged king to Cordelia, by the prevailing tragic development produces a conception of drama completely removed from realism and properly definable in symbolic terms.

Having thus introduced the term 'symbolism', which will play a considerable part in the argument which follows, it is time to limit strictly the ground covered by its meaning. The term itself, as applied to Shakespeare, is liable to two kinds of misuse, one of which is considerably more dangerous than the other. The first of these follows from the temptation to read into these reiterated themes a personal, 'biographical' significance, to associate in particular the emphasis undeniably laid on the father-daughter relationship with hypothetical events in the author's own life. Such interpretations rest neither on known facts nor, which is more important, on a proper understanding of the nature of the creative process at work in Shakespeare's mature plays. More serious, in so far as it reflects a legitimate definition of the symbolic concept, is the second misunderstanding. Symbolism, as we commonly know it, assumes an imposition of ideas more or less abstract upon the immediate perception of experience, an imposition, to put it crudely, of the 'Let A equal B' type. Nothing could be more foreign to the nature of drama, and —more particularly—to Shakespeare's handling of it as a normal extension of poetry. Far from representing an imposition of abstract conceptions, the type of symbolism to be observed in these comedies grows out of poetic experience as its unforced, spontaneous expression. In the course of the great tragedies, poetry, characters, and plot become increasingly complementary and interdependent facts of an underlying organic unity; the plot of *Macbeth* is not the less dramatic for having become the vehicle for a profoundly personal intuition of the relations of good and evil. The fullgrown symbolism of the last plays is only a development from this situation. Shakespeare's power of uniting poetry and drama is now such that the plot has become simply an extension, an extra vehicle of the poetry. His experience has come to require not only verbal richness and complexity, not even simply deep insight into human motives and the sources of moral impulse, but this type of 'symbolic' incident as part of his purpose; and his elaboration of the poetry of each play has become so complete, so homogeneous, that such 'symbols' fit naturally into it. The essence, in short, of Shakespearean 'symbolism' lies in the fact that it springs out of the poetry as an extension of the word as spoken on the stage; that is why abstract profundities are so misleading in discussing it.

If this view of Shakespeare's development of poetic drama is substantially true, it follows that the tendency towards 'symbolism' will be most immediately reflected, at each stage, in the changing quality of his verse. A comparison between two passages, separated from one another by more than ten years of intense creative activity, will indicate how this can be confirmed. Shakespeare's early blank verse is, generally speaking, appreciably less the expression of an unmistakable personality than that of Marlowe. It differs from the work of his predecessors mainly in superior control and in a more consistent texture. *Richard II* is a typical work of this period, and this is a typical extract from that play:

> I have been studying how I may compare
> This prison where I live unto the world;
> And for because the world is populous,
> And here is not a creature but myself,
> I cannot do it: yet I'll hammer it out.
> My brain I'll prove the female to my soul,
> My soul the father; and these two beget
> A generation of still-breeding thoughts,
> And these same thoughts people this little world
> In humours like the people of this world,
> For no thought is contented.   (v. v.)

The opening statement of the comparison suggests a line of thought which, though in itself conventional, might have been used in later plays—in *Hamlet*, for example—as the starting-point for a series of reflections of universal human validity. Here, however, there is very little question of tragic feeling. Shakespeare is less concerned with his hero's unhappy situation than with the development of a rather sententious comparison. The verse obviously reflects this superficial quality. The stresses fall according to pattern, and once we have grasped the run of the rhythm, it falls pat to the accustomed ear. The virtues of the lines are not compatible with delicate or direct feeling; they are virtues of artificial construction, turning on the connected succession of ideas, from parents to their 'generation', and from that to

4

the vast extension of metaphor implied in 'people this little world', followed by the characteristic taking up of 'people' in the next line. This is not great verse, and certainly not great Shakespearean verse. It is important chiefly as an exercise in the writing of balanced and connected blank verse, an exercise which helped to ensure that, when the great flood of associated ideas and sensations which characterize Shakespeare's mature poetry came to demand expression, his verse forms should not break down into incoherence under the strain.

The development of this relatively superficial instrument into a potent means of expression that we can now agree to call, in the special Shakespearean sense, 'symbolic' was already far advanced at the time of writing *King Lear*. This is particularly apparent in the type of poetry normally associated with Cordelia in the later scenes of the tragedy, of which the Gentleman's account of her sorrow (IV. iii) is perhaps especially typical. As he puts it—

> . . . patience and sorrow strove
> Who should express her goodliest. You have seen
> Sunshine and rain at once; her smiles and tears
> Were like a better way; those happy smilets
> That play'd on her ripe lip seem'd not to know
> What guests were in her eyes: which parted thence
> As pearls from diamonds dropp'd. In brief,
> Sorrow would be a rarity most beloved,
> If all could so become it.

The logic of this passage is clearly not that of factual description. Few of the comparisons used to convey the quality of the queen's grief have direct visual connection with the scene described. 'Sunshine and rain', 'ripe lip', 'guests', 'pearls', and 'diamonds' are all connected with one another and with Cordelia less as visible attributes than as expressions of the sense of value, conveyed through intimations of richness and fertility, which they impart. It is this sense, pervasively present, which imposes unity upon apparently conflicting elements. The struggle between the queen and her passions is a strife between two emotions—'patience' and 'sorrow'—equally natural and worthy in her, each contributing, beyond the conflict, to a 'goodly' expression of her nature. Her behaviour, in fact, is so normal in its spontaneity that it reflects the balance of 'nature' in 'sunshine' and 'rain', each pointing to the single harmonious effect which presents itself as 'a better way', an indication of possible redemption; and this, in turn, causes us to feel no surprise when 'happy smilets' make their appearance, just below, as indicative of Cordelia's mood. 'Sunshine and rain', moreover, by a different thread of associations, leads directly to the suggestion, in 'ripe', of the maturing crops, and 'guests' hints at the bounty which expresses itself in hospitality; and the prevailing sense of the whole passage is gathered up in the further phrase 'pearls from diamonds dropp'd'. These are 'rarities', and sorrow itself thus borne is less a manifestation of tragic weakness than a rarity enriching human nature, part of a harmony calling for its external manifestation less in continued exposure to suffering than in the symbol of healing reconciliation.

The tremendous expansion of poetic range visible in Shakespeare's mature verse is not, of course, an isolated phenomenon. It is accompanied naturally by parallel developments in the presentation of motive and character. These, in turn, are best discussed in terms of the linguistic resources which made it possible to express them and, in due course, to integrate them into the unified emotional pattern of each play. The passage already quoted from *Richard II*, and the suggested comparison in terms of dramatic impact with Marlowe, indicates only part of the truth about the early plays. If Marlowe's writing is still more powerful, more emphatic in its effect, Shakespeare's shows almost from the first a wider range, greater resources of imagery, and, above all, a closer adaptation to varied dramatic needs. The result is an instrument perhaps less obviously personal, but superior in theatrical possibilities, as may be seen already in a play as early as *Richard III*. The central figure of this historical tragedy, though clearly owing something to the characteristic Marlovian blend of rhetoric and irony, is possibly the first of Shakespeare's tragic figures to emerge from the conventions of contemporary melodrama with a genuine force of personality. His opening definition of his own character is expressed with a linguistic resource that is already typical:

> . . . I, that am not shaped for sportive tricks,
> Nor made to court an amorous looking-glass;
> I, that am rudely stampt, and want love's majesty
> To strut before a wanton ambling nymph;
> I, that am curtail'd of this fair proportion,
> Cheated of feature by dissembling nature,
> Deform'd, unfinish'd, sent before my time
> Into this breathing world, scarce half made up,
> And that so lamely and unfashionable
> That dogs bark at me as I halt by them;—
> Why I, in this weak, piping time of peace,
> Have no delight to pass away the time,
> Unless to spy my shadow in the sun,
> And descant on mine own deformity:
> And therefore, since I cannot prove a lover,
> To entertain these fair, well-spoken days,
> I am determined to prove a villain,
> And hate the idle pleasures of these days.   (i. i.)

The speech, based though it is on the established dramatic conventions of envious villainy, represents a toning-down of Marlowe's rhetorical overtones in the interests of a less grotesque irony and a firmer delineation of character. Although a certain stilted quality survives in the movement of the verse (there is a sense, common in Elizabethan stage heroes and villains, of the speaker playing up to a dramatically acceptable picture of himself[1]), the general effect is

---

1. We have only to read certain speeches of Othello to realize that this sense survived in Shakespeare's mature tragedies, to become an important part of the make-up of his tragic heroes.

7

remarkably concise and pointed. Richard's state of mind is conveyed primarily through a series of sharp visual touches directly expressed in the vision of himself as 'strutting' ludicrously before a 'wanton, ambling nymph', as being 'barked at' by the dogs as he passes before them, as 'spying' his misshapen shadow in the sun, and through the sustained contrast, implying contempt and repudiation, between the 'sportive tricks' and exigencies of 'these fair, well-spoken days' and his own situation, 'deform'd, unfinish'd', 'scarce half made up', lame and 'unfashionable'. In this way, by making envy the vehicle for a criticism which is felt, by its very directness, not to be altogether unjustified, the speaker is humanized, transformed from the abstract incarnation of a traditional vice exploited for melodramatic effect into something like a person whose nature is twisted indeed by his exclusion from 'love's majesty' (the phrase stands out forcibly by contrast with the sneer that follows it), but who retains in the cool, pungent run of his comments a definite human plausibility. The creation of character, indeed, is not to be regarded as the unique, or even principal, end of Shakespeare's dramatic creations, in which plot and motive, themselves handled with greater flexibility and insight, tend increasingly to find their proper context in a more ample artistic unity which embraces and illuminates them; but in the delineation of personality beyond the limits of convention his language first attained some sense of its full possibilities.

The stages by which this capacity to convey personality with concrete objectivity is assimilated into a broader conception of dramatic unity can be traced through Shakespeare's great series of tragedies. They are, in fact, steps in the sublimation of the tragic conflict, which was achieved by a process of concentrating the different and contradictory elements of experience into clearly-defined conflicting groups seeking their expression through action. This concentration, or projection into a dramatic pattern, was not immediately attained. In *Hamlet*, for example, when for the

first time the elements of the tragic antithesis find expression
in a fully-drawn character, the necessary clarity of definition
is still absent; Hamlet, hesitating between the recognition
of a duty which impels him to act and the absence in himself
of a conviction that action can be adequately motived, dies
with his father revenged but without his spiritual dilemma
ever really finding a solution. The inspiration of the play,
introspective and exploratory, is reflected in verse which
habitually returns upon itself, splits up into a series of
parentheses, of arguments and counter-arguments, more
often than it moves to a decisive conclusion:

> So, oft it chances in particular men
> That for some vicious mole of nature in them,
> As, in their birth, (wherein they are not guilty,
> Since nature cannot choose his origin),
> Or by the overgrowth of some complexion,
> Oft breaking down the pales and forts of reason;
> Or by some habit that too much o'erleavens
> The form of plausive manners;—that these men,
> Carrying, I say, the stamp of one defect,
> Being nature's livery, or fortune's star
> Their virtues else (be they as pure as grace,
> As infinite as man may undergo),
> Shall in the general censure take corruption
> From that particular fault . . . (i. iv.)

Without diminishing the greatness of *Hamlet* or denying its
essential place in the unfolding of the Shakespearean pattern
we may doubt whether verse of this kind is really fully
dramatic. The space between the beginning and end of the
process of reasoning, between the 'particular men' with
which it opens and the conclusion 'shall in the general
censure take corruption', is probably too great to be fully
sustained on the stage across the series of semi-speculative
parentheses which separates them. Such verse is the work
of a poet who is still more concerned to clarify his own ideas
and impressions than to give them a rounded and external

9

expression; and indeed it has often been felt that none of the intensely analytic and subjective speeches which chiefly characterize Hamlet's thoughts really harmonize fully with the motives of the melodramatic action upon which they are imposed. The tragic conflict of the play is still essentially an internal one, which the author himself was concerned to clarify; that is why the clash of personalities representing opposed motives, which later became a fundamental feature of Shakespeare's tragic technique and which we may believe to be essential to a fully-realized drama, never really exists in this most subjective of plays.

This does not mean, of course, that there are not aspects of *Hamlet* that show the dilemma of the central figure, the blight that so mysteriously spreads itself over his nobility, finding reflection in the external action. The tragedy of Hamlet is associated with the spread of an influence that can only be called corrupting, that springs, in despite of himself, from the infirmity with which he struggles in his own nature until it affects those around him, involving them almost without exception in a process of moral decay. If the speech just quoted is as far from clarity as the speaker's own condition, it is none the less true that the most intimate emotions of the play—the bitter rejection of Ophelia based upon repulsion against the vision of an errant humanity 'crawling' ignobly 'between earth and heaven', the contrast between the 'grace' of the murdered king and the vision of the usurper,

> like a mildew'd ear,
> Blasting his wholesome brother   (III. iv),

the profound ambivalence, poised between rejection of sin and the intimate infection which the expression so insistently reveals, of the reproaches addressed by Hamlet to his mother—radiate from a central contradiction first revealed at its heart, and here powerfully if incoherently expressed. The spread of a palpable, *sensed* corruption at the expense of 'virtue', of the purity of motive which Hamlet, in abstract, unrelated idealism, seeks to maintain is a dominating feature of the action. Something is indeed 'rotten in the state of Denmark' as this play reveals it; and the fact that Hamlet protests against this rottenness, that his projected action aims at putting an end to it, cannot obscure its connection with the infirmity in his own soul. The interrelation of the personal theme with the development of the external action, although it ends less in clarification than in obscurity, is none the less an important feature of the play. [1]

In the tragedies which followed *Hamlet* the elements of conflict become at every stage more clearly grouped into sharply defined spheres. As we study these plays, we find ourselves ever more keenly aware of the existence in them of a cleavage of outstanding importance: that between, on the one hand, 'reason' making for the acceptance of 'degree', an ordered scale of values resting on an accepted conception of good, and, on the other, the impulses of egoistic passion making for anarchy. The dramatic projection of this cleavage into a clear-cut clash of opposing forces brings with it a corresponding clarification in the presentation of the protagonists, and in particular of the tragic hero. In *Othello*, the conflict of values operates on the individual alone with sexual passion as its foundation. Where Hamlet unites a vast number of impulses and feelings, often contradictory and conflicting, in the utterances of a single man, Othello is fully and continuously a person. He is, indeed, the first of a series of Shakespearean tragic heroes whose sufferings are explicitly related to their own failings, but who manage in spite of these failings to attain true tragic dignity. Like Antony and Coriolanus after him, he dramatizes as 'nobility' much that reflects in him an innate incapacity to cope with life; and, as in their case, the very weakness which becomes obvious to all around him, and by which Iago engineers his downfall, is turned into true tragedy. The bringing to the

1. The tendency to modify the coherence of plot and character by a new conception of unity, which expresses itself in an interwoven texture of imagery, can be traced in earlier plays. I have tried to study its existence in *Henry IV—Part II* in my *Approach to Shakespeare* (1938), pp. 29–37, and to relate it to Shakespeare's mature work.

surface of this intimate flaw is, indeed, a principal purpose of the entire action. The dramatic construction of *Othello* turns upon the close, intricate process of analysis by which the two contrasted characters of the Moor and his Ancient are at every moment dovetailed, seen for what they are as opposed but strictly related conceptions. This is a type of drama in which motive is presented with as much assurance as in the great historical plays; but the objectivity which had there mainly illustrated a detached political study is now controlled by the presence of a more ample poetic unity, the expression of an intense tragic emotion.

Only in *Macbeth*, however, do the full consequences of this more intimate fusion of character and action become apparent in their relation to the poetic unity which emerges from the play. As usual, the new development makes itself felt through a fresh quality in the verse. When the thought of evil first enters Macbeth's head, immediately after his first meeting with the Witches, the disjointed intensity of his utterance is new in Shakespeare's work:

> This supernatural soliciting
> Cannot be ill; cannot be good; if ill,
> Why hath it given me earnest of success
> Commencing in a truth? I am thane of Cawdor;
> If good, why do I yield to that suggestion
> Whose horrid image doth unfix my hair
> And make my seated heart knock at my ribs
> Against the use of nature? Present fears
> Are less than horrible imaginings:
> My thought, whose murder yet is but fantastical,
> Shakes so my single state of man that function
> Is smothered in surmise, and nothing is
> But what is not.   (I. iii.)

As the realization of a psychological state of considerable complexity this is superbly conceived. There is nothing accidental about the telescoped syntax in the last few lines; that strange juxtaposition of 'thought' and 'murder' conveys perfectly the birth of the horrible project in the tangled chaos of ideas. The rest of the speech suggests even more. It anticipates the whole disturbance of natural 'function', of 'the single state of man', which is implied in the very thought of such a crime; it expresses with magnificent nervous directness the shaking of the foundations of a harmonious personality. The speech, in short, is a *physical* apprehension of ambiguity, a disordered experience express-ing itself in terms of a dislocated functioning. And yet, keen as it is, the almost bestial sensitivity conveyed through the unfixed hair and the hammering of the heart is, morally speaking, quite meaningless. Divorced from its proper place in 'the use of nature', the most intense feeling has only a quality of hallucination—this is the full force of words like 'horrible imaginings' and 'fantastical'. Feeling is 'smothered in surmise', and the keen senses are directed only to a muffled fumbling among uncertainties.

It is at this point that we begin to see how the personal situation of Macbeth is related, more completely than that of Hamlet (whose characteristic turn of thought is by comparison self-centred, even abstract) ever was, to the train of events which his action has set in motion and which finally annihilates him. The fertile poetry of Duncan, based on so delicate and so full an organization of the 'gentle' senses, stands out against Macbeth's incoherence with the force of a deliberate contrast. It depends, indeed, upon a right ordering, which is absent in Macbeth from the moment he conceives the murder, of 'the single state of man'. Harmony in the individual is balanced by harmony in the Scottish *state* under its lawful king. Macbeth's poetry, on the contrary, reflects the result of a breach wilfully intro-duced into this single state. The result is a discontinuity in him between the senses and the mind, between the mind and the conscience (note how the speech opens with a vain fumbling at the meaning of 'good' and 'ill'), and between these gaps nothing but an intense and growing awareness of their existence. It is indeed here that the development of the external action throws light decisively on the inner drama of the protagonist. The overthrow of Duncan's just and bountiful rule by the baseless impulse of his murderer is an act which transcends the individual sphere, in the same way as the latter's career is related at each step to a public development which at once follows from and illuminates it. In the great tragedies of Shakespeare's maturity, the protagonists and the action which they initiate stand in the closest mutual relationship. The moral drama of the central figure finds full dramatic projection in the external events which he himself has, by an act of the will, set in motion; and the events in turn acquire coherence and meaning through the relationship which binds them at every stage to the tensions which constitute the tragedy of the hero. With character and plot thus brought into unity, and both subjected to the vast unifying range of Shakespeare's mature poetry, the possibilities of drama are extended to achievements otherwise inconceivable.

With *King Lear*, in so many ways Shakespeare's central masterpiece, these possibilities are at last fully realized. The integration of plot and character is more complete than ever before. There is a very real sense, indeed, in which the whole action of the tragedy might be described as a projection of the conflicting issues supremely present in the mind of the central figure. As father, Lear produces in his daughters contrasted reactions which reflect different and contradictory facets of his own mind; the firmness with which Cordelia clings with an unadorned simplicity to the position which she rightly regards as sanctioned by 'nature' is as clearly hereditary as the passionate devotion of her sisters to the selfish ends which they have proposed to themselves. As king, his wilful impulses liberate forces of social anarchy which are related to those which have split apart the family unit and which, likewise, nothing less than utter extinction can ultimately contain. From the conflict whose dual aspect is thus concentrated in one mind the various issues of the play radiate as partial reflections of a common

14

image, at once contributing depth and variety to the central situation and deriving from it the subsistent unity which alone can give the complete story its full meaning. In none of Shakespeare's mature plays is the correspondence between action and motive, the external event and the inner meaning, so exactly and so significantly achieved.

The story thus intimately related to the development of the central figure is, largely as a consequence of this relationship, more deliberately conceived as a pattern than any which had preceded it. Both aspects of Lear's position, the personal and the social, contribute to the unity of a tragedy whose various stages correspond, in the external action, to a closely-knit development. The first stage in this development, occupying roughly the first two Acts, deals with the entry of uncontrolled passion as a disruptive force into Lear's mind and with the consequent overthrow of ordered balance in himself, in his family, and in the state of whose unity he has been hitherto the royal guardian. In the second stage, which covers the central part of the play, personal and social disorder find in the tempest to which the protagonists are exposed a symbol which at once reflects and transcends it; the elements at war, besides corresponding to the conflict in Lear's distraught person, act through the intense suffering which they impose upon him with the force of a self-revelation to become the necessary prelude to spiritual re-birth. That re-birth, however, though momentarily achieved in the personal order in the third and final stage, cannot affect Lear's external fortunes. His reconciliation with Cordelia, presented in a scene (iv. vii) which marks a decisive advance in Shakespeare's progress towards the poetic symbolism of his final manner, is followed almost immediately by their final defeat and death against a background of almost unrelieved disaster. The personal and the social themes, hitherto so closely united, now separate to produce the concluding catastrophe, and the tragedy, after touching unprecedented heights in its treatment of the personal issues, is rounded off in a mood of Stoic acceptance.

15

From the point of view of Shakespeare's adaptation in the last plays of the resources of poetic 'symbolism', the scene of Lear's awakening is, as we have said, particularly interesting. It is full of a 'symbolism' which is not imposed upon the dramatic development but springs from and completes it. Given the extraordinary freedom, the breadth of reference which characterizes the verse of *King Lear* throughout, it is only a step forward to introduce effects that are not strictly necessary to the factual development of the drama, but which the unprecedented control of the poet succeeds in welding organically into the total effect. 'Sleep' has already been used in *Macbeth* as such a 'symbolic' value; and Shakespeare now adds music, with its associations of harmony, and 'fresh garments',[1] suggesting the purification accomplished in Lear by past sorrow through sleep. Cordelia prays for her father's 'restoration' in language which relates the musical symbol of harmony to the restoration of health to the torn and divided personality:

> O, you kind gods,
> Cure this great *breach* in his abused nature!
> The *untuned* and *jarring* senses, O, wind up
> Of this child-changed father. (IV. vii.)

By such means, Shakespeare succeeds in transforming Lear's suffering, making it a condition of his revival. We can feel this in his first exclamation on awaking:

> Thou art a soul in bliss; but I am bound
> Upon a wheel of fire, that mine own tears
> Do scald like molten lead. (IV. vii.)

This looks back to the 'burning shame' which, in an earlier scene,[2] had 'stung' him and kept him from Cordelia. Lear's difficulty in believing that he really sees his daughter before him indicates both the depth and the remoteness of what he has passed through; the suggested idea of resurrection

---

1. Both these symbols are prominent in *The Tempest*.
2. Act IV, Scene iii.

16

('You do me wrong to take me out o' the grave') contributes to the same effect. Lear still suffers on the 'wheel of fire', but his grief no longer springs from division, from the 'embossed carbuncle' in his own 'corrupted blood'[1] which produced Regan and Goneril; it has become such that it can contemplate 'a soul in bliss'. For the length of this scene, Shakespeare has succeeded in balancing the suffering which dominates the first part of the play with a corresponding harmony, fulfilled in Cordelia's prayer for 'benediction' and in Lear's answering confession of his fault:

> I know you do not love me; for your sisters
> Have, as I do remember, done me wrong:
> You have some cause, they have not.

This is the central reconciliation; the natural relation of child to father is the resolution of the ruin originally caused by 'blood', the action of passion, in the unity of the family and extended thence to the social state of man. Shakespeare's 'symbolic' technique has woven Lear's suffering, by transforming it, into the fabric of 'restoration'.

The relevance to the last plays of the foregoing account of the broad conception of *King Lear*, and of some of the steps in Shakespeare's previous work which led up to the most inclusive of his mature creations, should now be sufficiently obvious. What we have traced is, in effect, the growth in the work of its greatest exponent of a balanced conception of poetic drama. According to this conception, none of the elements into which a play is commonly and, up to a point, conveniently divided—neither 'character', the analysis of motive, 'poetry', nor even 'plot' or action itself—can be considered as existing in its own right. The relative importance of each of these factors varies in different plays, but the prevailing tendency—and with it the end of poetic drama as a whole—is towards an ever closer identification. The personal conflicts of the tragic hero are projected into the dramatic action, itself conventional, the result of a process

1. Act II, Scene iv.

of artistic selection, which reflects them; and both are unified as expressions of an inclusive creative impulse by the threads of related imagery, repeated or contrasted, which underlie the complete development.

From this state of affairs, it is an easy and natural step to the deliberate abandonment of realism which is apparent in the last plays. Leontes' lunacy in *The Winter's Tale* is scarcely more improbable, psychologically speaking, than the impulse which leads Lear to divide his kingdom among his daughters; neither is Hermione's 'statue' much less credible, in terms of normal experience, than the 'leap' from Dover cliff by which Gloucester aims to end the torture to which he is subject. It is true that the examples from *Lear* reflect a type of drama in which psychological analysis, and the interplay of character and action, are more relevant than they are in the later comedy; but the tendency is none the less away from realism, towards a conception of the art of the theatre in which character and action alike are real in relation to the poetic unity to which they belong, and finally to that alone. To describe this unity as 'symbolic' is not to deny these plays the concreteness proper to great poetry, which they possess indeed to a high degree, but which is not to be confused with the realistic imitation of life. It is simply to say that the characters and situations of Shakespeare's final comedies are more exclusively conditioned than ever before by the poetic emotion, that the plays themselves are to be regarded accordingly as expanded images, and that these images in turn attain their full expression by moulding to their purpose the conventions of the stage. A study of such plays as *The Winter's Tale* and *The Tempest* reveals the full meaning of the commonplace assertion that poetry and drama are in Shakespeare intimately fused into the unity of 'poetic drama'.

II

PERICLES, PRINCE OF TYRE

PERICLES is, by the common consent of criticism, a problematic play. As it stands, it is clearly in some sense a stratified construction, in which passages demonstrably in Shakespeare's latest manner are superimposed upon others relatively crude and undeveloped. It is doubtful, however, whether the theory of divided authorship, which has been argued on strong grounds and is, indeed, widely accepted, accounts fully for what reads in reality more like a failure in creative consistency. The relationship between the various layers which can be distinguished in the play is, on any theory, not a simple one. Whatever the defects of the supposedly non-Shakespearean scenes, they are bound to the finer episodes by a demonstrable unity of plan which recalls, in its deliberate and sometimes clumsy formality, the similar imposition of a moral pattern in *Timon of Athens.* Whether Shakespeare originated or, as we may reasonably prefer to believe, simply remodelled the material on which *Pericles* is based, assimilating some parts of an earlier, inferior play to other episodes entirely of his own creation, it seems likely that the play represents an early approach to the conception of drama which later produced *The Winter's Tale* and *The Tempest.* Conceived as an experiment in poetic symbolism, it shows the basic conceptions of the last comedies, still in the process of formation, striving to impose artistic unity upon an imperfect theme; and it is this fact, rather than the uncertain authorship of disputed passages, that constitutes the primary interest of the play.[1]

The existence in *Pericles* of a definite unity of purpose can be detected even in the early scenes whose connection with the later, more demonstrably 'Shakespearean' passages has been most plausibly questioned. It is to be felt consistently in the development of the general conception and occasionally—so we may believe—in detailed touches of verse and imagery. The early stages in the history of Pericles, up to the consummation of his marriage with Thaisa (II. v) are treated with a conventionality which, though crude in its expression, is beyond doubt perfectly deliberate. They could be described, without straining the text unduly, as steps in a symbolic pilgrimage in search of an ideal expressed in terms of devotion to chivalrous love, steps underlined at each important stage by the significant, if often archaically uncouth comments of Gower. The first stage in the pilgrimage brings Pericles to Antioch, attracted by the fame of a beauty whose attributes, celebrated by him in characteristically Marlovian cadences, are given a distinctively heavenly content. His appeal is from the beginning to the 'gods that made me man, and sway in love'; and to these same gods he ascribes the flaming in his heart of desire 'To taste the fruit of yon *celestial* tree' and so 'To compass such a boundless happiness.' The terms in which Pericles pursues his quest respond, in fact, to a recognizably allegorical conception of his story. 'Son and servant' to the will of the 'gods' who are so frequently invoked in the unquestionably 'Shakespearean' passages to follow, he seeks to satisfy desires which,

1. It is of interest to note that a theory to account for the textual problems presented by the play, recently put forward by Philip Edwards (*An Approach to the Problem of Pericles*, in *Shakespeare Survey* 5), would coincide with the argument here developed on non-textual grounds. Edwards holds that the 1609 Quarto is a debased text reconstructed by two reporters, 'the first responsible for the first two acts, the second for the last three'. From this he goes on to state that 'the problem that has to be solved is whether the different aptitudes of the two reporters are the *sole* cause of the difference in literary value between the two halves of the play, whether, in fact, the original play of *Pericles* was all of one standard, all by one author, and that the first reporter, in his crude attempts to rebuild a verse structure . . . has perverted language such as is found in the later acts'.

crudely expressed though they may be, are not irrelevant, in terms of moral symbolism, to the later development of the play.

The ambiguous response of Antiochus, equally conventional in expression, extends further the moral significance of the episode. The object of Pericles' pilgrimage, though a 'fair Hesperides' laden with 'golden fruit', is *dangerous* to be touch'd'; and, in his reaction to this evocation of a peril still unspecified, Pericles himself introduces, as a fresh but relevant element in the situation, the theme of mortality which is to be so repeatedly stressed in the later scenes of the play:

> Antiochus, I thank thee, who hath taught
> My frail mortality to know itself.

At this point, with the sense of romantic infinity balanced by the more sober considerations of traditional morality and both related to the symbolic quest for self-knowledge, the riddle proposed by Antiochus to cover his own guilt introduces an element of equivocation in the light of which Pericles reacts completely:

> . . . he's no man on whom perfections wait
> That, knowing sin within, will touch the gate.
> You are a fair viol, and your sense the strings;
> Who, finger'd to make man his lawful music,
> Would draw heaven down, and all the gods to hearken:
> But being play'd upon before your time,
> Hell only danceth at so harsh a chime. (I. i.)

The stressing of moral responsibility is here accompanied by the evocation, admittedly crude, but still typical of Shakespeare's last plays, of musical harmony. Perfection, which Pericles has hoped to attain through dedication to a worthy object of love, is conceived in terms of 'lawful music', of the blending of parts in a unified conformity to law which is in

21

turn a reflection of the heavenly order; but this turns to harshness, and to the thought of 'hell', when surrender to 'sin' disrupts the propriety of order and wrests 'sense'—a word in which the meanings of consciousness and sensual impulse are subtly blended [1]—from its established context. With this apprehension further reinforced by the fear of the absolute power which he has offended, Pericles returns to Tyre with his vision of happiness apparently irreparably obscured. In the following scene, the poison thus introduced injects itself, as a disturbing element, into his psychological make-up—

> . . . the passions of the mind,
> That have their first conception by mis-dread,
> Have after-nourishment and life by care   (i. ii)—

and drives him, after the destruction of his peace, to the decision to leave his power in the hands of Helicanus and to abandon Tyre.

At this point, and after the visit to Cleon at Tarsus (i. iv)—which lays the foundation for the later abandonment of Marina, but is scarcely otherwise assimilated, poetically speaking, into the emotional development of the play—Pericles is exposed to the action of the elements. This exposure is anticipated by Gower's clumsy couplet:

> He, doing so, put forth to seas,
> Where when men been, there's seldom ease,

in which the action of the tempest, foreshadowing one of the main conceptions of the later action, is clearly interpreted in terms of moral trial. The entry of Pericles, after the wreck of his ship, produces a monologue more distinctively Shakespearean than anything so far encountered in the play. The pressure of the storm causes its victims to reflect,

---

1. For the second implication of 'sense' compare Angelo's—
    She speaks, and 'tis
    Such sense, that my sense breeds with it. (*Measure for Measure*, ii. ii.)

in terms which recall similar passages in *King Lear*, upon the helplessness of man:

> Wind, rain, and thunder, remember, earthly man
> Is but a substance that must yield to you;
> And I, as fits my nature, do obey you.   (II. i.)

If this passage was not written by Shakespeare himself, it is evidently the work of a writer to whom the spirit of the great tragedies was present, and it is reasonable to assume at least the awareness of a collaboration in the symbolic purposes of the later part of the play. The action of the elements cause Pericles to consider, even more explicitly than at the court of Antiochus, the limitations of his mortal nature, which is, indeed, a necessary prelude to self-knowledge and which the whole of this part of the action is concerned to stress; whilst the concluding nostalgic assertion of his desire to find peace in death—'Here to have death in peace is all I'll crave'—recalls similar passages in the later scenes of *Timon of Athens*.

The conversation with the fishermen, which follows, leads directly to the introduction of the next stage in the development of the symbolic pattern—the recovery by Pericles of his father's armour, expressly described as part of his 'heritage' and as restored in 'calm' by the same 'rough seas' that, although they 'spare not any man', can yet in due course 'give again' what they previously took to themselves.[1] The armour so recovered is given a definite symbolic significance as the instrument by the aid of which Pericles is to pass through trial by combat to the marriage with Thaisa which is the first step in the restoration, on a moral basis enriched by subjection to suffering, of his princely fortunes. His words upon finding himself newly clothed in it have,

---

1. The restoring function of the sea in these plays, with its peculiar spiritual quality, is most strongly affirmed in Ariel's:

> . . . remember,—
> For that's my business to you,—that you three
> From Milan did supplant good Prospero;
> Exposed unto the sea, *which hath requit it*,
> Him and his innocent child.   (*The Tempest*, III. iii.)

whatever be their actual authorship, an authentic Shakespearean ring:

> By your furtherance I am clothed in steel;
> And, spite of all the rapture of the sea,
> This jewel holds his building on my arm.

The connection of the 'jewel' with the concept of 'value'—'Upon thy value I will mount myself'—and of 'virtue'—'I'll show the virtue I have borne in arms'—suggests at least the symbolic sublimation of the chivalrous theme, and has as such its place in the unfolding conception; it is, indeed, taken up and developed, in anticipation of the tournament, by Thaisa's father, Simonides, in the following scene (ii. ii):

> . . . princes are
> A model, which heaven makes like to itself:
> As jewels lose their glory, if neglected,
> So princes their renown if not respected.

Once more a contemporary commonplace, of the type in which this part of *Pericles* abounds, is being taken up into the subsistent poetic structure of the play.

The response of Pericles to this implied challenge is to enter the tourney as the 'mean knight' whose emblem, whilst recalling the rigours of fortune through which he has passed, is that of hope, the 'withered branch, that's only green at top'. Thus, armed in sober confidence, he wins the hand of Thaisa from all competitors. The use made of symbolic incident of this kind, though perfunctory, is scarcely more so than that which introduced the 'armed head' and the 'bloody child' into *Macbeth*.[1] Pericles' victory calls forth, in the banquet which follows (ii. iii), a corresponding generosity from Simonides, who expresses in characteristically Shakespearean terms the bounty which is a proper attribute of true kingship:

> Princes in this should live like gods above,
> Who freely give to every one that comes
> To honour them,

1. See *Macbeth*, iv. i.

24

and thus provides Pericles with a compelling motive both to
recall his father's past munificence and to anticipate his own
future restoration to princely glory:

> . . . now his son's like a glow-worm in the night,
> The which hath fire in darkness, none in light.

This part of the play, with its effort to give symbolic exaltation to the chivalrous theme, ends with the consummation
of marriage between the pilgrim prince and the daughter of
Simonides and with the simultaneous arrival of the news
that Antiochus has received at the hands of the 'gods' just
vengeance for his reversal of 'nature' (ii. iv). Helicanus,
left in Tyre as regent, hails the news by calling upon
Pericles' 'noble subjects' to search for their lord, upon
whose return, he says, they 'shall like diamonds sit about
his crown'.

At this point, with the preliminary foundations of the
action laid, the spirit of the play is subjected to a decisive
transformation, by which the bare allegorical structure is
filled out for the first time with a vivifying subtlety of poetic
treatment. This new development takes place precisely at
the point in which the story offers the closest parallel to that
of *The Winter's Tale*. Returning by sea to take up his
inheritance in Tyre, Pericles is overtaken by a tempest during which Thaisa dies in childbirth and her body, thrown
overboard at the request of the sailors, is washed ashore at
Ephesus, where it is restored to life by the operations of the
learned Cerimon; the new-born daughter, meanwhile, preserved from the perils of exposure to the elements, is left at
Tarsus in the charge of Cleon, whose city Pericles himself
had formerly saved from the consequences of famine. It is
clear that the set of related events thus placed, as its turning-
point, at the centre of the play contains all the typical
contrasts—between tempest and succeeding calm, birth and
death, mortality and healing—which go to make up the
symbolic unity of the last plays; they provide, from now on
in increasing measure, a framework for the pattern of inter-

dependent imagery by which the play attains its full poetic life.

This pattern begins to take shape when Pericles evokes, in terms that once more remind us of *Lear*, the tempest by which his ship is threatened. The storm is ascribed to the 'gods' whose power to control it is admitted, and this assertion of overruling purpose is followed by an invocation to Lucina, 'divinest patroness, and midwife gentle', which introduces, against this background of elemental conflict, the theme of birth through travail. The nurse Lychorida, in turn, gives dramatic substance to this theme by announcing the queen's death and, together with it, the arrival of a living infant, expressly described first as 'this piece of your dead queen' and then, even more openly, as 'all that is left living of your queen'. The birth of Marina thus becomes a token of the continuity, now asserted by Pericles, which unites death and birth, tempest and following calm, in a single process:

> Now, mild may be thy life!
> For a more blustrous birth had never babe:
> Quiet and gentle thy conditions! for
> Thou art the rudeliest welcome to this world
> That e'er was prince's child. Happy what follows!
> Thou hast as chiding a nativity
> As fire, air, water, earth and heaven can make,
> To herald thee from the womb: even at the first
> Thy loss is more than can thy portage quit,
> With all thou canst find here. Now, the good gods
> Throw their best eyes upon it. (III. i.)

The whole speech, with its balanced blend of contrasted emotions, reflects its position at the turning-point of the symbolic action. Pericles prays that the life of his child may be 'mild' and the conditions of her future existence 'quiet and gentle', precisely because its birth has been unprecedently 'blustrous' and its 'welcome to this world' the 'rudeliest' that ever met 'prince's child'. In the latter part of his

26

invocation, this set of contrasts is related to Pericles' own
recent experience; the ideas of 'loss' and value (implied in
'portage') are brought together and, although the sense of
suffering naturally predominates, the concluding invocation
to the 'good gods' looks forward to the compensating
development of the future.

Before this can receive its dramatic expression, however,
the death so recently announced needs to be introduced
fully into the symbolic pattern. The dialogue with the
sailors by which this is achieved is set against a background
of tempest evoked in prose that clearly recalls, in its touches
of evocative detail, the similar scene in *The Winter's Tale*;[1]
whilst Pericles, responding to external pressure with a
corresponding growth in moral insight, combines the
patience expressed in

> Courage enough: I do not fear the flaw;
> It hath done to me the worst[2]

with tender concern for the well-being of this 'fresh, new
sea-farer'. Death and birth, the new and the old, are now
seen to be more closely connected than ever in a single,
continuous process. When, as a final tribute to the storm,
the sailors insist that the 'ship be cleared of the dead', the
symbolic action is taken a decisive step further; for the
burial of his wife at sea is not only a sacrifice on the part of
the prince, but is seen to imply the elimination of death as
prologue to its poetic transformation. The shift of emphasis
begins to make itself felt in Pericles' dispositions for the
funeral. Thaisa's death, though the result of the 'terrible
child-bed' to which she has been exposed, has found issue,
beyond the suffering which it has involved, in the creation
of a new life; and, in view of this, even her burial, conceived
as the sacrifice of her corpse to the 'unfriendly elements',

---

1. Compare the phrase: 'an the brine and cloudy billow kiss the moon' (*Pericles*, III. i) with 'now the ship boring the moon with her main-mast' (*The Winter's Tale*, III. iii).

2. It is perhaps worth recalling Edgar's similar acceptance of 'the worst' as a turning-point or prelude to moral reaction in *King Lear* (IV. i).

becomes subject to a process of mutation reflected in the motion and texture of the verse:

> . . . nor have I time
> To give thee hallow'd to thy grave, but straight
> Must cast thee, scarcely coffin'd, in the ooze;
> Where, for a monument upon thy bones,
> And aye remaining lamps, the belching whale
> And humming water must o'erwhelm thy corpse,
> Lying with simple shells.   (III. i.)

This deliberately poetical recalling of the body's consignment to the sea, destroyer and preserver, aims at giving the idea of death a transforming quality of remoteness, at making it, in the words of Ariel in *The Tempest*, 'suffer a sea-change' to which the supporting indication of expanding moral understanding will give the necessary substance.   The imaginative quality conveyed in the use of 'ooze' to indicate the sea,[1] in the transmuting musicality of '*humming* water', and in '*aye remaining* lamps' is a fit introduction to the burial of Thaisa with her 'casket and jewels', whilst the mention of the 'satin coffer' and the rich 'spices' by which her body is, symbolically speaking, preserved from the temporal action of the elements and disposed for the coming resurrection contributes to the creation of a subtle effect of harmony which will be taken up in due course into the final scenes of reconciliation.

The following scene transports the action to the house of Cerimon at Ephesus (III. ii). The position of Cerimon, like so much in this play, is clearly intermediate between the preceding tragedies and the symbolism of the final comedies. From the first he is surrounded, in the words of his attendant Gentleman, with indications of overflowing opulence that take up images already associated with the burial of Thaisa and are to play an important part in the scenes to come; we are told that he has 'rich tire' about him, and his

---

1. Compare Alonso's use of the word: 'Therefore my son i' the *ooze* is bedded' (*The Tempest*, III. iii) for a somewhat similar effect.

repose is described in terms of '*golden* slumber'. His felicity, however, is of the kind that, although 'thereto not com-pell'd', is 'conversant with pain', compatible with a mature grasp of moral realities. In point of fact, Cerimon occupies in *Pericles* a position intermediate between that of the physicians who ministered to spiritual infirmities in *Macbeth* and *King Lear* and that of Prospero in *The Tempest*, whose studies gave him power over nature and an insight into the true character of things. Cerimon himself, besides affirming in his first important utterance that 'virtue' and 'cunning', moral and intellectual understanding born of deep and pro-longed dedication to the search for truth, are superior to 'nobleness and riches', even asserts that the type of aware-ness after which he is striving confers 'immortality' upon the seeker, makes 'a man a god'. His own studies are as much spiritually as medically conceived. They concern the '*blest* infusions' that dwell in the properties of nature and tend to the cure of deep-seated 'disturbances'; they proceed, in fact, from a contemplative depth that recalls that of Prospero and aim, like the operations of the doctors in the tragedies, at restoring the broken moral harmony of human nature.

To the figure thus conceived the coffin of Thaisa, recov-ered in accordance with the prevailing symbolic design from the sea, is brought in. Its appearance is surrounded, as befits Cerimon, with characteristic evocations of splendour; it emerges from 'the sea's stomach o'ercharged with gold' and is steeped in the pervading presence of sweet odours:

CERIMON: Soft! it smells most sweetly in my sense.
2nd GENTLEMAN: A delicate odour.
CERIMON: As ever hit my nostril. . . .
          Shrouded in cloth of state: balm'd and *entreasur'd*
          With full bags of spices.

The combination of sensuous and verbal opulence with the effortless flow of verse that can take these splendours in its stride, preserving the sense of natural exchange with true dramatic effect, is, stylistically speaking, one of Shakespeare's major triumphs in his late plays. First fully achieved, perhaps, in *Antony and Cleopatra*, it is now being turned to a deliberately symbolic effect. The general impression left by the account of the coffin is one of incalculable wealth, reinforced by the wording of the enclosed 'passport' with its mention of 'This queen, worth all our mundane cost', and surrounded by invocations to the 'gods' into whose keeping the corpse was committed when cast upon the waters. Against a background thus assimilated to the poetic spirit of the play, Cerimon proceeds to exercise his vocation, spiritual not less than medical, by restoring Thaisa to life. With this end in view he introduces fresh strands into the developing pattern of imagery, calling first on fire as the symbol of life re-born—'Make a fire within'—and then, like the Doctor in the reconciliation scene of *King Lear* (IV. vii), invoking the healing harmonies of sound:

> The rough and woeful music that we have,
> Cause it to sound.

The music, 'rough and woeful' in recognition of the tragedy that has led to Thaisa's death, serves at the same time as an anticipation of peace restored and as a prelude to the coming resurrection.

The resurrection itself is, as in the parallel case of Lear, a gradual process, during the course of which the returning tide of life is first hailed by the bystanders of the scene in terms of the manifestations of renascent nature—

> . . . see how she 'gins to blow
> Into life's flower again!—

and at last confirmed in the re-opening of her eyes to the light. Her revival is greeted by Cerimon with a speech in which fresh intimations of value and beauty, of the kind already indicated, but only now allowed complete expres-

sion, give a fuller, more universal content to the dramatic
symbol:

> She is alive; behold
> Her eyelids, cases to those heavenly jewels
> Which Pericles hath lost,
> Begin to part their fringes of bright gold;
> The diamonds of a most praised water
> Do appear, to make the world twice rich. Live,
> And make us weep to hear your fate, fair creature,
> Rare as you seem to be.   (III. ii.)

In this speech, a new, transhumanizing element (so to call it)
enters explicitly into the verse, giving its full symbolic
quality to what has now become a poetry of resurrection.
This is perhaps the first time in Shakespeare that the full
range of his mature poetry is lent to an effect so deliberately
remote, so charged with a quality that can truly be described as supernatural, and yet so free from any suggestion
of abstraction or strain. The connection with the central
themes of the play is immediately apparent. Thaisa, once
'lost' to Pericles in her death, is again *alive*, and the first sign
of her restoration is a renewal of value by which her very
physical attributes are transformed.   Her eyelids have
become 'cases' to the 'heavenly jewels' of her eyes, jewels
which were formerly the most valued treasures of Pericles
and which their loss has made doubly precious to him. The
eye-lashes on these lids have become, by the same process of
transmutation, 'fringes of bright gold' and the eyes themselves 'diamonds of a most praised water', whose influence
in their resurrected beauty is able to enrich, even more than
in her first life, the world which had already celebrated their
loveliness; their effect, in fact, is now 'to make the world
twice rich'. The beauty of Thaisa, thus deliberately exalted
above common realism, is of a 'rarity' that has now only to
wait for the final reconciliation to Pericles to exercise its
power as the key to a new life.

The time for this reconciliation, however, is still distant.

31

The next scene (III. iii) shows Pericles resigned to what he still believes to be his irreparable loss:

> We cannot but obey
> The powers above us.

The need for acceptance, conformity to purposes still only dimly apprehended in the course of exposure to tragic experience is an essential part of the conception on which each of Shakespeare's last plays is built. Such resignation, however, is not final. It is rather a necessary prelude to the restoration of a harmony made potentially richer by exposure to adversity. Already, in the stress of the very tempest that robbed him of Thaisa, his daughter Marina, herself symbolically named, has been born. Pericles now leaves her in the hands of Cleon, so that she may receive from him 'princely training' and 'be manner'd as she is born', stand out by her possession of the civilized virtues in a society whose courtly spirit has already been indicated (I. iv) and whose shortcomings will soon be revealed. The Act concludes (III. iv) with Thaisa learning from Cerimon of her situation and balancing Pericles' vow to leave his hair uncut until his daughter's marriage by assuming 'a vestal livery' in the temple of Diana. With this pair of resolutions duly adopted, and waiting upon the future development of events, this central stage in the play, poised between past tragedy and future reconciliation, is brought to a close.

Most of the action of *Pericles* covered by the fourth Act shows, by comparison with what has gone immediately before, a partial decline in emotional tension and poetic mastery. The reasons for this are not easy to define. It could be argued, indeed, that the greater part of the action at this point belongs to an earlier version of the play, perhaps only occasionally touched by Shakespeare to bring his material into a minimum of concordance with his general purpose. The argument, however, needs to be advanced with caution. The contrast between Marina's innocence and the trials to which she is subjected in the brothel is excessively facile and sentimental, but its spirit, and some of its phrasing, can be paralleled in earlier plays. The first exchange between Pandar and Boult (IV. ii) and the final discussion between the latter and Marina (IV. v) recall, at times closely, the scenes in *Measure for Measure* which present social dissolution as a background to the central moral conflict. Their purpose, indeed, is not dissimilar. Like the prostitutes of Vienna, the 'unwholesome wenches', 'pitifully sodden',[1] of the Mytilene brothel are conceived as victims, subject to creatures themselves conscious of the iniquity of their trade ('the sore terms we stand upon with the gods') but powerless to react against adverse circumstances[2]; the physical infirmities which accompany the exercise of their 'profession' are as much morally as bodily significant, symptoms of a process of social disintegration to which the universal force of 'appetite' subjects them and against which only the consistent purity of Marina stands out in flawless integrity. The weakness of these scenes, indeed, lies precisely in the excessive clarity of the contrast. Marina, unlike Isabella, does not answer to the realistic conception of drama which still prevails at this stage in the presentation of her background. Her motives are not analysed, and still less subjected to the possibility of conflict; they are inflexibly simple, self-consistent, and therefore, in terms of the dramatic objectivity with which Boult, Pandar, and their like are presented, artistically incompatible. The fault lies in the attempt to adapt the realism of Shakespeare's earlier manner to symbolic purposes still in the process of elaboration; but the presence of this inconsistency does not alter the fact that the whole episode is conceived as a necessary stage in the development of the action to which it belongs.

The same can be said of the remaining scenes in this part of the play. The episode (IV. iii) in which Cleon reproaches

1. Act IV, Scene ii.
2. Note, for example, the implications of Boult's remark: 'What would you have me do? go to the wars, would you? where a man may serve seven years for the loss of a leg, and not have money enough i' the end to buy him a wooden one?' (IV. vi).

Dionyza for having instigated and, as he thinks, carried out the murder of Marina reminds us, in argument and expression alike, of similar exchanges between Macbeth and his wife at the time of Duncan's murder. Like Lady Macbeth, Dionyza reproaches her husband for his lack of spirit—

> I do shame
> To think of what a noble strain you are,
> And of how coward a spirit—

and when he, like Macbeth, argues that this 'proceeding' does not flow 'from honourable sources', the tone of her reply strikes a note familiar in the earlier tragedy:

> Be it so, then:
> Yet none does know, but you, how she came dead,
> Nor none can know, Leonine being gone.

Whether these similarities proceed from mere recollection of Shakespeare's undoubted work, or whether they point to the presence of his own hand (admittedly working on a more perfunctory level of execution) can only be a matter for conjecture. There can, in any case, be no doubt that this part of *Pericles* shows the chief protagonists exposed to adversity and the possibility of spiritual growth as a prelude to the final reconciliation. To all of them can be applied the words dedicated to Pericles by Gower:

> He bears
> A tempest, which his *mortal* vessel tears,
> And yet he rides it out   (IV. iv);

by these lines the tempest symbol which is one of the constant underlying factors of the play is related once more to the tragic situation of man and so asserts its relevance to this part of the action.

In the concluding episodes, however, which bring the principal strands of the play finally together in a harmonious close, the main symbolic line is once more taken up in full poetic mastery. The pattern of dramatic events leading to

34

the final resolution is familiar in all Shakespeare's late plays, and may be described as an effort to give a more definite symbolic content to the type of reconciliation first treated in *King Lear*, when the aged king, after having been exposed to the chastening and purifying action of the elements, is restored to Cordelia.[1] Here, however, factual possibility is given a purely secondary place, and the episode needs to be read in terms far removed from the ordinary considerations of realism. The sufferings of Pericles, though still related to the pressure of the tempest, have not been presented in any detail and their impact upon character has not been stressed; storm and the succeeding calm are now merely elements in what is essentially a symbolic structure to which a complex skein of interdependent images will give life and justification. Plot, in short, exists in *Pericles* as a function of imagery, and imagery, in turn is directed to the elaboration of a kind of dream in the course of which normal human qualities, detached from their customary attributes and elevated above their usual status, undergo a process of poetic sublimation to become symbols of a moral re-birth. The awakening of Pericles, and his restoration to his wife and child, belong in fact not to the realm of tragedy as commonly understood or even as previously practised by Shakespeare himself, but to that of the essentially unrealistic conception of the conclusion of *The Winter's Tale* of which it may fairly be regarded as an experimental anticipation.

The last stage in the play opens with the visit of Lysimachus, the governor whose moral transformation by Marina we have already witnessed, to Pericles upon his ship at Mytilene. The stricken king lies in 'a close pavilion on deck, with a curtain before it', which emphasizes his isolation from the surrounding world and makes the approach to him, like that of Leontes to the 'statue' of Hermione in *The Winter's Tale* (v. iii), a gradual and step-by-step approximation. As a first stage, Lysimachus is informed by Helicanus of his master's tragic story, and of the 'disaster' that, 'one *mortal*

1. Act IV, Scene vii.

night' (the frequent recurrence of this adjective in the play perhaps helps to underline the universal symbolic implications of the action), brought him to his present plight; he then hails him, in characteristic terms, as 'royal sir' and invokes for him the protection of the 'gods'. Having in this way prepared the ground for what is to follow, Lysimachus goes on to refer to the presentation of Marina as a possible means of restoring Pericles to speech. His account of her is couched in terms of the 'sweet harmony' which—according to him—is calculated to revive the 'deafen'd parts' of Pericles and to bring them back to normal hearing; the themes of harmony and restoration are thus introduced directly into the main action. When Marina finally appears, Lysimachus hails her as an instrument of healing in terms carefully chosen to build up, by the further introduction of significant strands of imagery, the elaboration of the central theme. Her nobility is stressed, for we are told that she came of 'a gentle kind and noble stock', and each of these adjectives, with their associations of breeding and human solicitude, will have their part to play in the final effect; and so, as a proper counterpoise, is the 'bounty' which she may expect as a natural consequence of the 'goodness' of her 'kingly patient' if she restores him to normal life. Lastly her own faculties, like those of Cerimon before her, are given the proper note of healing spirituality by being described as 'sacred physic'. Thus called upon, Marina accepts the task of restoring Pericles and enters his seclusion as Lysimachus invokes once more the approval of the 'gods'.

She begins, significantly, by singing to Pericles, for 'music' is here, as always, the necessary prelude to restoration. The effect upon him is not immediate; but when she goes on to speak directly to the stricken prince, invoking her subjection to a 'grief' equal to his own and referring to her noble but 'forgotten' parentage, Pericles is moved for the first time to break his silence with words whose halting incoherence records the first, tentative groping towards a restored life. Thus we are brought, step by step, to the presentation of the

central symbolic situation, when Pericles finally brings himself to ask Marina—

> What countrywoman?
> Here of these shores?—

and meets with a reply in which fact and symbol are at last
fully blended:

> No, nor of any shores:
> Yet I was mortally brought forth.

The contrast between Marina's mortal birth and the remoteness from common circumstance implied in 'nor of any
shores' is indeed of fundamental importance in assessing her
place in the play. From now on, she clearly fulfils a double
function. She is at once 'mortal', the issue of Pericles' own
flesh and blood, and the instrument of entry into a new,
transfigured life; the conditions of her birth both link her to
'mortality', and so to the strain and suffering symbolized in
her past subjection to the elements, and exalt her, through
their very remoteness, to the spiritual freedom of a fresh
creation. Through her, past and present, death and life,
temporal servitude and spiritual freedom are fused in a
single organic process tending to the affirmation of a new
state of being.

The gateway to this new state is, as Pericles now realizes,
the 'grief' imposed upon him by his tragic past and now
accepted as at once the natural consequence of mortal frailty
and the necessary condition of moral growth. This growth
through subjection to suffering is openly related to the
central birth-symbol when Pericles himself comments:

> I am great with woe, and shall deliver weeping,

indicating the transformation of his grief into fertility
through the incarnation, in the figure of Marina before him,
of the daughter whom he still believes he has lost and,
through her, of his 'dearest wife'. The description which
follows, with its wonderful range of symbolic imagery, brings

37

us at last to the vision of a new and transformed humanity which is the true end of the whole play. Nowhere in Shakespeare's late plays, not even in *The Tempest*, is the 'brave new world' of a human semblance transfigured by entry into the divinely sanctioned state of 'grace' more splendidly conveyed. Marina's brows, like those of Thaisa as Pericles remembers them, are 'square' and her stature, like that of the Greek goddess whom she now explicitly recalls, 'wand-like straight'; whilst in the following account of her as '*silver*-voiced', with eyes '*jewel*-like' and '*richly* cased' in their orbs, the perfection of her physical attributes becomes a symbolic echo of spiritual value. Finally, as the natural consummation of this process of poetic exaltation, Marina's attributes, thus raised to a quasi-divine similitude, shed their bounty over the surrounding world. Compared to Juno, her perfections become an inexhaustible incitement to lesser beings to transcend their imperfections: she—

> . . . starves the ears she feeds, and makes them hungry,
> The more she gives them speech.

By the end of the passage, the transformation of Marina into a source of renewed life is substantially complete.

To the spectacle thus miraculously presented before his eyes Pericles, still feeling his way back to renewed life, responds by an exercise of faith based upon the assurances of his reviving memory. This response, indeed, is the indispensable prelude to his restoration. He calls upon Marina to tell her story, promising her to believe even what still seems impossible; for the truth of the words she speaks is guaranteed, for him, by the echo it calls forth from the depth of his past experience and, as he puts it,

> thou look'st
> Like one I loved indeed.

As Marina replies, and the tide of memory flows back in a process which reminds us even more strongly than what has gone before of the gradual restoration to life of Hermione in

38

The Winter's Tale, his desires convert themselves step by
step into reality. First she tells Pericles that her name is
Marina, then that her father was a king; and when he feels
himself, as it were, mocked by this miraculous rehearsal of
his abandoned hopes, she comes finally to the full revelation:

PERICLES: Where were you born?
And wherefore call'd Marina?
MARINA: Call'd Marina,
For I was born at sea.

By this declaration of her origins, Marina finally assumes her
full place in the symbolic pattern. Connected by her birth
'at sea' with the tempest that bore Pericles apart from
Thaisa and confirmed their separation in her supposed
death, Marina, having passed unscathed through the trials
to which her early separation from her father exposed her,
now returns to him as the harbinger of harmony restored.
With the response aroused in Pericles by the contemplation
of her transfigured humanity, the necessary conditions for
the final reconciliation are at last established.

In complete possession of a truth which thus gives meaning
to his own past, and after receiving the confirmation of
Lysistratus, Pericles at last gives full and harmonious
expression to the re-birth in himself of natural emotion.
The stages of his final awakening are conveyed with an
exquisite tenderness. As Lear, when restored to Cordelia
(IV. vii), called for a pin to put himself to the test through
physical pain in order to discover whether he was in fact
alive, so Pericles calls upon Helicanus to 'strike him', give
him 'a gash'—

Lest this great sea of joys rushing upon me
O'erbear the shores of my mortality,
And drown me with their sweetness.

At this point and after Marina's recent declaration, the
references to the 'sea' and to 'mortality' are more than ever

39

relevant. Their emotional content has now been finally transformed; for the sea to which Pericles' wife and child had formerly been exposed, and which has so far served as a symbol of tragic suffering, has now become a 'sea of joys' which threatens, by its very vastness, to overthrow his weak 'mortality' and to cause a death conceived in terms of 'sweetness'. Against this background, Pericles calls Marina to himself in words which express, with full explicitness, the symbolic kernel of the whole play:

> O, come hither,
> Thou that beget'st him that did thee beget;
> Thou that wast born at sea, buried at Tarsus,
> And found at sea again.

What is here asserted, under the guise of the play's poetic symbolism, is nothing less than a concept of spiritual resurrection. Its instrument is Pericles' own child, formerly begotten as the fruit of a marriage that was itself the result of search in pilgrimage, and now, in the moral sphere, the instrument of his re-birth. Marina, recently described in terms that confer a certain status of divinity upon the human, has brought her father the intuition of a new and deeper life; and this she has been able to do as a result of her own experience, the pattern of which involved her birth in tempest, her death and burial, her exposure to human malevolence, and finally her triumphant resurrection—once more at sea—as symbol of a re-integrated and regenerated humanity.

Having thus declared this fundamental truth, Pericles calls upon those around him to give thanks to the 'holy gods' whose provident action has from the beginning shaped his story. He also recalls, through Marina, her mother and his 'lost' wife, who, in Marina's words,—

> did end
> The moment I began.

In this mood of enlightened conformity, Pericles is ready formally to acknowledge his child and to assume—in clear symbolic reference to his new spiritual state—'fresh garments'; once more there is an obvious parallel with the re-awakening of Lear.[1] Like Lear again, his first gesture on being restored to his position as father is to respond to Marina's kneeling to him by embracing her and giving her his blessing; and finally, as a background to restored harmony, his speech becomes penetrated, insistently and joyfully, by the 'music of the spheres' which fills her enraptured imagination. This 'heavenly music', in turn, brings Pericles the sleep which is the necessary prelude to lasting restoration, and with it the conclusion of the episode.

The last scene (v. iii) brings the chief protagonists together before the altar of Diana at Ephesus; the final reconciliation of Pericles with his wife, of which Marina is once more the instrument, takes place in the presence of the 'gods' to whom she has, in the intervening years, dedicated herself. Pericles begins by recalling the death of Thaisa 'in childbed' and the bringing forth of their 'maid-child'; the self-dedication of Marina to Diana is also referred to, as are the 'better stars' which have preserved her from adverse 'fortunes' and restored her finally to her father's care. Hearing her own story thus repeated, Thaisa faints and Cerimon, taking up the prevailing symbolic imagery, describes how he found her 'early in blustering morn' upon the shore with 'rich jewels' in her coffin, and how, having restored her, he placed her in the holy temple. Thaisa's recovery from her swoon is also, and simultaneously, the awakening into a new condition. Like Pericles before her, she gropes her way towards the truth, leaning for enlightenment upon her obscure understanding of the central symbolic situation by which

---

1. Compare Cordelia's words to Kent:
> These weeds are memories of those worser hours:
> I prithee, put them off,
and the Gentleman's reference to Lear himself:
> . . . in the heaviness of his sleep
> We put fresh garments on him. (IV. vii.)

birth and death, united in common exposure to adversity, are seen as related aspects of a single process issuing in a new life:

> did you not name a tempest,
> A birth, and death?[1]

With this, and the showing of the ring given her as symbol of union by Pericles' father (who also, it will be remembered, bequeathed his son with the armour in which he faced adversity), her husband is convinced. In the light of the harmony thus restored, his 'past miseries' are seen as 'sports', and his happiness is such that only in terms of death can its absolute, *final* quality find expression:

> O, come, be *buried*,
> A second time within these arms.

Marina, in turn, feels her heart leap 'to be gone into my father's bosom', kneels, and is presented by Pericles to her mother with the pregnant simplicity of 'Flesh of thy flesh, Thaisa'. It is significant, indeed, of the play's intention that, even in this moment of achieved spiritual harmony, physical normality is given its full and essential part. The central balance of filial prayer and answering paternal benediction having thus been established, the healing function of Cerimon ('through whom the gods have shown their power') is given its proper spiritual context, and Helicanus for the last time affirms his loyalty. With the concluding betrothal of Marina to Cerimon, the pattern of reconciliation in *Pericles* is finally complete.

---

1. Compare *The Winter's Tale:* 'thou mettest with things dying, I with things newborn' (III. iii).

III

CYMBELINE

CYMBELINE, second to *Pericles* in the series of Shake-speare's last plays, is also, though in a rather different manner, an unequal piece. The presence in it of diverse and even contradictory artistic purposes seems to point, as in the earlier play, to an experimental origin. Beyond that, however, the parallel breaks down. Whereas the avowedly 'Shakespearean' passages of *Pericles* stand out clearly from the inferior matter which surrounds them, in *Cymbeline* the theory of divided authorship, though in part feasible, rests on no clear-cut distinction in style or treat-ment. The more pedestrian passages of the play are firmly embedded in the general structure, and its inequalities sug-gest less a stratified construction by different hands than the work of an author feeling his way, with incomplete clarity of purpose, towards a fresh use of the dramatic conventions which lay to his hand.

The attempt to give symbolic validity to conventional matter is evident in the broad lines of the plot. The theme of loss and reconciliation, though less clearly defined than in *Pericles*, is doubly present in the new story. Cymbeline, king and twice-married father, loses his two sons, Guiderius and Arviragus, who are replaced at court by Cloten, the upstart son of his unnatural queen; at the same time, in his determination to marry his daughter Imogen to Cloten, he obliges her to question his parental authority and to expose herself, in defence of her innate perception of the true

43

'value' of Posthumus, to the state of nature. The two stories, after being developed separately in the early action, are brought together at Milford, where they become inter-dependent and mutually revealing before being gathered together, in the final episodes, into a wider context of patriotism and loyalty. Restored to civilized life and to their father's embrace, Cymbeline's sons bring with them the virtues of barbaric honesty which they have shown throughout their exile; and these virtues, in turn, restored to their proper place in association with the integrity of Imogen and Posthumus, which their exposure to tragedy has served to confirm, are finally resumed into the order of true courtliness.

It is, indeed, as an attempt to use conventionally familiar material of the type evidently present in the theme just outlined and to give breadth of reference to the conception of dramatic poetry already developed in *Pericles* that we should read the later play. More closely connected than its predecessor with the theatrical taste of the day, which favoured sentiment and the idealization of the simple life on lines popularized by John Fletcher,[1] *Cymbeline* none the less shows Shakespeare trying, with partial success, to turn these conventions to his own ends. The result is a play which, although notably uneven in execution, represents a stage of transition between the highly personal symbolism of *Pericles* and the greater scope, the reference to wider fields of human experience, successfully achieved in *The Winter's Tale*. In relation to the later masterpieces *Cymbeline* is a strangely incoherent and incomplete performance; but, read as the successor to Shakespeare's earlier experiment in dramatic symbolism, it shows him reaching out towards a more ample social content and a more inclusive conception of poetic drama.

I

The relation between romantic convention and the under-lying purpose of *Cymbeline* only emerges gradually in the

1. Points of contact with *Philaster* have often been noted.

course of the early action. It is best approached, in the first place, through a consideration of linguistic quality. The opening scenes of the play are distinguished by the presence of a definite vitality of speech, itself the reflection of a deeper content, from the sentimental conceptions of Fletcher. The clash of loyalties occasioned by Imogen's forced betrothal to Cloten, which serves as point of departure for the action, is given a definite universality, firmly and objectively defined, in the opening words of the play:

> . . . our bloods
> No more obey the heavens than our courtiers
> Still seem as does the king. (I. i.)

The arbitrary act of the monarch, occasioned by the blind passion that binds him to his second wife, is thus set by his own courtiers against a background of the obedience properly owed by 'blood', or instinct, to the 'heavens': an obedience, however, which is already felt to be subject to strain, to 'seem' rather than to be, and which soon gives way to a more explicit contrast between the mask of duty and the compulsion of true feeling:

> . . . not a courtier,
> Although they wear their faces to the bent
> Of the king's looks, hath a heart that is not
> Glad at the thing they scowl at.

The complexity of expression, imposed in a kind of verbal counterpoint upon the plain sense, is, as in so much of Shakespeare's mature writing, an indication of underlying purpose. The deliberate intricacy of the double negative ('*not* a courtier . . . that is *not* glad'), the balancing of opposites in 'glad' and 'scowl', the sense of dissembling implied in 'wear their faces',[1] all point to the presence of a

1. For another instance of Shakespeare's interest in the connection, liable to various degrees of ambiguity, between 'face' and feeling, we might quote Sonnet xciv: 'They are the lords and owners of their faces.'

deep-seated dislocation of natural feeling. The bond which binds individual conduct, through proper obedience to established authority, to the cosmic order, accepted though it may be on the surface with an appearance of conformity, is in fact subjected to a sense of pervasive strain which will soon find its counterpart in the external action. The return to normality through the final integration of natural simplicity to courtly virtue, and the subordination of both to a higher loyalty, is the true theme of the play.

In accordance with this general plan, Imogen's repudiation of Cloten, whose parody of true courtliness can only be acceptable to Cymbeline's passion-distorted vision, implies her choice of a superior conception of humanity, at once supremely natural and truly civilized. This conception inspires, in the same scene, the description of Posthumus, whom the king formerly endowed with—

> all the learnings that his time
> Could make him the receiver of; which he took,
> As we do air, fast as 't was minister'd;
> And in's spring became a harvest; liv'd in court—
> Which rare it is to do—most praised, most loved;
> A sample to the youngest; to the more mature
> A glass that feated them; and to the graver
> A child that guided dotards.   (i. i.)

It is worth noting that the association, which underlies this passage, of virtue with lineage in a single process of spontaneous, overflowing fertility, has been carefully prepared for from its opening words. The process is, once more, definable in terms of related imagery. 'I cannot delve him to the root': the Gentleman's answer to his companion's question concerning Posthumus' name and birth relates lineage to a conception of natural growth ('unfold his measure', just above, suggests something of the same feeling) and, a little further on, death and normal fulfilment in fertility are combined in a single, enriching process:

46

> ... their father,
> Then old and fond of issue, took such sorrow
> That he *quit being*, and his gentle lady,
> Big of this gentleman, our theme, *deceased*
> *As he was born.*

The description of Posthumus' mother as 'gentle', combining nobility of birth with unassuming moral distinction, the deliberate muting of the harshness of physical dissolution implied in 'quit being', and the familiar association of birth and death in the final words, are all clear anticipations of the symbolic world of *The Winter's Tale*. Born as his parents died,[1] Posthumus is more than an individual example of the courtly virtues. He stands, through the possession of these, for a conception of 'value' which, fostered by his upbringing and the action of time, is to be an essential point of reference in the development of the action.

With the universal intention thus indicated, the sense of the main description of Posthumus' courtly education is evident. For the first time—and the last, until the end of the play—nature and civilization are united in spontaneous harmony. The virtues celebrated in him are those of true courtliness, fostered by a 'learning' imbibed as naturally as air and proceeding, in the normal course of youthful development, to its proper 'harvest'. In a world in which, as events will show, true virtue is indeed a rarity, the 'outward' of Posthumus reflects the merit of the 'stuff within'; he has become thereby an example to all ages and conditions, a mirror of the finer human qualities which Imogen, in loving him and rejecting Cloten, has appreciated at their proper worth.

The integrity of Imogen's love, her fitting response to the virtues enshrined in Posthumus, receives poetic expression in their interview, to which the opening exchanges have served as an introduction. The tone is one in which romantic sentiment is modified, though with less than complete con-

---

1. Like Marina before him, and (supposedly) like Perdita in *The Winter's Tale*.

sistency, by the introduction of a pervading symbolism to stress the conception of *value*, of surpassing worth. The expression of emotion is built deliberately round the central image of the jewel, which will shortly receive external projection as a symbolic element in the plot. Imogen refers to her 'dearest husband', about to be separated from her by banishment, as 'this jewel'; she confers upon him at the moment of parting a diamond which 'was my mother's' and receives in return the bracelet which is 'a manacle of love'. The external symbols of value, in themselves normally associated with romantic passion, serve to focus around their rarity intense expressions of emotion, in which the separating action of time is balanced against the sense of achieved timelessness—

> Should we be taking leave
> As long a time as yet we have to live,
> The loathness to depart would grow—

and living dedication gains added point by being set, in terms of religious sanction, against the evocation of mortality:

> You gentle gods, give me but this I have,
> And sear up my embracements from a next
> With bonds of death!

The poetry, though more diluted with romantic sentiment, recalls the relevant portions of *Antony and Cleopatra* in its easy freedom and intensity of phrase. A similar impression of timelessness and transcendent value is conveyed by Posthumus' reference to Imogen's 'so *infinite* loss', and this infinity is in turn balanced against the intense immediacy implied in 'sense'—

> Remain, remain thou here
> While sense can keep it on!—

and confirmed, a little further on, in Imogen's firm retort to the enraged Cymbeline: 'I am *senseless* of your fears'.

The whole of this part of the action is steeped, in fact, in an impression of value, of 'rarity'—Imogen herself refers to the 'touch more *rare*' which 'subdues' all 'pangs' and 'fears'— in which the action of time, itself apprehended as implying a kind of refinement of the sensual, is set against the infinite delicacy, at once tenuous and intense, of experienced love.

It is this emotional affirmation of value, this 'rarity', indeed, which, together with its context in courtly convention, is subjected in the following scenes to analysis. After having received further expression in Imogen's dialogue with Pisanio (i. iii), it is first emphasized by contrast with the aristocratic pretensions of Cloten—a court parody of the truly 'natural' man, enslaved to his base passions [1]—and then exposed to the intrigues of Iachimo. The arrival of Posthumus in Rome (i. iv), with which the prevailing mood is switched from integration to analysis, introduces a contrast essential to the play. Fittingly expressed in prose, the scene introduces the convention of Italianate court cynicism, which is allowed to play with critical detachment, or the appearance of it, upon the values incarnated in Posthumus' idealization of Imogen. The malevolence of Iachimo, his fundamental attitude of negation, should not obscure his part in expanding the moral content of the action. His opening words, which balance the theme of courtly reputation—given due weight in his recognition of Posthumus' 'worth' and 'crescent note'—against a refusal to be carried away by mere 'admiration', indicate this part of his function perfectly. That function is both destructive and, within limits, exploratory. Like Iago and Edmund before him, Iachimo, perverse as he undoubtedly is, illuminates part of the truth. His outlook, founded on a clear-sightedness which only its self-sufficiency, its refusal to look beyond its own assumptions, turns into a principle of destruction, isolates aspects of the central situation which need to be taken into

---

1. The short and rather perfunctory scene between Cloten and his two attendants (i. ii) emphasizes the disparity, so unlike the consistency already observed in Posthumus, between outward pretension and the poverty of the 'stuff within'.

account; and, by so doing, it produces a reaction which eventually leads to a deeper, more inclusive understanding. The separation of evil impulse under the guise of critical detachment, and the final assimilation of its findings into a wider field of awareness, is an essential feature of the development from the Shakespearean tragic process to the reconciliation aimed at in his last plays.

This assimilation, however, belongs to the complete pattern of *Cymbeline*, and is not at this early stage immediately discernible. The primary purpose of this Roman dialogue, poised in the calculated intricacy of its prose between convention and analysis, is an exploration of the conception of 'value' intuitively accepted by Imogen and Posthumus as the basis of their relationship. As it opens, Philario and Iachimo divide between them the possible attitudes to Posthumus' reputation. For Philario, whose judgement is based on friendship and a family bond of gratitude, [1] Posthumus is 'without and within'—the stressing of this consistency is, in the light of earlier expressions, a notable indication of the play's continuity of purpose—an incarnation of the perfect gentleman; for Iachimo, on the other hand, a dispassionate weighing of the facts as they appear to him introduces a persistent doubt, a reducing of this supposed 'value' to interest and pretension. Iachimo, in fact, sees Posthumus' virtues not as illuminating social existence, as the crown of human living, but as conditioned by it, tainted by its inescapable hollowness. His devotion to Imogen, regarded hitherto as the supreme proof of his moral excellence, becomes from this new standpoint a proof of imperfection; for, to a critical eye, it seems to imply that 'he must be weighed rather by her value than his own', whilst the very 'approbation' of those that welcomed the match can be explained in terms of a desire to 'fortify' the weak judgement of Imogen, 'which else an easy battery might lay flat, for taking a beggar without less quality'. The intricate

---

1. 'His father and I were soldiers together: to whom I have been often bound for no less than my life.'

verbal pattern thus woven round the central situation has, in fact, beyond its obvious purpose as a reflection of sophisticated 'Italianate' cynicism, a strictly analytic content. To Iachimo, absolute 'value' of the kind postulated in love by Imogen and Posthumus is inconceivable. His intelligence, acute in its limitations, plays upon such 'value' and the virtue which is its moral expression, reducing both alike to a mixture of sentiment and interest; and, if his attitude is rootedly negative, if such a phrase as 'how *creeps* acquaintance' clearly reflects the speaker's tendency towards systematic debasement, under-valuation, it is none the less true that his position needs to be taken into account, to be first isolated in its expression and then assimilated, through the positive reaction it will eventually produce, into the final pattern.

To this clash of contrary attitudes to 'value', the tangible symbol of the ring, already introduced in the earlier verse-scene, serves as a point of focus. Around it, indeed, the moral and material values with which the play is ultimately concerned are subtly interwoven. Posthumus is ready to defend his belief in his mistress' virtue in terms of tangible worth, and Iachimo uses this very readiness to insinuate that the two conceptions of value, the moral and the material, are in fact identical, that the one is only to be conceived in terms of the other. In this he is helped, if not justified, by a strain of romantic rashness (if we may call it so) in Posthumus, which is indicated from the first in his preparatory exchange with the Frenchman. What strikes the latter, in remarking upon an incident in Posthumus' earlier career, as an unjustified disparity between the 'mortal purpose' of a challenge and the 'slight and trivial' nature of its cause, is at once acknowledged by him to have been the product of impulse in a 'young traveller' and confirmed by what he now considers to be his 'minded judgement'. The distinction at once asserts a valid principle—for Posthumus' adoration of his mistress is clearly intended to be ratified by his mature evaluation—and indicates a possible danger; for, although it is undoubtedly true, as he asserts later, that there is a fundamental difference between 'what may be sold or given' and what is 'only the gift of the gods', the assumption that the two values are connected, that the one may properly be discussed in terms of the other, is perhaps a little too easily made. Certainly it gives Iachimo his opening. To Posthumus' sweeping assertion that his jewel and the object of his love stand alike unparalleled in his estimation—'I praised her as I rated her: so do I my stone'—the answer inspired by his rooted relativity is, as far as it goes, indisputable: 'I have not seen the most precious diamond that is, nor you the lady'. The attempt, whether successful or not, to turn romantic commonplace to the ends of moral analysis, is undoubtedly present. The romantic love of Posthumus, far from being, as he believes, a final and sufficient relationship, needs to be subjected to a destructive process which will eventually bring it to full maturity. 'She your jewel' and 'this your jewel', thus brought together in the subtleties of court conversation, represent in their identification a knot of contrasted interpretations of value which the play, in so far as it is consistent with its deeper purposes (which is only in part), will be concerned to unravel.

With the two conceptions of 'value'—the romantic and the critical, so to call them—thus contrasted, the rest of this, the first stage in the development of the play, deals with the undermining of the former by the latter. Iachimo's next appearance (I. vi) brings him face to face with Imogen, and so with the chance to apply his 'philosophy' in practice. His attack rests, characteristically, upon the contrast between inward quality and outward features, the evident perfection of that part of his intended victim 'that is out of door' and the possible 'rarity' of the mind with which she is furnished. The distinction enables him to apply his peculiarly dissolvent, disintegrating procedure in a way that contributes to the total analysis of 'value' with which the play as a whole is particularly concerned. If both aspects correspond in Imogen (as Posthumus holds), then she is indeed 'the Arabian bird', unique and unassailable. It is essential to Iachimo's way of thinking, however, to believe that this cannot be so. In this, once more, he reminds us of earlier plays. Like Iago and Edmund before him, Iachimo, apparently dispassionate but in reality enslaved to his own sensuality, finds true virtue inconceivable. In his attack upon Imogen, the overflow of physical imagery, product of

> the cloyed will,
> That satiate yet unsatisfied desire, that tub
> Both filled and running   (i. vi),

which is for him the reality of love is at once intense and deeply repellent. This is a speaker to whose cynical intelligence passion seems sterile, even disgusting, but to whom no justifying conception of value is conceivable as a check to the senseless promptings of temporal desire. The conviction that no such conception is valid, the product of an intelligence at once critical and rooted in the instincts it despises, is the key to Iachimo's place in the symbolic structure of the play.

The scene which follows is at once important and oddly unsatisfactory. It reminds us, in its conception, of the episode in *Macbeth* (iv. iii) in which Malcolm first tries the loyalty of Macduff by stressing his imagined villainies and then, undoing his own words, brings out his deepest allegiance. Both scenes are symbolically rather than realistically conceived; both have their function as turning-points balancing in opposed poetic intensities the contrasted themes of their respective plays, and both—it is only fair to say—fail to relate these purposes to a convincing dramatic action. In the case of *Cymbeline*, the impact of the episode is further complicated by a definite derivative note in the poetry, a use of language which repeatedly recalls themes used in earlier tragedies without really equalling them in intensity or conviction. This is particularly apparent in the treatment of Iachimo's resentment against the physical embodiment, in Imogen, of a purity which he finds inconceivable. He begins, in accordance with the constant theme of the play, by ascribing to Posthumus a madness, an incapacity to 'distinguish' or 'make partition' between evident value and its parody, between 'fair and foul'; but, as he proceeds, his detachment fails and the characteristic expressions of repulsion, 'apes and monkeys' and the desire that, surfeited, 'vomits emptiness', come to the surface as reflections of his own sensuality. Ascribing to Posthumus sentiments formerly held by Iago—

> . . . that man, who knows
> By history, report, or his own proof,
> What woman is, *yea, what she cannot choose*
> *But must be*—

he falls into the disgust imagery typical of so many earlier plays, but felt here a little too easily and with something less than the full Shakespearean immediacy. The intention, it seems, is to pervade the scene with the sensuality with which Imogen's 'honour' is threatened, to reflect a world in which she lives indeed but in isolation and subject to continual perils. There is even a moment, when Imogen herself responds by referring to the 'Romish stew' and the 'beastly mind' of the stranger who is seeking to abuse her, in which the prevailing animality of Iachimo seems on the point of turning her otherwise serene utterance into unbalance; but the shift in tone is unprepared for, without relation to any justifying complexity of character,[1] and stands in strange contrast to her prevailing integrity as a sign of the imperfect assimilation so evident in this play. The development, indeed, is not insisted on. Iachimo recognizes his error, falling back on a description of Posthumus which reminds us, in its evocation of intangible perfection, of a kind of divinity which the subject's own behaviour is shortly to qualify:—

1. Such as we may detect, tentatively, in the strained expression of Isabella's virtue in certain scenes of *Measure for Measure*.

He sits 'mongst men like a descended god:
He hath a kind of honour sets him off,
More than a mortal seeming.

At the end of the exchange, Imogen has repelled easily
enough Iachimo's direct assault, but is powerless to meet
the guile by which he plans to steal from her in sleep the
'proof' of his conquest; and, as a result of her defencelessness,
she is faced in due course, not only with her father's passionate resentment, but with the anger of her disillusioned lover.

The following scenes at Cymbeline's court add little to
themes already announced. A background to Imogen's
betrayal, and a comment on the worthlessness of courtly
pretension divorced from true 'value', is provided (ii. i) by
the contrast between Cloten's claim to external nobility and
a rooted coarseness which becomes grotesque in the eyes of
his attendants and expresses itself most characteristically in a
persistent underlining of the animal, the purely physical
element in passion. Cloten's stressing of his 'nobility' and
his preoccupation with 'rank' turns, in his own words, to
the image of the strutting 'cock' that 'nobody can match';
and this, in turn, is associated with a gross sensuality of
expression essential to the character. His companion
insinuates this by taking up his use of 'rank' with the pungent
aside 'To have smelt like a fool', and by balancing 'cock'
with 'capon' and a clear suggestion of the 'cox-comb'; and,
finally, his preoccupation with possible 'derogation' leads to
a comparison between empty claims to eminence and a folly
which, being absolute, cannot 'derogate'. The climax to the
repeated physical suggestions which underlie the whole
episode appears in the Lord's concluding assertion that
Cloten is more 'hateful' than the 'foul expulsion' of Imogen's
husband. In this play on the double sense of 'expulsion'—
for, of course, the sense of banishment is also glanced at—
Cloten is presented to us in his true light, as the leavings of a
society which has no place for the virtues previously celebrated in Posthumus, less concerned with true value than

with the external accidents of assumed nobility. Against this background the hope is expressed that the 'heavens', upon whose sanction true 'honour' depends, will 'hold firm' and 'keep unchecked' its 'temple' in the fair mind of Imogen.

From this point, it is natural to pass on to the scene (II. ii) in which the 'temple' itself is finally subjected to direct siege by the furtive entry of Iachimo into Imogen's bed-chamber. Symbolically speaking, of course, the climax of the incident lies in the theft of Imogen's bracelet, the function of which as a point of focus for the poetic development has already been indicated. Poetically, however, the scene, like so much in the play, hesitates between the full symbolic integration of its theme and a prevailing decorative spirit. It is worth noting that the tragic implications of Iachimo's speech are persistently diluted by reflections which, while they recall images and themes derived from the great tragedies, are less immediate than, in a very real sense, literary elaborations. His opening evocation of sleep in

> . . . man's o'erlaboured sense
> Repairs itself by rest

might be taken to recall *Macbeth*, and, in the light of this, the further description of Tarquin 'softly' pressing the rushes,

> ere he waken'd
> The chastity he wounded,

confers a more definite sinister quality upon the criminal stealth of Iachimo's intrusion. Set against it, and typically 'poetic' in tone, is the association of Imogen with Cytherea, followed by a series of images which immediately takes us back to *Othello:*

> fresh lily!
> And whiter than the sheets! That I might touch,
> But kiss; one kiss! Rubies unparagon'd,
> How dearly they do't! 'T is her breathing that
> Perfumes the chamber thus.

To read these phrases as counterparts, in some sense, of 'that whiter skin of hers than snow', of Othello's 'One more, one more' and 'balmy breath' is to be aware, unquestionably, of a fundamental modification of purpose. Tragic urgency and the firm grasp of character seem, in short, to have been both diluted into something very like an excess of decorative poetry. And yet the excess itself—it is necessary to add—is possibly part of a deliberately chosen effect. Imogen's honour is set here, temporarily, in a setting of opulent artifice which is foreign to its nature and in which the sophisticated sensuality of Iachimo is unquestionably at home. Her marriage with Posthumus will only be consummated after she has been removed from Cymbeline's court, exposed to 'nature' and a variety of trials; but, meanwhile, her very virtues are set against a background, beautiful indeed, but steeped in convention, particularly calculated to set Iachimo's sensuous instincts sharply on edge.

Seen in this light, it is not without meaning that the central incident, the assault on Imogen's honour, is also wrapped in a pervading sense of decoration. Her eyes are 'lights'—

> canopied
> Under those windows, white and azure, laced
> With blue of heaven's own tinct;

the sleep in which she lies is 'ape of death' and her sense—

> a monument,
> Thus in a chapel lying!

The introduction of a literary parallel with 'the tale of Tereus', and the reference to the open book by Imogen's side, contribute to the same deliberate effect. They convey a sense of artificiality and opulence which correspond to a contrived quality of feeling. Iachimo's sensuality, which habitually dwells, for all its appearance of intensity, on the surface of things, is as much at home in this elaboration as Imogen's virtue is obscured, in a sense stifled by it; the liberation of her integrity by removal to another environment, and the exposure of her enemy which naturally accompanies it, are essential features of the full development of the play. Seen in this way, what otherwise appears as stylistic insecurity has its own importance in the complete conception.

The following episode (II. iii), with Imogen's repudiation of Cloten, develops further the contrast between true 'honour' and its parody, the respect given to place and courtly advancement. As usual in *Cymbeline*, the working out of the contrast in terms of imagery is something less than fully realized. Cloten, in yet another conversation with his attendants—there are surely too many of these in the play, making a point that scarcely needs so much elaboration—carries on the familiar contrast between 'heat' and 'cold' in terms of success in passion. His vulgarity serves as a background to the exquisite sophistication, itself a little too self-conscious to be truly natural, of the 'lark' song which echoes, in its deliberate artifice, the spirit of the preceding scene and which, in turn, he shows by his comments that he does not appreciate; the same music which, if it 'penetrate' the ears of Imogen, Cloten is willing to praise, is otherwise a 'vice' in his ears, a mere matter of 'horse-hairs and calves-guts' which his crude masculinity rejects. The determination, which follows, to bribe Imogen's attendants, couched once more in familiar Shakespearean language—it reads, indeed, not unlike a repetition of much in *Timon of Athens*—stresses the extent to which he, unaware of the true nature of his case, is prepared to use court corruption as an instrument to gain his end:

> 'Tis gold
> Which buys admittance, oft it doth; yea, and makes
> Diana's rangers false themselves, yield up
> Their deer to the stand o' the stealer; and 'tis gold
> Which makes the true man kill'd and saves the thief;
> Nay, sometimes hangs both thief and true man: what

Can it not do and undo? I will make
One of her women lawyer to me, for
I yet not understand the case myself.   (II. iii.)

The manner of expression here has its significance for the
general conception. The idea of chastity is bound up with
an allusive, self-conscious artifice—'Diana's rangers'—which
is again not without relation to Iachimo's recent words in
Imogen's bedroom. Decorative as it is in feeling, it conceals
the corrupt motives which underlie Cloten's own barely
disguised animality; and this in turn naturally accepts the
idea of corruption (*'false* themselves'), turns on the related
ideas of legality and bribery, involves 'thief and true man'
alike in a promiscuous confusion of values. Here, once more,
we are in the presence of the artificial, egoistic and brutal
world from which Imogen needs to be removed before her
love for Posthumus can realize its full human possibilities.
   Cloten's following dialogue with Imogen, to which all
this leads, reminds us that her 'honour', though helpless in
sleep and bound, in her present surroundings, to the
intrigue which is an inescapable aspect of court sophistication, is fully able, in her waking hours, to defend itself. It
also stresses, through the attendant Lady's opening words to
Cloten, that true gentility needs to be distinguished from
the external adornments which so often replace it in common
esteem. When Cloten describes himself as a 'gentleman' and,
further, as 'a gentleman's son', he provokes the comment:

That's more
Than some whose tailors are as dear as yours
Can justly boast of.

The matter of clothing, indeed, is not raised by accident.
The superficial courtliness of Cloten is exposed by his
denunciation of Posthumus, in verse of some complexity, as
'a base wretch' in whom lack of fortune is a certain sign of
lack of desert. 'Bred of alms and foster'd with cold dishes',

he is—so Cloten argues, reflecting the attitude of the society
which has accepted his own claim to aristocracy—no proper
match for a princess, and one, moreover, specially bound by
her station to the duty of 'obedience'. The argument, in
Shakespearean terms, is not without force, as may be
gathered from the closely-knit writing in such a passage as—

> . . . to knit their souls,
> On whom there is no more dependency
> But brats and beggary, in self-figured knot;

but it is invalidated by the essential coarseness of he who
proposes it, whose relation to true courtliness is properly
assessed by Imogen when she subordinates him, in a phrase
which will be echoed persistently from now on, to the
'meanest garment' of her lover.

Cloten's pretensions having thus been sufficiently placed
by the mere fact of contact with Imogen, we return (II. iv)
to Posthumus in Italy, and to the introduction into his soul
of the poison associated with Iachimo. With this introduction, the first stage in the play's development will be completed. Once more, the circumstances of Imogen's betrayal
are surrounded, in the telling, with a quality of sensual
artifice which links them with Iachimo's particular brand
of courtliness. The account of her bed-chamber, with its
direct evocation of Cleopatra at Cydnus, reads like a deriva-
tion from Enobarbus' famous description, and has, perhaps,
something like the same function in the play. The emphasis
is throughout on 'workmanship and value', on the artistic
counterfeit of true life:

> never saw I figures
> So likely to report themselves; *the cutter*
> *Was as another nature, dumb;* outwent her,
> *Motive and breath left out.* (II. iv.)

To grasp adequately the relation between this artifice and
the human value to be ascribed to Imogen's honour is to

be in possession of one of the main themes of the play. The 'golden cherubins' on the roof of her bed-chamber, the 'two winking Cupids' of silver, the chimney-piece with 'chaste Dian bathing', and the tapestries 'of silk and silver' are all elaborate counterfeits, seen through the self-conscious, artificial vision of a courtier, of 'nature'. Iachimo, as befits him, responds sensually to their opulence, but the perfection he evokes is not meant to obscure the fact that 'motion and breath' have been here 'left out', have no part to play in an essentially lifeless effect. Without claiming that the point is consistently made, we may say that the setting of courtly opulence in which Imogen has so far moved—and which is associated, above all, with the betrayal of her trust—is intended as a contrast to the firm simplicity which will only emerge fully in the hour of her misfortune.

Whether or not this reading be entirely justified, the description leads directly to the assertion of the central 'symbolic' theme, the 'wedding' of Imogen's bracelet to Posthumus' diamond. The ease with which Posthumus is convinced of his mistress' betrayal reminds us, in a certain sense, of the similar behaviour of Othello when confronted by the 'proof' of Desdemona's 'faithlessness'; but, it is necessary to add, his behaviour is not supported by any similar rigour in the dramatic analysis of character. Posthumus, indeed, seems to hesitate, as always, between a realistic and a symbolic function, seems not to belong fully either to the spirit of the earlier plays or to that of the final comedies. His dramatic mode of being, whilst recalling both, is neither that of Othello nor of Leontes; we are neither convinced by his declared motives nor ready to regard detailed motivation as irrelevant to a character not conceived as actor in a realistic tragedy. The commonplace rant with which he states his conviction of betrayal—

> Let there be no honour
> Where there is beauty; truth where semblance; love,
> Where there's another man—

lacks that justification in terms of motive which alone could make it plausible, and the further direct echoes of *Othello*—

> I will kill thee if thou dost deny
> Thou'st made me cuckold.

> O, that I had her here, to tear her limb-meal!—

suffer from a similar lack of defined dramatic purpose. As a character, Posthumus is, to say the least of it, inadequately conceived; as participant in a symbolic action, his behaviour too frequently raises questions of motive which should have been felt to be irrelevant, and his expression is too derivative, too reminiscent of earlier figures conceived on different lines, to carry complete conviction. Perhaps that is another way of saying that he, like the play to which he belongs, stands at a transitional moment in Shakespeare's artistic development, in which old themes have yet to be fully assumed into a new dramatic conception.

In so far as a clear purpose can be said to emerge from this part of *Cymbeline*, this scene and Posthumus' following monologue (II. v) seem to be intended to convey the entry into his mind of a sensual poison which springs finally from Iachimo's cynical evaluation of human motives. The soliloquy which brings this part of the action to an end—'We are all bastards!'—clearly aims at giving universal force to a particular experience in which motive, as in Leontes, counts for little. The image of the 'coiner' and his 'counterfeit' is of universal rather than particular application, as is the final catalogue of vices and the denunciation of woman which accompanies it; but it is impossible not to feel that the universal purpose is in great part invalidated by the presence of a feeling of particular resentment, and the whole passage reads—in spite of a number of remarkable verbal felicities: 'as chaste as unsunn'd snow', '*yellow* Iachimo'—rather as the repetition of themes more convincingly developed elsewhere than as a fresh dramatic creation. Be that as it may, it does certainly mark the attempt to work out an important stage in the main symbolic design. Posthumus is now, in a very real sense, assimilated in outlook to Iachimo, affected by the poison that corrupts human relationships in their courtly context. He casts doubts upon his own paternity and evokes the comparison with Diana—introduced not for the first time into the play—only to give it the validity of appearance, of mere *seeming*. His very memories of Imogen's behaviour become affected, in the telling, with a strangely ambiguous note:

> Me of my lawful pleasure she restrain'd,
> And pray'd me oft forbearance; did it with
> A pudency so rosy, the sweet view on't
> Might well have warm'd old Saturn.   (II. v.)

Imogen, thus described, becomes a figure of hypocrisy, restraining her lover from his 'lawful pleasure' at the same time as she planned his betrayal; her very 'pudency', touched with sensuality by the choice of the epithets 'rosy' and 'sweet' which accompany it, has the power to 'warm' the unnatural instincts of the aged Saturn. Posthumus' relations to Imogen have, in short, been corrupted by exposure to court sophistication and cynicism. He, and Imogen, will have to be taken out of that context, exposed to the natural simplicities, before any true process of recovery can be initiated.

II

The central part of *Cymbeline*, involving the integration of the various symbolic themes, is mainly concerned with the events that lead up to the meeting of Imogen, Cloten, and the lost sons of the king at Milford Haven. At this point, and as a result of their expulsion from the civilized world, the story of the two lovers meets that of Guiderius and Arviragus in a common exposure to 'nature'. Before this takes place, however, the 'civilized' society of Cymbeline's court is itself placed in a context more ample than any so far

63

suggested, asserting its dignity in patriotic affirmation. It is the Queen, oddly enough, who expresses the reaction of her subjects to Caesar's demand for tribute in verse remarkably free and rich in associations. The force of her reference to the Roman ships as 'ignorant baubles', the sense of power conveyed in her anticipation of their fate—

> . . . on our terrible seas,
> Like egg-shells moved upon their surges, crack'd
> As easily 'gainst our rocks   (III. i)—

the final felicity of 'Britons *strut* with courage': all these, allied to the ease with which sense is played against the restraints of structure in the typical late Shakespearean manner, point to the introduction into the play of a fresh theme of primary importance. To this spirit, even Cloten, with his downright prose, is able to offer a certain response, and Cymbeline himself rounds off the new mood when he refers, with a fine gesture of repudiation, to—

> Caesar's ambition,
> Which swell'd so much that it did almost stretch
> The sides o' the world,

and invokes that freedom under the law of which he is, in spite of his own passion-impelled excesses, the royal guarantor. From now on, all the personal fortunes traced in the action, themselves moving as they are to a point of concentration, need also to be seen against this further background, the full significance of which will only be apparent at the end of the play.

The following scene (III. ii) between Imogen and Pisanio returns to a more sentimental strain, but sets both lovers definitely on the path to Milford. Imogen's reaction to Posthumus' letter is, like so much in *Cymbeline*, strangely poised between sentimental elaboration and true immediacy of feeling. The effect of emotion overtaking coherence is, at certain moments, beautifully conveyed:

> Then, true Pisanio,—
> Who long'st, like me, to see thy lord: who long'st—
> O, let me bate,—but not like me—yet long'st,
> But in a fainter kind:—O, not like me;
> For mine's beyond beyond: say, and speak thick,—
> Love's counsellor should fill the pores of hearing,
> To the smothering of the sense—how far it is
> To this same blessed Milford.   (III. ii.)

The breathless intensity conveyed by the repetitions of 'long'st' and the insistence on 'not like me', the contrast with a fuller power of emotion implied in 'fainter', the suggestion of infinity in 'mine's beyond beyond' are all beautifully realized, as is the keen sense of an overpassing of common experience indicated in 'the smothering of the sense'. The immediacy, however, is not altogether sustained. Just below, the expression of emotion is reduced, in a way not less typical of *Cymbeline*, to something very like a literary quibble in—

> Tell me how Wales was made so happy as
> To inherit such a haven,

when the clearly implied fusion of the ideas of 'heaven' and 'haven' is scarcely justified in terms of intensity of feeling. The whole speech, indeed, hesitates between passion and artifice. If passion makes itself felt in the immediate evocation of Imogen's breathlessness, it is literary convention that prevails in—

> . . . that is my lord Leonatus!
> O, learn'd indeed were that astronomer
> That knew the stars as I his characters,

and in her first apostrophe to his unopened letter:

> Good wax, thy leave. Blest be
> You bees that make these locks of counsel!

This stylistic contrast is typical of the play, and perhaps we may hold, whilst admitting it to be a sign of weakness, of inconsistent purpose, that it incorporates part of its true meaning. The poet himself, indeed, was not necessarily entirely conscious of this. The verse of much of *Cymbeline* reads like an effort to break through convention, or to use convention for the expression of a deeper artistic purpose, of which the romantic forms are simply in a sense the vehicle. Imogen herself, according to our reading of the early action, is in some sense an incomplete character. She needs to discover her true moral being, and the full implications of her love for Posthumus, by being taken from her court surroundings to another world in which the social artifices are not so prominent; and it is perhaps part of the play's effect—though less than fully conscious—that this growth in moral insight should find expression in a corresponding intensification of poetic content.

Be that as it may, the next scene (III. iii) introduces the world of 'nature', the environment of Belarius and his two adopted sons. It also raises once more the problem of the relationship between true feeling and literary convention which is characteristic of *Cymbeline*, and perhaps one of its main themes. For the 'nature' which is set in contrast to court artificiality is itself artificially conceived, and this is one of the complicating features of the play. The spirit which impels Belarius to draw his moral from every aspect of his surroundings—as when he contrasts the low entrance of the cave, through which his wards have to stoop, with the 'gates of monarchs'—

> . . . arch'd so high that giants may jet through
> And keep their impious turbans on, without
> Good morrow to the sun,

or when he remarks—

> Consider,
> When you above perceive me like a crow,
> That it is place which lessens and sets off—

suggests that Shakespeare, in the writing of this play, was caught up to some extent in the conventions he was trying

to use. The complexity of tone, balanced between senten-
tiousness and sincerity, may be said, however, to correspond
to the state of the action, which is still manifestly incomplete. The relationship between 'civilization' and 'nature',
indeed, is not of the kind that can be projected into a simple
contrast. If the contrast exists, it reflects a mutual incompleteness. Advantages balance disadvantages on either side.
The court world which produced Iachimo and the Queen
also gave their proper background to Imogen's essentially
royal virtues; and, if these have to be removed from their
corrupt setting to find themselves in contact with 'nature',
the shortcomings of 'nature' itself are equally clear, through
the operation of instinct, to Cymbeline's transplanted offspring. Arviragus and Guiderius, in the same scene (III. iii),
balance in their discussion with their father a realization of
the advantages of the simple life, which he has a little
theoretically enlarged upon, against a sense of its limitations.
On the one hand, indeed,

> Haply this life is best,
> If quiet life be best;

on the other, Arviragus acknowledges himself to be 'beastly'
and feels his simplicity as a confinement:

> our cage
> We make a quire, as doth the prison'd bird,
> And sing our bondage freely.

Simplicity, in other words, has limitations of its own, and
freedom under conditions of primitive life involves the
'bondage' of the higher, specifically civilized faculties. These
will only be awakened in Cymbeline's sons when they are
restored to free loyalty and to a proper relationship with
the father they have lost. This, in turn, will imply their
assimilation into the wider pattern of the action, at once
patriotic and (as we shall see) universal, in which the personal
issues of the play are finally to be resolved.

The confronting of Imogen with Posthumus' letter

(III. iv) evidently falls into place here in the symbolic structure of the plot. By it, she is finally torn from past security, exposed to a process that will either confirm her faith or finally destroy it. Her opening speech stresses the note of uncertainty, the shaking of values hitherto secure and regarded as the foundations of normal existence; when she refers to the countenance of Pisanio as reflecting the state of—

> a thing perplex'd
> Beyond self-explication,

or when she voices, even before reading the letter, her fear of the effect upon Posthumus of his stay in 'drug-damn'd Italy', she is clearly on the edge of a new stage in her development. The moralizing tone with which she greets the shock produced by his letter, though itself related in intention to the main theme, is less happy. The rhetorical evocation of 'slander' is, like so much else in this play, a little less than fully personal, rather more the product of a habit of writing and feeling common in contemporary drama than would be necessary to give the emotion its proper weight; the same applies to the anxiety to meet death with which she urges Pisanio to carry out his master's instructions. That Imogen's desire to die is accompanied by a sense of the reversal of proper values is apparent, indeed, from the incidence in her speeches of certain flashes of distinctive linguistic vigour. 'Sinon's weeping' did 'scandal' many 'a holy tear', and the result of Posthumus' betrayal is a sense of disillusionment which is felt to have universal implications, a state in which 'Goodly and gallant shall be false and perjured'; but the reference to her heart as 'the innocent mansion of my love', the conventional sadness of

> The scriptures of the loyal Leonatus,
> All turn'd to heresy,

and, a little below, the facile effect by which she offers herself to death—'The lamb entreats the butcher: where's thy

68

knife?'—all reflect a decorative tendency which is in harmony with the spirit of much of the play. *Cymbeline* is, among other things, an attempt to turn established conventions to individual use, and the stylistic insecurity discernible in many of its more emotional passages corresponds to an impurity that was only finally surpassed in the consistency of *The Tempest* and *The Winter's Tale*.

The general effect of this episode, indeed, is one of a conventional structure imperfectly, though persistently, animated by flashes of intensely realized poetic feeling, such as those which emerge in relation to the play's underlying pattern in Imogen's comparison of her own state with that of her lover:

> Thus may poor fools
> Believe false teachers: though those that are betray'd
> Do feel the treason sharply, yet the traitor
> Stands in worse case of woe.
> And thou, Posthumus, thou that didst set up
> My disobedience 'gainst the king my father,
> And make me put into contempt the suits
> Of princely fellows, shalt hereafter find
> It is no act of common passage, but
> A strain of rareness: and I grieve myself
> To think, when thou shalt be disedged by her
> That now thou tirest on, how thy memory
> Will then be pang'd by me. (III. iv.)

Here too there is an element of convention in style and theme alike. The opening lines state a moral commonplace, of the kind that could be applied with conventional propriety to Imogen's situation, and the rhetorical gesture a little further down—'no act of common passage', 'a strain of rareness'—reads like a memory of Cleopatra's speech over Antony's corpse in the monument'[1] without evoking, to any corresponding degree, a feeling of true tragic urgency. On the other hand, the stressing at this moment of Imogen's

1. *Antony and Cleopatra*, IV. XV.

69

'disobedience' against her father and king is not accidental; this is an act which is clearly intended, natural and right though we must feel it to be under the circumstances, to cause tragedy and division. At the end of the speech, the immediacy of phrasing observable in the central contrast between 'disedged' and 'tirest on', together with the following 'pang'd', is anything but weak or conventional. This is one of the flashes of intense feeling which repeatedly illuminate the utterances of this play, without pervading it sufficiently to convey an impression of entirely consistent and coherent life.

The rest of the scene, in which Pisanio advises Imogen to assume a boy's disguise and in which his plan is accepted, adds little to the deeper meanings of the play. The situation is a conventional one and, though it is handled with occasional flashes of remarkable felicity—such as the famous reference to Britain 'in a great pool a swan's nest', and the description of Imogen's forced transformation in terms of 'waggish courage', 'saucy' and 'quarrelous as the weasel'—it is hard to detect a real unity of developing purpose. The following scene (III. v), which returns to Cymbeline's palace, has also relatively little to offer. It serves to recall once more the patriotic background which will have its part to play in the final resolution, and returns explicitly, in Cloten's prose soliloquy, to the contrast between the 'garment' and the inner man, relating the former this time to the characteristic operations of lust. In terms of plot, the main purpose is to bring the various protagonists a step further towards their meeting at Milford; Cloten believes that the achievement of his revenge, to be executed in terms of particularly brutal animality, is there, and Pisanio opposes this by invoking upon Imogen 'heavenly blessings' and anticipating that her pursuer will not meet her. The tendency to elaborate unduly the external development of the action, without infusing into it a sufficient degree of symbolic transformation, is indicative of the transitional nature of the inspiration in *Cymbeline*.

The meeting, which follows, between Imogen and the 'adopted' sons of Belarius (III. vi), though clearly important in the structure of the play, is likewise uneven in conception and treatment. The main theme, the acceptance of primitive conditions by a heroine born to court life, is once more superficially handled, fails to resolve its conventionality in terms of a deeper purpose. Imogen's opening speech, which seems occasionally to echo themes familiar in *King Lear* and other tragedies, evidently seeks to relate the action to a significant moral development. The emphasis on her exhaustion and the very phrase 'I have made the ground my bed', the assertion of her 'resolution' as a counterpoise to despair, the relating of her experience of poverty to a more universal uncertainty in 'Foundations fly the wretched' (although 'foundations', as has been observed, carries the subsidiary sense of 'hospitals' and cure, taken up by Imogen herself when she adds 'such, I mean, Where they should be relieved'), the moral contrast between 'poor folks', whose very afflictions, 'a punishment or trial', should guarantee the truthfulness still more inexplicably lacking in 'rich ones': all this reminds us in certain respects of Edgar's similar reduction to 'unaccomodated' beggary, whilst failing to produce any similar sense of coherence, of relation to a central moral exploration consistently developed. 'Famine', we are told, makes 'nature' valiant, before it 'overthrows' it. 'Hardness' is mother of 'hardiness', and 'plenty and peace', by contrast, breed 'cowards'; but Imogen's resolution, when Guiderius and Arviragus appear, is scarcely stressed as the new factor it should be, and the scene tapers off into sentiment of a more conventional kind. The emphasis on the sexual confusion, sensed if not understood by the brothers, is scarcely an adequate background for the overtly universal moral drawn by Imogen in conclusion, as she looks back on her recent experiences:

> Great men,
> That had a court no bigger than this cave,

That did attend themselves and had the virtue
Which their own conscience seal'd them—laying by
That nothing-gift of differing multitudes—
Could not out-peer these twain.   (III. vi.)

Once more, in reading this passage, we are faced with a discrepancy, frequent in *Cymbeline* and perhaps the fundamental problem of the play, between expression and effectiveness. The language, concise and compact, is that of the mature tragedies, and the sentiments expressed are related, by means of it, to that exploration of moral realities which is characteristic of Shakespeare at his best; but the themes stated are not adequately developed, fail to make themselves felt in the course of an action that remains basically conventional.   Nowhere is the provisional quality of the inspiration of *Cymbeline* more clearly apparent.

The following scenes carry the situation at Milford to its climax.   The first of them (IV. i) incorporates Cloten once more into the central action and takes up the contrast, already developed with reference to him, between the external 'garment' and the inner man.   Cloten, in fact, is the unpolished human animal, dressed up as a courtier and given the external circumstances of rank.   His very likeness, in physical terms, to Posthumus—stressed by the fact that the latter's clothes fit him perfectly—emphasizes the vainness of his pretensions.   Cloten is sure of his similarity, or superiority, to Posthumus in physique, in 'fortunes', in 'the advantage of the time', in 'birth', and in martial prowess; the inability of these qualities, or the imaginary possession of them, to impress Imogen is a sign of his failure in moral understanding and the cause of his resentment.   That resentment, typically, breeds the brutality expressed in his final anticipation of the way in which, having killed Posthumus, he will treat his mistress:

Posthumus, thy head, which now is growing upon thy shoulders, shall within this hour be off; thy mistress enforced; thy garments cut to pieces before thy face: and

72

all this done, spurn her home to her father, who may haply be a little angry for my so rough usage; but my mother, having power of his testiness, shall turn all into my commendations.   (IV. i.)

The final admission, conceived in a spirit of sardonic irony which characterizes much of the prose scenes of this play, that Cloten's power rests on the accident of birth, which is sufficient in his eyes to justify his brutality, is a clear indication of the intention which underlay the creation of the character.

The following scene (IV. ii) is clearly intended, in its length and elaboration, to be of central importance. Its intention, which is to use the romantic circumstances of Imogen's sickness and death as means for setting the personal issues of the play against a common subjection to 'mortality', is stressed from the first. Imogen's opening words expressly relate the conception of brotherhood—more conventionally relevant in the relationship, still unknown to her, which binds her to Guiderius and Arviragus—to that of death. 'Are we not brothers?' asks Arviragus, and receives in reply the observation—

> So man and man should be;
> But clay and clay differs in dignity,
> Whose dust is both alike.

The relevance of this to Cloten's recently expressed pretensions is obvious enough; less so, but equally to be considered, is the suggestion of the true meaning, symbolically speaking and in the play's general structure, of Imogen's own exposure to tragic circumstance. Through it she is learning, in a process of moral growth, how far beneath the surface appearances of courtliness lie the true sources of a 'nobility' which 'nature' possesses indeed, but which needs to be confirmed and deepened by exposure to tragic experience before being assumed into a more ample, civilized order; and, through this development, she will attain to a true brotherly relationship as well as to the confirmation of her love for Posthumus. Meanwhile, it is precisely the failure of the merely sociable to sustain her that is stressed in her attitude—

> society is no comfort
> To one not sociable.

The whole episode, indeed, rests on an atmosphere of moral commonplace to which the development of the action and its poetic unfolding are meant to contribute poetic life. 'Nature', following Belarius' aside, 'hath meal and bran, contempt and grace', and Imogen's sojourn in his cave will lead to a more discerning separation of the one from the other.

The entry of Cloten, and the threats with which he approaches Guiderius, revive once more the theme of true nobility as the gift of 'nature', in opposition to its appearance, symbolized in the possession of gorgeous clothes. 'Natural' nobility may not be—indeed, *is not*, as the course of the action will amply show—the crown of human virtue, but, when confronted with Cloten, it is seen to be, in a very true sense, its foundation. Cloten demands to be recognized by his possession of surface splendour—'know'st me not by my clothes?'—before seeking to intimidate his opponent by declaring himself to be 'son to the queen'; Guiderius replies by stressing the necessity of correspondence between inner worth and the pretensions of origin:

> I am sorry for't; not seeming
> So worthy as thy birth.

The fight which follows, leading to the elimination of Cloten, serves as a decisive evaluation of the value of his claim to nobility.

The final removal of Cloten is followed immediately by the playing of the 'solemn music' which announces the supposed 'death' of Imogen, and with it the opening of one of the most deliberately worked passages in the whole play. Like so much in *Cymbeline*, the episode produces a peculiar sensation of mingled sentiment and tragic feeling which fails, in spite of its beauty (or perhaps because of the excess of it), to carry entire conviction. The phrasing is from the first pervasively sentimental. Arviragus' phrase—

> The bird is dead
> That we have made so much on,

the corresponding exclamation of Guiderius, 'O sweetest, fairest lily', and the deliberate aiming at emotional effect in the description of Imogen's expression in 'death'—

> Thus smiling, as some fly had tickled slumber,
> Not as death's dart, being laughed at,

are all clearly part of an effort to transmute the sense of tragic mortality by dissolving it in poetic harmony. Personal emotion is here set in an elaborate decorative framework, sound and image combining to create immediacy, to give feeling a sense of remoteness on the basis of which the desired effect of acceptance may be achieved. Such is the purpose which underlies Belarius' grave apostrophe to sadness—

> O, melancholy!
> Who ever yet could sound thy bottom? find
> The ooze, to show what coast thy sluggish crare
> Might easiliest harbour in?[1]—

and such too the intention of the following invocation by Guiderius:

> With female fairies will his tomb be haunted,
> And worms will not come to thee.

The tone of such passages presents a critical puzzle highly characteristic of *Cymbeline*. Their beauty, recognized though it may be, cannot fail to strike us less as a new creation than as an evasion of true tragic feeling; unlike the best of Shakespeare's mature verse, its aim is primarily

---

[1]. It is just worth recalling other appearances of the word 'ooze', with a similar suggestion of nostalgic melancholy, in *Pericles* and *The Tempest*. See pp. 28 and 252.

decorative, its relation to the situation described tenuous and remote. Were it not for the presence of similar passages in more successful plays of this period, such as *The Winter's Tale* and *The Tempest*, we might pass these off as imitations of the fashionable sentimentality of Fletcher. There is no reason, indeed, to prevent us from supposing that an influence of this kind exists; but, in view of the later successes, we shall probably do better to regard the feeling of these speeches as a first attempt to elaborate a type of poetry which, if not convincing in isolation, will later be an essential element in a fuller and more various effect. It is part of the symbolic technique of the last plays to absorb direct emotion into a more complex poetic harmony, and this seems to be Shakespeare's intention here in his handling of the romantic conventions; except that in this part of *Cymbeline*, unlike *The Winter's Tale*, the prevailing tone seems to be still that of a sentimentality which is its own justification, rather than that of a harmony in which tougher and more realistic states of feeling can find their context in reconciliation.

The impression of an incomplete security of purpose is heightened in the two central passages of the burial episode: Arviragus' catalogue of flowers, with its transmutation of personal feeling into tenuous romantic delicacy, and the famous dirge over Fidele's 'body'. The delicacy of feeling of the first strikes an unmistakable note:

> With fairest flowers,
> While summer lasts, and I live here, Fidele,
> I'll sweeten thy sad grave: thou shalt not lack
> The flower that's like thy face, pale primrose, nor
> The azured harebell, like thy veins; no, nor
> The leaf of eglantine, whom not to slander,
> Out-sweeten'd not thy breath. (IV. ii.)

The whole passage turns on a romantic balance of beauty and subsistent melancholy. The 'sweetening' effect of the 'fairest flowers' promised by the speaker are set against a

sense of temporal impermanence—'While summer lasts'—
and of the sadness associated with the grave; and, as
counterparts to the emotional background thus created, the
flowers—'*pale* primrose' and the 'azured harebell, like thy
veins'—are evoked to produce a sense of personality dissolved, poetically transmuted in death. The beauty of the
passage has obvious points of contact with Perdita's more
perfect flower speech in *The Winter's Tale*.[1] It leaves us with
a sense of evasion, even of dissatisfaction, to which Guiderius
himself gives expression when he makes his realistic comment:

> Prithee, have done;
> And do not play in wench-like words with that
> Which is so serious.

Throughout this part of *Cymbeline*, there are signs of a
certain effort to balance, in the utterance of the two
brothers, two contrasted attitudes to tragic experience.
Arviragus proposes to express tragedy in song, transmuting
feeling into harmonious dirges, whereas Guiderius says:
'I cannot sing: I'll weep, and word it with thee', stressing the
necessity for concordance between feeling and its expression:

> For notes of sorrow out of tune are worse
> Than priests and fanes that lie.

If the voice of 'nature' clearly speaks here, condemning the
fictions of courtly life and modifying his brother's more
decorative attitude, Belarius, recalling Cloten's death,
reminds us that differences of rank, though needing to be
set against the fact of the universality of death, have in the
world their proper relevance:

> . . . though mean and mighty, rotting
> Together, have one dust, yet reverence,
> That angel of the world, doth make distinction
> Of place 'tween high and low. Our foe was princely;
> And though you took his life as being our foe,
> Yet bury him as a prince. (IV. ii.)

1. Act IV, Scene IV.

Guiderius' reaction to this, characteristically blunt, speaks with the voice of 'nature':

> Thersites' body is as good as Ajax',
> When neither are alive;

but the following dirge envelops the whole in a quality of poetic remoteness, evoking indeed the elements of a tragic experience, but seeing them as it were from afar. The feeling behind the reference to the completed 'worldly task', and the following catalogue, taken together with the craving for peace in the oblivion of death, is evidently a residue of feeling present in the tragedies; but the mellow sensation behind 'golden', which will be repeated elsewhere in the play, combines significantly with a feeling for youth and innocence which has already been present in the early part of the scene, and lends a note of peaceful 'consummation' to the whole.

This, however, is not the last word in this scene. When Imogen wakes, after the departure of Belarius and his 'sons', her first words give a moral quality, itself typical of the play, to the rites we have just witnessed:

> These flowers are like the pleasures of the world;
> This bloody man the care on't.

The speech thus introduced, however, leaves us yet again with a sense of imperfect concordance between action and expression, between a quality of feeling that recalls the great tragedies and external events which fail to correspond to them. Imogen's statement that she has awakened, as it were, from the dream of simple life in which she was a 'cave-keeper', aims at a universality of human reference which recalls, for a moment and imperfectly, the phrasing of *King Lear*:

> 'Twas but a bolt of nothing, shot at nothing,
> Which the brain makes of fumes: our very eyes
> Are sometimes like our judgements blind.

78

The feeling, however, is not sustained. When Imogen passes from general moral statement to face her particular tragedy —the death, as she believes, of Posthumus—her words, instead of rising to the occasion and giving concrete application to the universal abstractions already formulated, slip into melodrama, into an incoherence which is justified by the situation but adds little to its poetical development:

> Damn'd Pisanio
> Hath with his forged letters—damn'd Pisanio—
> From this most bravest vessel of the world
> Struck the main-top.

This is rather a normal, ample gesture of Elizabethan verse drama than a contribution to the poetic integration of the main theme.. It gives way, as the scene ends, to the entry of the Roman Lucio and the carrying of the plot a stage further by the incorporation of Imogen, disguised as Fidele (the name has, of course, a certain symbolic association, but one has only to compare it in function with those of Marina, Perdita, and Miranda to see how relatively insecure in conception is *Cymbeline*), into the Roman army. The episode at Milford has played its part in the development of the general theme; what now follows is the incorporation of the values there expressed into a wider range of action and, more particularly, the assimilation of 'natural' virtue through patriotic dedication and further exposure to death into a more ample field of harmony.

III

If the central part of *Cymbeline* has been marked, as we have tried to show, by a concentration of the various strands of the play upon Milford, where different conceptions of life, conventionally represented, are brought into contact and in some sense tested, the final episodes broaden out again into an inclusive harmony, itself once more projected through familiar conventions, in which these conceptions finally fall into place. This amplification is mainly achieved by a repetition of significant images, at first introduced in apparent isolation but later taken up again and extended until they throw light on the whole action. One of these recurrent themes, indeed, is first tentatively stated in the words of the Soothsayer who accompanies the Roman army at the moment of coming upon 'Fidele'; his vision of 'Jove's bird, the Roman eagle' vanishing in the sunbeams, though only partially interpreted here, is destined to be repeated as an essential element in the final effect.

For the moment, however, it is announced without development, and the action turns back (IV. iii) to the tensions in Cymbeline's court which, though indicated from the first, have been thus far mainly concealed but are at last coming into the open. The King, who has played no part in recent events, now re-appears, moved by the 'fever' and 'madness' of his queen, brought on in her by Cloten's absence and now faced by him together with the loss of Imogen; and all these trials have to be borne at a time when 'fearful wars point' at him. There is a suggestion of spiritual stress, of exposure to trial as a prelude to restoration, in Cymbeline's despair—

> it strikes me past
> The hope of comfort—

a situation, however, which only moves him to propose the torture of the faithful Pisanio. The moment, in fact, is dangerously poised between the blindness of passion and an awakening to its destructive effects. 'The time', as Cymbeline further remarks, 'is troublesome', and the announced landing of the Romans clearly indicates that the decisive crisis is at hand. This crisis will be the prelude to the final resolution, but meanwhile the prevailing state of confusion is reflected in Pisanio's own observation that he is bound to remain 'perplex'd in all' and in the spirit of his statement—

> Wherein I am false I am honest; not true, to be true.

It is stressed, lastly, that the resolution of this state of ambiguity lies in the unfolding of events. 'The heavens still must work', the obscure developments to come are explicitly ascribed to powers beyond human control, and meanwhile Pisanio rests on the certainty of a loyalty which stands firm under the most adverse circumstances. 'All other doubts, by time let them be clear'd': the sentence with which he concludes his speech, deliberately commonplace, reflects the state in which this moment finds him.

The last scene of this Act (IV. iv) takes us a stage further by drawing Belarius and his two 'sons', hitherto secluded in the state of nature, into the main action. Indeed, the debate as to whether they should, or can, stand aside is the principal theme of the episode. 'The noise is all about us', as Guiderius states at its opening; the question now is, whether to withdraw from the new developments, as Belarius wishes ('Let us from it'), following a counsel of prudence, or to plunge into a danger which may be a prelude to a fuller life. The two young men, for slightly different motives, favour the opposite course to that proposed by their guardian. Arviragus stresses the point of view that the 'pleasure' of life can only be found by those who refuse—

> to lock it
> From action and adventure;

Guiderius, speaking more practically, argues that isolation is, in fact, impossible, that the only choice before the brothers is to enter the main action as it is developing around them, or to be treated either as enemies to the Romans or traitors to their British foes. Belarius himself relates this choice to the main analysis of the differing implications of 'nature' when he admits the crudity and incompleteness implied in the 'natural' life; he refers to the 'want of breeding' which accompanies and limits its 'certainty' and describes his adopted children as—

> hopeless
> To have the courtesy your cradle promised,
> But to be still hot summer's tanlings and
> The shrinking slaves of winter. (IV. iv.)

Once again, the insertion of the decorative element does less than full poetic justice to the symbolic conception; but the words 'breeding' and 'courtesy' here imply the turning of aristocratic convention to a more positive, civilizing purpose. It is evident that we are to regard the life of these two young men as hitherto incomplete, lacking in the proving which is brought by the risks of war and the graces which accompany the courtly civilization to which they were born. This is made explicit in Guiderius' repudiation of the suggestion that the challenge facing them should be evaded—

> Than be so
> Better to cease to be—

and in the parallel comment of Arviragus—

> I am ashamed
> To look upon the holy sun, to have
> The benefit of his blest beams, remaining
> So long a poor unknown.

The reference to the 'sun', as somehow embodying the supreme religious values in this play, gives a further depth to the conventional theme of fame, reputation more obviously contained in these lines. It connects with other similar references to contribute to an effect of fundamental importance in the final resolution. The Soothsayer has already (iv. ii) described before Lucio his vision of the Roman eagle vanishing in the 'sunbeams' of the West, and it is not perhaps altogether fanciful to connect the repetition of the image with the characteristic sense of rich mellowness already implied in the famous dirge:

> Golden lads and girls all must,
> As chimney-sweepers, come to dust.

The epithet 'golden' and the evocation of sunset splendour, though not directly connected, belong to a common set of feelings, the full value of which will only become clear in the final poetic treatment of the allegorical theme. Meanwhile, the 'quiet consummation' of death, characteristically transmuted in terms of poetic imagery, is already in the process of being linked to a dramatic action that tends, through the crisis of approaching war, to a similar rounding-off in harmony. Cymbeline's sons are about to discover their princely 'blood' and, as a result of the discovery, to take up their position in a loyal order of true courtliness and inclusive peace.

The last Act of *Cymbeline*, whilst maintaining the inequalities so typical of the play as a whole, has some of its most interesting passages to offer. In fact, with the possible exception of the opening, nothing in the whole action reads as so distinctively Shakespearean. The main symbolic structure leading up to the final reconciliation is clear enough, as is its aim of absorbing personal vicissitudes into a more universal inclusiveness. To this conception, the 'death' of Imogen already belongs. It implies, as we have seen more especially in connection with the dirge, a certain liberation, and to it now corresponds the captivity of Posthumus and the tone of his meditations in prison:

> Most welcome, bondage; for thou art a way,
> I think, to liberty.   (v. iv.)

Both attitudes, in so far as they reflect a spirit of tempered acceptance, are proper preludes to the battle in which Posthumus and the sons of Cymbeline, joined in action, alike find their natural place, fighting against the foreign invader in the orbit of patriotism. Patriotism, however, is not itself the last word. The Britons, though they defeat the Roman invader, are finally absorbed into an order more than patriotic, and accept the payment of tribute which is the sign of a unity that surpasses the national. The play ends, indeed, not on a note of victory contrasted with defeat, but on one of reconciliation, coupled with an ample gesture of thanksgiving. To the Soothsayer's declaration of the relevance of supernatural purpose—

> The fingers of the powers above do tune
> The harmony of this peace—

Cymbeline, restored to true self-knowledge and to his position as royal symbol of unity, replies with a gesture of forgiveness and a final offering of thanks:

> Laud we the gods;
> And let our crooked smokes climb to their nostrils
> From our blest altars. (v. v.)

In no part of the play, perhaps, is the link which binds it to the development of the final Shakespearean conception, in spite of its conventional foundations and uneven execution, so fully realized.

The working out of the design thus sketched is, of course, something less than consistent. The first step (v. i) is the re-introduction into the action of Posthumus, for some time past displaced by Imogen and by the sons of Cymbeline in the development of the play. The Posthumus of the opening soliloquy is, characteristically, a chastened figure and his words echo a definite moral tone which is, at this stage, intentional and proper. The 'bloody handkerchief' he bears with him is a reminder of his own folly, now recognized and kept firmly in view:

> . . . bloody cloth, I'll keep thee; for I wish'd
> Thou should'st be colour'd thus.

This leads, in turn, to a new sense of submission to the purposes of the 'gods', in obedience to whom alone lies the possibility of 'blessing':

> do your best wills,
> And make me blest to obey!

Meanwhile, however, Posthumus has his part to play in the external development, and this part, as befits his own situation and moral state, is a mixed one. Having returned to Britain from exile, with the 'Italian gentry' (among whom, of course, as we are reminded in the short battle scene that follows, is counted Iachimo, the author of his sorrows), he has to maintain his patriotism in disguise; and this action

itself is felt by him to be a prelude to the death which he
sees as the only issue from his predicament:

> . . . so I'll die
> For thee, O Imogen, even for whom my life
> Is, every breath, a death.

The disguise itself which Posthumus has assumed is given by
him a moral interpretation in terms of achieved sincerity:

> To shame the guise o' the world, I will begin
> The fashion, less without and more within.

'The guise o' the world' is, in a general sense, the set of
assumptions which has governed the court action of the
play, and which Posthumus has learnt to estimate at its
proper value in the light of his own experience. The tone of
his whole meditation, thus deliberately couched in terms of
a self-knowledge tragically won, is a proper prelude to the
development which follows.

The short battle scene which ensues, deliberately formal-
ized in the familiar Shakespearean manner, adds little to the
sense of the play. It serves, however, to show for a moment a
Iachimo whose new attitude in some way parallels the latest
state of Posthumus, a Iachimo freshly possessed of 'heaviness
and guilt' and newly aware of the contrast that separates
nobility truly worn from the possession of mere external
titles:

> . . . knighthood and honours, borne
> As I wear mine, are titles but of scorn.   (v. ii.)

It is not, however, until the next appearance of Posthumus
(v. iii) that we are aware of having reached a new and
decisive stage in the development of the conception. As
usual, the entry of a renewed urgency is immediately reflected
in the handling of language and rhythm. The description of
the battle incidents, as placed in the mouth of Posthumus,
is, to the most cursory reading, superbly realized, intensely
alive in its free, supple adaptation of the resources of speech

to the blank verse construction. Against the suggestion, as a background, of divine control, indicated in 'the heavens fought', the speaker builds up, in a sustained accumulation of linguistic and rhythmic power, a fine impression of vast and impressive action. The first lines stress, by a deliberate intensification of phrasing, the magnitude of the original defeat of the British, transforming it into a superhuman tide of adversity by which they are carried, their wings 'destitute', their army 'broken', 'all flying' towards the 'strait lane' which is to be the focal point, in space as in rhythmic development, of the whole episode. Against the helplessness thus conveyed, and balancing the British dejection with the corresponding confidence of victory, the Roman enemy is evoked with superb concreteness in all his exultation, 'full-hearted' and 'lolling the tongue with slaughtering'. The sense of an irresistible tide of action is wonderfully conveyed, at the peak of the Roman success, by the fine carry-over of the blank verse rhythm in the description of the victims—

> struck down
> Some mortally, some slightly touched, some falling
> Merely through fear;

and this, in turn, culminates once more in 'the strait pass', where the critical moment of moral crisis is beautifully indicated in the complex final reference to—

> cowards living
> To die with lengthened shame.

By this culminating phrase the action is carried to its decisive turning-point in the 'lane', and with it to the affirmation that life dishonourably saved in defeat is a form of death which calls for redemption by a reaction on the moral as well as the military level.

The reaction, indeed, is given substance, saved from the danger of appearing a mere abstraction, in the second part of Posthumus' description. After the short question suitably

86

interposed at this focal point by the Lord, his account proceeds, again through a complete adaptation of the resources of imagery and verse-movement, to a decisive reversal of the original ebbing rhythm. It opens with a more detailed description of the crucial 'lane', of the 'ancient soldier'—whose 'honesty' is stressed—and of the two 'striplings' who stood in its defence. In their reported words to the routed British troops, the verse for the first time ceases to ebb, reflects in its change of movement a repeated emphasis on the idea implied in the call, thrice-repeated at this point, to 'stand':

> To darkness fleet souls that fly backwards. Stand;
> Or we are Romans, and will give you that
> Like beasts which you shun beastly, and may save
> But to look back in frown: stand, stand!

The pattern of words and rhythms at this point responds admirably to the purpose in hand. The first line flows naturally to its culmination in 'backwards', and then takes this up, balances it in the single, isolated syllable of contrasted command. The threat of the very death which the soldiers are seeking 'beastly' to escape, but which will come upon them 'like beasts', emphasizes the balance of physical situation and decisive moral choice; and, in the light of this, the earlier 'backwards' is balanced by a 'back' that now implies the opposite of flight, and leads finally, with a decision emphasized by repetition, to the final firmness of 'stand, stand'. The accumulation of phrases, in other words, whilst recalling that of the early part of the speech, is now built up round the idea of resistance and leads finally to the reversal of former tendencies implied in 'Part shame, *part spirit renewed*'. From this moment, the rhythm of recovery makes itself felt irresistibly to the end of the description:

> Then began
> A stop i' the chaser, a retire; anon
> A rout, confusion thick: forthwith they fly

Chickens, the way which they stoop'd eagles; slaves,
The strides they victors made: and now our cowards,
Like fragments in hard voyages, became
The life o' the need: having found the back-door open
Of the unguarded hearts, heavens, how they wound!
Some slain before, some dying, some their friends
O'erborne i' the former wave: ten chased by one
Are now each one the slaughter-man of twenty;
Those that would die or ere resist are grown
The mortal bugs o' the field.   (v. iii.)

At this point, and henceforth, the reversal of the previous
ebb is direct, decisive. The verse grows superbly from the
opening check implied in 'stop', in which the reversal of the
original retreat is finally concentrated, through the 'retire'
of the pursuer whose forward progress dominated the earlier
stages of the battle, to the accumulated effect of 'rout' and
'confusion thick'. Confusion itself, indeed, is here given controlled expression in verse, subordinated to the development
of a coherent artistic purpose. The beautifully telescoped
syntax of the following reference to—

Chickens, the way which they stoop'd eagles; slaves,
The strides they victors made,

at once adds breathless immediacy to the change of fortunes
and relates it to the new rhythmic development of the
whole; intensity and the breathlessness of the moment are
beautifully combined in a single comprehensive effect. To
this splendid rhythmic control corresponds an equal vigour
and immediacy of speech, conveyed in phrases such as 'fragments in hard voyages' and 'the life o' the need', as well as
in the grotesque power of—

having found the back-door open
Of the unguarded hearts.

With language and verse movement thus marvellously fused
in a single, forward-flowing impression, the way is at last

open for a full expression of the rhythm of recovery, and the speech attains complete freedom of movement in the cumulative power of the final lines.

> Some slain before, some dying, some their friends
> O'erborne i' the former wave;

carried on the crest of a developing rhythm, the intense, bold imagery bears the speaker on to the final, triumphant gesture of—

> Those that would die or ere resist are grown
> The mortal bugs o' the field.

'A narrow lane, an old man, and two boys.' The central situation, further invested by the Lord's wondering comment with a symbolic overtone of its own, has thus become the point of departure for a process by which rout has been turned into recovery, confusion into restored harmony.

The moral state of Posthumus, meanwhile, is not overshadowed by this new development of the action. His sense of loss, related now to the recognition of his own folly, bears fruit in an intensified craving for death:

> I, in mine own woe charm'd,
> Could not find death when I did hear him groan,
> Nor feel him where he struck.

In this spirit, and having played his part in turning the fortunes of the battle, he returns to his Roman disguise and is arrested accordingly by his triumphant compatriots. In the following scene (v. iv), the death and imprisonment themes are further integrated into the structure of the play. Posthumus, accepting his bondage in a spirit of penitence for his treatment of Imogen, regards it as a liberation:

> Most welcome, bondage! for thou art a way,
> I think, to liberty.

This attitude to death, 'the sure physician', rooted though it is in Elizabethan convention, further balances fittingly the

spirit of the dirge already sung over the 'corpse' of the 'dead'
Imogen. Both, in fact, have been exposed to trials which
involve the contemplation of death, and both, according to
the symbolic intention of the play, will emerge from them
enriched in terms of moral experience. Posthumus here
declares himself more 'fettered' by the accusations of his
own conscience than by the external fact of his imprisonment;
liberation he sees in the acceptance of mortality and of the—

> gyves,
> Desired more than constrain'd,

which are its external equivalent. The 'penitent instrument',
in fact, which is now the mainspring of his reflections, is
coupled with a sense of the 'mercy' of the 'gods' and of his
own mortal dependence:

> For Imogen's dear life take mine; and though
> 'Tis not so dear, yet 'tis a life; you coin'd it:
> 'Tween man and man, they weigh not every stamp;
> Though light, take pieces for the figure's sake:
> You rather mine, being yours; and so, great powers,
> If you will take this audit, take this life,
> And cancel these cold bonds.   (v. iv.)

What is being stated here is something very like an adaptation to the circumstances of the action of the Christian view
of atonement. Springing from the deep sense of mortality
which Shakespeare shares with other writers of the age, the
argument proceeds, after admitting the inequality between
the 'value' of Imogen, murdered as an indirect consequence
of the speaker's own behaviour, and his repentance, to stress
their common dependence upon the 'gods' in restoration of
the balance. His life, though less 'dear' than Imogen's, has
been equally 'coin'd' by the 'gods', and in their common
dependence at least there is an implication of equality.
' 'Tween man and man, they weigh not every stamp'; in
their common need for mercy, at least, men are equal, and
the processes of divine forgiveness can properly ignore the

discriminations and evaluations of relative guilt which are a necessary part of the 'cold bonds' of human justice.

The peculiar vision which appears to Posthumus in his following dream, though it falls naturally enough into place at this point as a supernatural intervention, is one of the puzzles of the play. The verse, taken as a whole, is poor enough to make the theory of interpolation plausible, and yet there is no denying that the episode, like much in the early part of *Pericles* and like the masque in *The Tempest*, is firmly integrated in the structure of the play. The appearance of Posthumus' parents with his two brothers is, indeed, made the occasion for a recapitulation of the significant points in his past history. His birth as an orphan is first recalled, and with it a sense of human helplessness implied in the mother's—

> . . . from me was Posthumus ript,
> Came crying 'mongst his foes.

Perhaps it is not altogether fanciful to see here a certain parallel, in symbolic intent, to the 'bloody child' in *Macbeth* and to the 'untimely' birth of Macduff. In both cases, we may hold that the particular situation has an undertone of universal reference. Be that as it may (and it would clearly be rash to press the parallel), Posthumus appears in these lines as being at once 'a thing of pity' and the inheritor of a great lineage; for we are told of him that—

> Great nature, like his ancestry,
> Moulded the stuff so fair,
> That he deserv'd the praise o' the world,
> As great Sicilius' heir.

This dignity, a natural projection of the conception of lineage, equally naturally, according to the lines which follow, sought its 'parallel' and found it in Imogen, to whose perfection alone he could appear as a 'fruitful object' in the full comprehension of his 'dignity'. Like, in other words, responds to like, enhancing the stature of human nature and suggesting fertility as its proper consequence; but this union is, in the nature of things, itself exposed to trials, and so Posthumus came to be 'mocked' with an unconsummated marriage, exiled and separated from Imogen by force of circumstance and the pressure of evil. The instrument of divorce was Iachimo, scornfully described in comparison with the full nobility of his victim as 'slight thing of Italy', but nevertheless able to cast his blight upon superior excellences, to 'taint' his 'heart and brain' and to plunge him, by a mocking irony, into 'needless jealousy'. Against the consummation of this injustice, Posthumus' ancestors plead by recalling their own patriotic actions and by pointing to their prolongation in their descendant's recent prowess on the field of battle; these, they assert, are titles of merit which call for recognition in the form of divine 'graces'.

To the prayers of Sicilius and his family corresponds the descent 'in thunder' of Jupiter, which we may reasonably find a crude piece of stage machinery, but which itself contributes to the interpretation of the action. Jupiter's utterance is, in its best moments, suitably grave, weighted, and it stresses the moral issues with which the whole scene is concerned. The god asserts in no uncertain terms his providential control of the incidents under consideration:

> No care of yours it is; you know 'tis ours.

This control is unequivocally directed to moral ends, and the trials through which Posthumus and Imogen are still passing are deliberately related to divine purposes which need to be seen in terms of controlling love and moral development:

> Whom best I love I cross; to make my gift,
> The more delay'd, delighted.

If this, like so much else in the scene, reads like commonplace, it is precisely such commonplace that Shakespeare's last plays came in increasing measure to relate to a rich particularity of experience, to vivify. Jupiter's utterance is, basically, a clear assertion of purpose, summed up in the affirmation that Posthumus' trials 'well are spent', and that his marriage with Imogen, having been consecrated in his own temple, will bear fruit in fulfilment and happiness:

> He shall be lord of lady Imogen,
> And happier much by his affliction made.

The relative crudity of the theatrical apparatus which accompanies this vision cannot blind us to the fact that it has an essential part to play in the development of the main conception. Whatever may be thought of its expression (and we may concede the possible presence of another hand without denying a measure of Shakespearean adaptation), there can be no doubt that the words of Sicilius immediately after Jupiter's withdrawal are impregnated with a sense of supernatural 'grace' that is entirely in line with the spirit of the last plays:

> He came in thunder; his celestial breath
> Was sulphurous to smell: the holy eagle
> Stoop'd, as to foot us: his ascension is
> More sweet than our blest fields: his royal bird
> Prunes the immortal wing and cloys his beak,
> As when his god is pleased.   (v. iv.)

The feeling conveyed in '*celestial* breath', '*holy* eagle' and '*sweet* ascension', in '*blest* fields' and '*immortal* wing' is, cumulatively speaking, unmistakable. It belongs to the imagination that put into the mouth of Banquo the description of Macbeth's castle at Inverness,[1] or evoked, in *The Winter's Tale*, the holiness of the 'sacrifice' to the oracle in Delphos in terms of 'sweet air', 'delicate' climate, fertility, and the 'celestial' quality—'ceremonious, solemn, and unearthly'—of the offering.[2] Royalty, holiness, and immortality are fused in a vision of transforming 'grace' which will, in due course, be taken up, on the plane of the

---

1. Act I, Scene vi.
2. See *The Winter's Tale*, Act III, Scene i.

main action, in the splendid, sun-drenched vision which
rounds off the concluding scene; the presence here of the
'holy eagle' already serves to connect this utterance with the
Soothsayer's vision (IV. ii) and the final unravelling of the
action. That this is mature Shakespearean verse, and that it
belongs to the symbolic conception of the play, is not seriously open to question.

The full implications of this complex scene are still, however, to be completed. Posthumus wakes from his dream
with a sense of disillusionment, of return to a world of harsh
and conflicting realities still bounded by death and mutability. The tone of moral commonplace which dominates
his thought at this stage makes itself felt once more:

> Poor wretches that depend
> On greatness' favour dream as I have done;
> Wake, and find nothing.

The fabric of dreams has still to be integrated into the plane
of reality, although the speaker's disillusionment is already
modified by the sense of his lack of deserving:

> Many dream not to find, neither deserve,
> And yet are steep'd in favours; so am I.

Looking back on his dream in the light of a reawakening to
reality, Posthumus can still see it as a '*golden* chance' (the
choice of adjective is significant, because it has already
appeared in the dirge and will be taken up in the final contemplative vision of the sun's life-giving rays) with which
he has been favoured without understanding, as yet, the
reason. In this spirit, he is presented with the apparition of
the 'rare' book which contains, couched in oracular terms,
a key to the final resolution. It is remarkable that Posthumus, presented with this new revelation, returns once more
to the 'garment' theme so prominent in earlier scenes. He
prays that the fair appearance of the book be not a decep-
tion, a 'garment' to confer nobility, or the shadow of it,
upon matter intrinsically unworthy; and, as he does so, he

94

refers explicitly to that gap between appearance and reality which is a dominating feature of court life:

> let thy effects
> So follow, to be most unlike our courtiers,
> As good as promise.

Posthumus in prison is still in a state of trial, still occupied in sifting true moral worth from its shadow, still balancing appearance and substance against the sense of imminent death; and, accordingly, it is proper that the revelation now enigmatically offered comes to him not as enlightenment but as puzzlement and obscurity, a further instance of the apparently inconsequent fabric which goes to make up the dream of living:

> 'Tis still a dream; or else such stuff as madmen
> Tongue, and brain not: either both, or nothing:
> Or senseless speaking, or a speaking such
> As sense cannot untie. Be what it is,
> The action of my life is like it.

The dream quality which characterizes so many utterances in Shakespeare's last plays is here bound up, linguistically speaking, with a sense of complexity, of intricate uncertainty, which makes it something more than the merely poetic statement which it has so often felt to be. Just as Prospero's famous vision of the dream fabric of our experienced world[1] proceeds from his 'beating brain', is balanced against the imminent brutality of Caliban's design upon him in a way that forces reality upon us, so here the vivid energy of phrasing in 'tongue, and brain not', and the intricate knottiness of 'senseless' opposed to 'sense' and 'speaking' to 'speaking', corresponds to the felt pressure of reality. Of that pressure, Posthumus' imprisonment and impending death is, indeed, an external expression. The moment has come for self-examination, for the unravelling of complex and contradictory themes; the final resolution, strongly indicated

1. *The Tempest*, Act IV, Scene i.

in Jupiter's words, and more obscurely present in the attitude of Posthumus himself, is still bound up with fantasy and dream.

The final grave prose dialogue with the Gaoler, saturated in a sense of death that is at once characteristic of the age and profoundly personal, rounds off this fine scene in a most fitting manner. It has, indeed, its own contribution to make to the complete sense of the episode. The elements that go to make up the Gaoler's 'philosophic' attitude to mortality are, of course, Elizabethan commonplaces, used as such by many inferior writers; a phrase like 'he that sleeps feels not the tooth-ache' bears with it an air of self-conscious dramatic truism which can easily be paralleled, at least in feeling, among Shakespeare's lesser contemporaries. Once again, however, as in the use made of the barely less familiar 'dream' metaphor just considered, convention is put to a profoundly personal use. What really matters in the whole dialogue is the delicate and deeply individual balancing of contrary attitudes, the setting of death conceived as liberation—an emotion itself deeply, genuinely felt—against an equal sense of the uncertainty which the contemplation of mortality inspires: 'look you, sir, you know not which way you shall go'. The attitudes which go to make up the scene are, in fact, various, plausible, and—above all—mutually enriching. The Gaoler hesitates between the conceptions of death as release, as implying freedom from the burden of life, and as obscurity, entry into the unknowable; and to this Posthumus himself seems to oppose, with profoundly human effect, a feeling akin to religious conviction, which naturally accompanies the new and distinctively moral outlook which characterizes his utterances throughout this part of the play: 'there none want eyes to direct them the way I am going, but such as wink and will not use them'. The confidence thus implied, however, is no more than part of the whole effect. The essential tone of the dialogue—and it is here that the distinctively Shakespearean quality is above all to be sought—is one of balance, of poised alternatives. Posthumus' mood of religious acceptance is set against the quality of the Gaoler's prevailing scepticism, expressed above all in his clear statement of the spiritual alternatives that face the prisoner:

> . . . you must either be directed by some that take upon them to know, or take upon yourself that which I am sure you do not know, or jump the after-enquiry on your own peril.

The alternatives as here stated are an acceptance of spiritual authority, itself given a certain sense of pretension in 'some that *take upon them* to know', an admission of the helplessness of individual judgement ('take upon yourself that which *I am sure you do not know*'), or a plunge into the unknowable which recalls, in its expression, Macbeth's frustrated impulse to 'jump the life to come'.[1] All these are, in the Gaoler's eyes, equally confessions of helplessness, for the only certainty is, in his own terms, 'how you shall speed in your journey's end, I think you'll never return to tell one'. In this balance of opposing attitudes, none accepted as final but each serving to add immediacy to its fellow, the genuine Shakespearean note makes itself unmistakably felt.

With the last scene of the play (v. v) the time has come to gather the various threads of plot and symbolism into a final unity. The threads, indeed, are numerous and closely interrelated. Posthumus and Imogen have to be restored to one another, and the King's lost sons united to their sister, Imogen, all under the embracing royal paternity of Cymbeline; whilst, in the public order, the liberties of the British realm have to be reconciled with the universal claims of Rome, and both alike subdued to a final harmony depending on the will of the 'gods'. The scene, in fact, uses the familiar mechanism of romantic reconciliation for symbolic ends of its own, working up through successive stages to a final, inclusive effect. The first stage is to bring Belarius and his charges before Cymbeline, who is still unaware of his true

1. *Macbeth*, Act I, Scene vii.

relationship to them, so that they may receive the recompense of knighthood conferred by his royal 'grace'; the second disposes of the queen and her machinations through her suicide in which, having been 'cruel to the world', she concludes 'most cruel to herself'. These, however, are no more than preliminaries. The entry of the Roman prisoners immediately below, accompanied by Imogen in disguise, carries the action a step further in preparing the ground for the final reconciliation; the first decisive sign of it is, perhaps, Cymbeline's unconscious recognition of his daughter:

> His favour is familiar to me. Boy,
> Thou hast look'd thyself into my grace,
> And art mine own.

The recognition, in turn, leads Cymbeline to offer 'Fidele' a 'boon' of his asking, which will, he believes, be used to redeem Lucius from the sentence hanging over him as the result of his defeat. In this way, the final political reconciliation is already anticipated; but, by one of those sharp turns in the action which Shakespeare so often uses to make his final harmonies more inclusive, Imogen turns aside from her 'master' to contemplate, in the sight of her ring worn by Iachimo,

> a thing
> Bitter to me as death,

and to request private conversation with the King. To the eyes of Belarius and his charges, meanwhile, the re-appearance of 'Fidele', last 'buried' by them at Milford Haven, amounts to a resurrection:

> BELARIUS: Is not this boy revived from death? ....
> GUIDERIUS: The same dead thing alive,

whilst simultaneously to Pisanio his recognition of Imogen is an anticipation that the action of time will eventually bring clarity, 'good or bad', to the whole action.

At this moment, indeed, the way is clear for Cymbeline to return and demand of Iachimo, with Imogen's prompting, an account of the diamond he wears upon his finger. The confession, stressing the contrast between the villain's 'Italian brain' and the 'duller Britain' in which it operated, leads to the self-revelation of Posthumus and to his admission of a guilt that now amounts, in his own eyes, to sacrilege:

> . . . it is I
> That all the abhorred things o' the earth amend
> By being worse than they. I am Posthumus
> That kill'd thy daughter . . .
>   The temple
> Of virtue was she; yea, and she herself.   (v. v.)

Finally, in his hysterical remorse, he strikes 'Fidele', and her fall is the occasion for Pisanio, hitherto a bystander, to come forward and declare the true identity of the victim. It is at this point that the spirit of the episode, hitherto mainly conventional, comes to life in Cymbeline's charged phrase:

> If this be so, the gods do mean to strike me
> To death with mortal joy.

The balance thus asserted between life and death, joy and mortality is clearly akin in spirit to the mood of the final scenes of *Pericles*. It raises the tone of the conclusion, in strictly poetic terms, to one of spiritual integration, in which sorrow, neither forgotten nor set aside, is transmuted into an element of deeper joy. With the mystery of her 'death' finally related to the behaviour of Cymbeline's queen, now herself eliminated, the way is open for Posthumus and Imogen to be reconciled, and this they are in lines pregnant with symbolic meaning and unmistakably belonging to the spirit of Shakespeare's last comedies. 'I was dead', says Imogen, and her words, beyond the mere recalling of a past event, bear a distinctive quality of marvel that itself implies the integration of the action on the symbolic level. In the light of her following question to Posthumus—

Why did you throw your wedded lady from you?—

his intense, broken exclamation, 'My queen, my life, my wife', combining the personal and familiar with the vivifying and the regally transcendent, is given its proper counterpart, and the embrace of the lovers surrounded by intuitions of a harmony more than purely personal:

> Hang there like fruit, my soul,
> Till the tree die!

The feeling, in fact, is so fine, so precious, that it can only be described in terms of 'soul', and by relating the spiritual suggestion to an evocation of the rich fertility of nature. Cymbeline, in turn, responds with words that stress the closeness and value of the reconciliation which has just flooded him with a re-birth of emotions long presumed dead; again like Pericles before him, he salutes his daughter as 'my flesh, my child', and the strength of his feeling is such that he senses himself reduced to the state of a 'dullard' by his incapacity to express it. Finally, and most typically of all, the reconciliation assumes its proper external form. Imogen, kneeling, requests the 'blessing' of her father, the tears of whose mingled happiness and grief become, in his own mind, 'holy water', a transmutation of mortal sorrow into spiritual joy. In the light of these new discoveries, the queen and her machinations have indeed become 'naught', the unwitting cause, as he now sees it, of the miracle taking place before his eyes:

> . . . long of her it was
> That we meet here so strangely.

The pattern of plot, thus filled out with a corresponding harmony of poetic imagery, thus assumes its complete, balanced form.

The spirit of restored unity which now dominates the

conclusion is still, however, incomplete. The action, indeed, after advancing so far, now turns back upon itself, in a manner not uncommon in Shakespeare, deviating to pick up the threads that have been left on one side. The occasion is the recalling of Cloten, through the reference to his mother, and the subsequent confession of Guiderius that he killed him at Milford. By this recapitulation, the theme of the contrast between true princeliness and external pretension, the 'inner' man and the mere 'garment', is taken up into the final synthesis. For Cymbeline, even in his state of awakening understanding, the forms of royalty still carry weight: hence his ominous observation 'He was a prince', and the refusal to heed Guiderius' evocation of Cloten's 'incivility' (the word, of course, carries a meaning of much more than rudeness, or mere lack of polish) as justification for his act. Shakespeare, however, accepting the conventions which underlie his story, aims at turning them once more to his own ends. For Guiderius, as Belarius asserts, is 'better than the man he slew', both in birth and in moral quality; the two orders, indeed, go together, and the discovery of the true situation at once satisfies the conditions of courtly romance and suggests a symbolic integration. That the device is crude, relatively unsupported by the weight of poetic richness which alone could give it full life, proves that once more Shakespeare is experimenting with established conventions, feeling his way to a fully personal use of familiar dramatic devices. His success is, as yet, manifestly incomplete, but the transforming purpose is clearly present.

It makes itself felt more strongly, indeed, in Cymbeline's reaction to the finding of his lost sons. Belarius prepares the way for the symbolic transformation of the discovery, in poetic terms, by invoking upon his charges, even as he delivers them to their father, 'the benediction of the covering heavens'; the notions of benediction and reconciliation are, throughout the last plays, closely connected, and Cymbeline's answering expression of grief at the very moment when the way is clear for the full expression of felicity—'Thou weep'st, and speak'st'—is also significant. The convenient recalling of the mole on Guiderius' neck belongs, of course, to the external commonplaces of romance which are rarely, in this play, completely assimilated; but it is followed by an intensification of the idea of recovered paternity in Cymbeline's exclamation:

> O, what am I?
> A mother to the birth of three? Ne'er mother
> Rejoiced deliverance more.

The lines clearly contain, though less firmly wedded to an adequate symbolic action, the various elements that contribute to the final emotional transmutation of Pericles' grief. Birth, and a certain implied re-discovery of the self, are here indicated; so is the suggestion of the pangs of 'deliverance' by which sorrow finds relief in compensating joy. In the light of this intensified feeling, the idea of the paternal blessing falls naturally into place—'Blest pray you be'—and is associated in turn with the restoration of natural order:

> That, after this strange parting from your orbs,
> You may reign in them now.

The completing dialogue with Imogen:—

> CYMBELINE: Thou hast lost by this a kingdom.
> IMOGEN: No, my lord;
> I have got two worlds by it—

with its characteristic sense of 'symbolic' overtone, of a poetic content that surpasses its apparent occasion, combines with a stressing of the sanctity of intimate family relationships—

> O, my gentle brothers . . .
> you call'd me brother,
> When I was but your sister; I you brothers,
> When ye were so indeed—

to produce at least a verbal sense of latent significance springing through to the surface; later plays will wed this sense
more adequately to a relevant plot, but the poetic conditions
for the full development are clearly present, at least in
potentiality. How far they can be taken will be seen in
The Winter's Tale and *The Tempest*.

At this point, the development of the action is at last
ready for completion. Cymbeline, once more king over
himself—since his discovery of the dead queen's machinations—and over the realm he has seen victorious, points the
way to a final act of religious affirmation, in which the consummation of marriage between Imogen and Posthumus will
be one with the rendering of thanks for victory achieved:

> Let's quit this ground,
> And smoke the temple with our sacrifices.

Once more, the ideas of sacrifice and worship anticipate a
fuller development in *The Winter's Tale*. With Iachimo's
confession of guilt and the forgiving gesture of Posthumus
the way is open for an act of religious integration which
will give its highest justification to the 'gracious season' into
which the action has at last entered.

This act is confirmed by the Soothsayer's final reading
of the prophecy enigmatically declared to Posthumus in his
dream. Once more, as so often in this play, commonplace
and even inferior material is made to serve ends felt to be
far superior in terms of poetic organization and emotional
power. The riddle itself, indeed, has possibilities in the
sense it conveys of fertility and expanding inclusiveness.
Cymbeline, the 'lofty cedar', is at last restored to the 'lopped
branches' for whose original loss his own passion was partially
responsible; and by this restoration or 'revival' (to use the
Soothsayer's own term, with its suggestion of life restored),
his 'issue', joined once more to 'the most majestic cedar', is
a guarantee for Britain of 'peace and plenty'. Nor is this,
even in political terms, all. Victorious Britain, through its
king, acknowledges its 'wonted tribute' to the universal

empire of Rome, reintegrates itself, in other words, in bonds of peace and equality, to a conception vaster even than its own vindicated patriotism; and finally both states are united in subjection to a spiritual vision, full of mellow, 'golden' richness, which is itself expressed in Shakespeare's best manner:

> The fingers of the powers above do tune
> The harmony of this peace.

'Harmony', indeed, on a scale of ever-increasing spaciousness, is the key-note of this conclusion. 'The Roman eagle', lessening herself, is gathered into the 'beams o' the sun', vanishes, is absorbed into a greater union; and the final reference, sustained by verse at once free, ample, and superbly concise, is to sacrifice and the praise of the 'gods'. In this final vision of consecration to a unifying purpose, the personal issues of the play, the love of Imogen for Posthumus maintained through trials and separation, and the integration of natural simplicity to the graces of civilized order, find in subjection to a universal unity, through the figure of Cymbeline as father and king, their proper integration.

IV

THE WINTER'S TALE

To pass from *Pericles* and *Cymbeline* to *The Winter's Tale* is to leave the field of experiment for that of finished achievement. In this play, in fact, the symbolic conception of drama that characterizes Shakespeare's final period attains its first, and possibly its most assured success. The word 'symbolism', as we have already had occasion to suggest,[1] needs to be used with care. It implies a prolongation of the normal resources of poetry and drama, and in no sense an abstract imposition upon them. The poetic mastery so evident in this play, the extraordinary range of imagery and superb control of rhythm, is there for all to see, has never been seriously denied; but equally important is the fact that both are consistently used to clarify character and motive, and that poetry and character alike are in turn taken up into a dramatic action perfectly balanced in its several parts. Behind the repeated stress laid on the fact that we are following a fable, a 'tale' not subject to the normal laws of probability, lies a consistent desire to make this action, this fable, the instrument for a harmonious reading of human experience. The unreality of *The Winter's Tale* is no mere escape, as some have argued, into a world of fancy. The various stages of the 'fable' correspond strictly to steps in the integration of a varied range of emotions from which neither tragic discord nor the sense of harmonious

1. See Introduction, p. 3.

fulfilment is excluded. The interplay of character and the sequence of events are alike significant, necessary to the complete impression conveyed by the play; but both are perfectly under the control of a dominant purpose, and their full meaning emerges from the closely-knit development of imagery which underlies them.

In order to appreciate this beautifully balanced construction, it is more than usually important to get away from the conventional divisions into which *The Winter's Tale*, in its printed form, is divided. This can best be done, perhaps, by regarding the various stages of the action as the successive movements, differing in feeling and *tempo*, which go to make up the unity of a piece of music. In accordance with this conception, the first movement (so to call it) deals with the tragic breakdown of the unity previously existing between the central figures of the play through the passionate folly of one man. As a result of this breakdown, Leontes loses his wife and son, turns on the friend of his childhood, condemns his new-born daughter to be exposed to the elements, and is finally overcome by the censure of the gods. The second movement, which follows, though short, is in a very real sense the turning-point of the whole action. Beginning in a tempest, which itself carries on, symbolically speaking, the idea of the divine displeasure, it sets against this background the discovery by the Shepherd of Leontes' new-born child, thus uniting the ideas of birth and death in a single episode, and connecting the tragic past with the happy future in an anticipation of the final reconciliation. Before this can take place, however, the third movement creates in the great pastoral scene an evocation of spring which at once confirms the new birth and exposes it to the maturing influence of adverse circumstances; Perdita and Florizel are pledged one to another, but the entry of Polixenes both unites the two fathers of the play in a common fault and confirms that the final reconciliation, still premature, can only take place at the court of Leontes. The fourth and final movement completes the balanced structure of the play by introducing with full effect the idea of penitence as prelude to restoration, by consummating the marriage of the two children and by achieving, through them, the reconciliation of their respective parents and the 'resurrection' of Hermione in all her gracious perfection. The rhythm of human experience, thus attuned to that of the seasons in their successive course, is rounded off in an inclusive harmony.

I (a)

The Winter's Tale, following the conception I have just outlined, deals with the divisions created in love and friendship by the passage of time and the action of 'blood' and of the final healing of these divisions. It turns, to put the matter in other terms, less upon a sequence of events in themselves barely probable, than upon an organic relationship between breakdown and reconstruction, the various stages of which coincide with the development of the plot. It is natural that a plot so conceived should bear within itself from the first the 'symbolic' elaboration essential to its purpose. This, indeed, becomes apparent, with characteristic Shakespearean economy, in the brief opening scene. The first sign of it is the prose statement by Leontes' counsellor, Camillo, of the close friendship which binds together his master and Polixenes, kings respectively of Sicily and Bohemia. Camillo's words, besides possessing us of the facts needed for an understanding of the following action, anticipate the obscurities which underlie them. Beneath the closeness of their intimacy, still unrealized but implicitly present, lie hidden seeds of division:

> Sicilia cannot show himself over-kind to Bohemia. They were trained together in their childhoods; and there rooted betwixt them then such an affection, which cannot choose but branch now. Since their more mature dignities and royal necessities made separation of their society, their encounters, though not personal, have been royally attorneyed with interchange of gifts, letters, loving

embassies; that they have seemed to be together, though absent: shook hands, as over a vast; and embraced as it were, from the ends of opposed winds. (i. i.)

As a mere exposition of fact, this would be elaborate to a fault. It is, however, more than that. The force of the passage lies in the combination under one set of images of two processes apparently contradictory—that of natural unified development existing side by side with that of widening division. The word 'branch' can imply either the unity of living growth or a spreading division within that growth. If the affection of the royal friends is such that it 'cannot choose but branch', this may mean either that it will continue to grow and bear fruit, or that it must inevitably separate and break down as it grows. In other words, though 'rooted' and deeply natural, it bears within itself the causes of future disunion. The concluding words return to the same idea, and the reference to 'opposed winds' further anticipates, not only the emotional storm in which the present unity is shortly to be tested, but also the actual tempest in which Leontes' daughter Perdita is lost and found, and which is to play, as we shall see, a decisive part in the whole construction. The final reference to the young prince Mamillius, who 'indeed physics the subject, makes old hearts fresh', points to the contrast between age and youth which will also form part of the central conception, and anticipates the healing quality to be exercised by the latter over the jealousies and divisions accumulated by the royal protagonists with the passage of time.

The opening scene, then, suggests how the plot will develop. There will be a conflict between Leontes and Polixenes, during which the harmony which has so far existed between them will be destroyed by a gratuitous act of passion-inspired folly. The friendship which unites the two kings is glimpsed for a moment in its past fullness through the opening exchanges between them, at the same moment as the threat to its permanence is again subtly anticipated. This is the true meaning conveyed by the beautifully balanced rhythms of Polixenes' first speech:

> . . . time as long again
> Would be fill'd up, my brother, with our thanks;
> And yet we should, for perpetuity,
> Go hence in debt: and therefore, like a cipher,
> Yet standing in rich place, I multiply
> With one we-thank-you many thousands more
> That go before it. (i. ii.)

To read this as no more than a conventional expression of royal gratitude is largely to miss the point of the whole utterance. The elaboration of the sentiment, such as it is, is of the same kind as that already discussed in Camillo's prose speech. It is perfectly deliberate, the result of a conscious poetic purpose engaged in creating a style suited to the ends it has proposed to itself. This style calls for a deliberate complexity, overlying the ease and freedom of the rhythmic structure, as a means of arriving at the elaborate pattern of interwoven images which imposes upon the action its subsistent unity. Polixenes' words suggest a relation between 'perpetuity' and the inadequacy imposed by the speaker's temporal condition, between the infinite 'debt' of gratitude and the limited possibility of expressing it, between the 'cipher' of conceivable utterance and the 'rich place' in which it stands as a symbol of emotional value. The balance between emotions that aspire to a certain infinity and the temporal basis on which they rest is here attained, held precariously, but with an implied suggestion of impermanence; and the following dialogue, with its hint of Polixenes' barely-defined 'fears' and his reference to the '*sneaping* winds' that may be blowing in his absence at home, blighting the normal sweetness of life, points obscurely to the coming break-down.

It is not long, indeed, before Shakespeare, developing still further both his plot and its deeper implications, gives us another key-passage, relates the friendship of the two kings to considerations of a more universal kind. Hermione's request to hear something of the past relationship between her husband and his friend leads to the following dialogue:

POLIXENES: We were, fair queen,
Two lads that thought there was no more behind,
But such a day to-morrow as to-day,
And to be boy eternal.

HERMIONE: Was not my lord
The verier wag o' the two?

POLIXENES: We were as twinn'd lambs that did frisk i' the sun,
And bleat the one at the other: what we changed
Was innocence for innocence; we knew not
The doctrine of ill-doing, nor dream'd
That any did. Had we pursued that life,
And our weak spirits ne'er been higher rear'd
With stronger blood, we should have answer'd heaven
Boldly 'not guilty', the imposition clear'd
Hereditary ours. (I. ii.)

The importance of youth and spring-time in this play is sufficiently obvious, and this passage first shows the reason for it. Shakespeare is using this description to point a contrast between spontaneous human emotion and the continual pressure of time—a friction clearly connected, by the way, with the 'metaphysical' ambiguity of certain of the Sonnets.[1] Time, in brief, which brings friendship to maturity

---

1. For an early, conventional expression of one of the central themes of *The Winter's Tale* it is perhaps worth quoting Sonnet XI:

> As fast as thou shalt wane, so fast thou grow'st
> In one of thine, from that which thou departest;
> And that fresh blood which youngly thou bestow'st
> Thou may'st call thine, when thou from youth convertest.

The reconciliation between Leontes and Polixenes, brought about by their children after their own age-inspired resentments have driven them to mutual hatred, could evidently be interpreted as a dramatic development of this generalized statement. The gulf between the Sonnet convention and the superb particularity of the play is evident, but a continuity of conception could be held to underlie both alike.

also threatens to destroy it, just as, in *Troilus and Cressida*,[1] it destroyed the love which developed with it. But Polixenes' speech adds something fundamental and peculiar to the last plays—the direct connection of this friction with sin, 'the doctrine of ill-doing'. The action of time is seen, at this stage in the play, as a corrupting action; experience, as it enters into the life of innocence, destroys the foundations of spontaneous friendship. The youthful freshness which is set against this inevitable deterioration is coupled by the speaker with an ominous ignorance of 'the doctrine of ill-doing'. Its beauty is nostalgic and pathetically defenceless ('Temptations have since then been born to's', as Polixenes puts it), an easy prey to the 'sneaping winds' whose imminence has already been suggested.

Polixenes' account, however, contains more even than this. The cause of Leontes' quarrel with him is, significantly enough, jealousy, the conviction that his friend has betrayed him with Hermione, who is known to be with child. Polixenes' introduction of the idea of 'blood', coupled with the birth of this obsession in his friend, gives the 'idyllic' poetry a fresh meaning by relating it to the problems raised by the nature of sexual passion. 'Blood', in fact, and the action of time are here fused into a single intuition; that is what is behind the contrast between 'stronger blood' and 'weak spirits'. The friendship between the two kings, which dates from childhood, has rested so far on the youthful state of innocence; based on a sentimental ignoring of the reality of the temporal process, it has assumed, with pathetic simplicity, that it was possible to remain 'boy eternal'. The realities of human nature, however, make this impossible. Boyhood is necessarily a state of transition. The development of the sensual life, 'stronger' than the innocence which preceded it, is necessary to complete maturity of the spirit. Without it, the ideal of pastoral innocence and eternal youth

1. I have attempted to discuss this aspect of *Troilus and Cressida* in my *Approach to Shakespeare* (London, 1938), pp. 51–57, and, at greater length, in *Scrutiny*, December, 1938, pp. 301–319.

is 'weak', though lovely. It is an ideal which at once depends upon its illusory timelessness and is vitiated by it; the continual action of time, here equated with the growth of a man into sexual maturity, gives the necessary fullness of the 'blood' to human experience, but also threatens it with exposure to the impersonal laws of mutability. The sensual life of man, whilst giving substance to his development, implies the subjection of his ideal innocence to the capacity for evil. Only through a conscious reaction to tragedy, and the consequent acceptance of deeper experience, can this idyllic state of childhood grow into an independent, conscious maturity.

For the moment, however, this harmonious development is nothing more than a remote possibility. Meanwhile, the capacity for sensual passion which time imposes upon man (whose instinctive reaction, as indicated by Polixenes, is an attempt to ignore it) bears a double interpretation. It may be good, if it leads to its natural fulfilment in the creative unity of the family, or evil and destructive, in the form of egoism and its consequences, jealousy overcoming all restraint of reason. In Leontes, it is the evil impulse which comes to the surface, destroying his friendship with Polixenes and leading him to turn upon Hermione with an animal intensity of feeling. That his jealousy, so often dismissed as the product of a dreary obsession, is in fact the moving force in this, the first stage in the development of the play, should by now be clear. The power of the verse in which it finds expression is, indeed, a sufficient guarantee of this:

Too hot, too hot!
To mingle friendships far is mingling bloods.
I have tremor cordis on me: my heart dances;
But not for joy; not joy.

But to be paddling palms and pinching fingers
As now they are . . .

112

They're here with me already; whispering, rounding
'Sicilia is a so-forth': 'tis far gone
When I shall gust it last.   (I. ii.)

Shakespeare's rhythms were never more impressive, never
more delicately adjusted to the breaks in an overwrought
consciousness, never more vivid in their ultra-sensual repulsion from the physical.   This is apparent in the superbly
palated 'gust', allying Leontes' loathing to the offending of
a highly sensitive taste; *Troilus and Cressida* is full of such
imagery, though the adaptation to the dramatic ends proposed
is there less completely realized.   The delicately broken line
—'I have tremor cordis on me: my heart dances'—could,
again, only have come from Shakespeare at the height of his
power.   Leontes plays his part in the play, at this stage, as
the 'embossed carbuncle'—to echo *King Lear*[1]—in the
organism of human relationships, as one by-product, per-
versely and destructively dynamic, of that organism's growth
through rising 'blood' to maturity.

   The entry of this new force, bitterly dissolvent in its
effects, into the unity precariously stated at the beginning
of the scene is, indeed, beautifully conveyed through the
various stages of the dramatic action.   The possibility of it
is anticipated, as we have seen, in Polixenes' own account of
his boyhood friendship with Leontes.   As he speaks, and as
Hermione presses him to postpone his departure, Leontes
stands aside in significant, foreboding silence; and only as the
poison slowly distils itself in his own mind, forces itself
forward into an overruling presence, does he advance,
dominating the scene with the power of his released emotion
and driving the action into its tragic development.   His first
entry into the discussion is a brief, abrupt question, uttered,
as it were, from the edge of the stage: 'Is he won yet?';
his second the implied contrast, more heavily charged with
menace, of 'At my request he would not'.   In his case, too,
developing thought takes the form of a comparison, strangely

1. Act II, Scene iv.

embittered in its expression, between present reflections and the memory of past experience. 'Never but once', he says, has Hermione previously spoken to better purpose; but that 'once'—

> was when
> Three crabbed months had sour'd themselves to death,
> Ere I could make thee open thy white hand,
> And clap thyself my love.

The type of feeling which can produce such a reference to 'three *crabbed* months' and follow it up with the peculiarly intense palating of '*sour'd* themselves to death' is clearly connected with the process of poisoning, the mounting bitterness that is taking possession of Leontes' mind; as in the case of Polixenes, past memories of untarnished happiness are being imperceptibly sullied, turned to present disillusionment. Before long, this same turn of emotion comes to the surface, in Leontes' first aside and dialogue with Mamillius, until it breaks out in violent, open repulsion. Even his preliminary admission that all *may* yet be as it seems conveys, in the manner of its expression, a profound sense of ambiguity:

> This entertainment
> May a free face put on, derive a liberty
> From heartiness, from bounty, fertile bosom,
> And well become the agent; 't may, I grant.

'Entertainment', 'free', 'liberty', 'fertile' are all words capable in themselves of a positive, healthy interpretation; but, in the mind of the speaker, freedom is associated with prodigality and liberty with licence, whilst fertility itself appears as the overflow of wantonness.[1] The broken rhythms and

---

1. It is perhaps worth noting the presence of a similar feeling in Othello's observation on Desdemona's hand:

> This argues fruitfulness and liberal heart;
> Hot, hot, and moist: this hand of yours requires
> A sequester from liberty, fasting and prayer,
> Much castigation, exercise devout;

intense, disjointed expression are all signs of a deep-seated dislocation which will come to the surface in the unfolding of events.

It is not an accident that the first outward sign of Leontes' condition is connected with the setting before him of his son. The continuity of the family relationship, by which the father is fulfilled in his child, is, as we shall see, one of the foundations on which the symbolic structure of *The Winter's Tale* rests. It is, therefore, proper that the disruption of Leontes' integrity should take the form in the first place of a doubt as to Mamillius' parentage. 'Art thou my boy?' is the question in which his unnatural moral state is first made clear to us. Both the fathers with whose relationship this scene is concerned see in their sons a reflection, transformed by youth, of themselves. Leontes, looking back over twenty-three years, sees his own lost youth reflected in his child:

> How like, methought, I was then to this kernel,
> This squash, this gentleman;

and, speaking of his own absent offspring, Polixenes is able to point a contrast between the innocence of youth, renewed as a consequence of his fatherhood, and the necessary disillusionments which accompany maturity:

> He makes a July's day short as December;
> And with his varying childness cures in me
> Thoughts that would thick my blood.

Already, in this statement of a parallel relationship, the age of the fathers is set against the youth of their offspring, 'December' against 'July', the vivid spontaneity of the state of 'childness' against the thoughts that, accompanying old

---

For here's a young and sweating devil here,
That commonly rebels. 'Tis a good hand,
A frank one.

(*Othello*, III. iv.)

Without pressing the parallel too far, a similar ambivalence in the use of such words as 'fruitfulness', 'liberal', and 'frank' may be conceded.

age, imply a certain spiritual infirmity and the thickening of the blood.

Once the doubt as to his parenthood has entered Leontes' mind—to be thrust aside, indeed, but to point none the less to the nature and extent of his infirmity—his degeneration into incoherence is expressed with a power that is not, indeed, to be judged in terms of realistic drama, but which is none the less intensely vivid. As he loses his integrity, as his unity of moral being is undermined by passion, so he moves from the periphery into the centre of the action, becomes not merely a marginal figure of foreboding but the prime mover in a descent into disaster. His language combines a growing failure to make the normal logical connections with an intensity of concentration upon isolated detail that takes the form, most obviously, of a new insistence upon the harsh directness of common speech. Mamillius is addressed as 'my bawcock', and the speaker clutches at the vivid, irrelevant detail with the immediacy of 'hast smutch'd thy nose?' before descending openly to a significant turn of imagery associated with the mating of cattle:

> We must be neat; not neat, but cleanly, captain:
> And yet the steer, the heifer and the calf
> Are all call'd neat.

Finally, an ironic contrast with chastity is indicated in the broken phrases which follow:

> Still virginalling
> Upon his palm!—How now, you wanton calf!—

where the original evocation of cleanliness is extended, by a purely verbal similarity, to the impressions roused in the speaker by 'virginalling' and the final transference of the 'wantonness' he suspects in his wife to the son, now described as the 'calf' which is the product of their union.

Having reached this stage, Leontes is ready to invert reality itself in the following of his released instincts. 'Affection', he affirms, makes 'possible things not so held', truth is confounded with dreams, and the 'unreal' is 'co-active' with the truth to the 'infection' of his peace of mind:

> Should all despair
> That have revolted wives, the tenth of mankind
> Would hang themselves. Physic for't there is none;
> It is a bawdy planet, that will strike
> Where 't is predominant. (I. ii.)

With the universalizing of his own infirm obsession into a not very impressive piece of Elizabethan commonplace, the infection of Leontes' mind is substantially complete. In the following exchange with Camillo, his concern is not to discover the truth, but to confirm what he holds in his own mind to be certain. In his perversity, indeed, and not unlike Othello before him, he craves for this confirmation as an alternative to the sense of chaos which is one of the accompaniments of unleashed passion; for, 'if this be nothing'—

> Why, then, the world and all that's in't is nothing;
> The covering sky is nothing; Bohemia nothing;
> My wife is nothing; nor nothing have these nothings,
> If this be nothing.

The whole of Leontes' behaviour has now become a frenzied building up of supposed certainties on 'nothing', on the baselessness of an irrational emotion followed to the limits of self-centred impulse. The consequences of this development, as they affect the world beyond him, soon make themselves felt in the choice offered to Camillo. To the loyal courtier, it is clear that his master's is a 'diseased opinion' and, as such, intensely dangerous; but the only effect of his protest is to provoke the accusation of lying and the command, based on royal authority, to poison Polixenes. Thus placed in a position where loyalties clash, Camillo's final comment stresses at once the irrationality of his master's behaviour, 'in rebellion with himself', and its extension implied in the determination to have 'all that are his so too'. As always, the introduction of passionate division in the mind of a king is followed by a split in the fabric of society, whose unity is only conceivable under a royal guarantee.

A full understanding of Leontes' position is considerably furthered by referring to the contrasted feeling in Polixenes, when he becomes aware of his former friend's suspicions. The imagery of disease has already been playing a part increasingly prominent in the development of the action, and has extended itself, in the process, beyond Leontes himself to those around him; perhaps the clearest indication of this is Camillo's observation:

> There is a sickness
> Which puts some of us in distemper; but
> I cannot name the disease; and it is caught
> Of you that yet are well.

As the knowledge of Leontes' suspicions, and of their implications for himself, penetrates into Polixenes' mind, he takes up this same sense of infection and sets it in contrast with the powerful symbols of loyalty associated with unsullied friendship:

> O, then my best blood turn
> To an infected jelly, and my name
> Be yoked with his that did betray the Best!
> Turn then my freshest reputation to
> A savour that may strike the dullest nostril
> Where I arrive, and my approach be shunn'd,
> Nay, hated too, worse than the great'st infection
> That e'er was heard or read.   (I. ii.)

The sensitive quality of these lines, based on a delicate balancing of opposed impressions, is worth noting. On the one hand, there is an insistence upon 'infection', allied to the odour of decay, which carries on Camillo's own line of thought; on the other, 'freshness' is associated with the idea of boundless value twice stressed, and given a specifically religious sanction, in the use of 'best'. This peculiar quality of 'freshness', with its persistent symbolic overtones, is as familiar in the great tragedies as the notion of contagious infirmity set against it. Lear, awakening from his madness, is dressed in 'fresh garments'[1] and, in *Macbeth*, 'infection' plays an important part in the account given of the 'healing benediction' of the English king,[2] in the Doctor's work at Dunsinane, and in the diseased disorder of the murderer's mind. The contrast, in fact, implies that Shakespeare is once more using his unrivalled control of sensual imagery to set forth, through Leontes' jealousy and the reaction it produces, a contrast between good and evil, between the fullness of human maturity crowned by 'grace' and the vicious and disintegrating savagery of uncontrolled 'blood'.

The mention of 'grace' reminds us that the behaviour of Leontes throughout this scene, and indeed in the whole play, is only fully comprehensible in a context provided by the concept of family unity. Of that concept, in its full moral significance, Hermione is the gracious symbol. 'Grace' is a word to note in Shakespeare's later plays. *Macbeth*, again, uses it to deliberate effect; it is associated with the sanctity and healing powers of Edward the Confessor, and Malcolm is revealed in his final restoration as an instrument of 'the grace of Grace'. Cleopatra's triumphant beauty on her throne is 'her strong toil of grace',[3] and the last comedies, from *Pericles* onwards, are full of the word. Its implications, which shift and develop in the intricate pattern of the plays, are hard to define. In *The Winter's Tale*, Shakespeare seems to reinforce the Christian associations already acquired in *Macbeth* with a deeply personal intuition of natural fertility, fulfilled in the intimate unity of the family. The play, indeed, contains a profound and highly individual effort to bring the impasse suggested by Shakespeare's exploration of the part played by 'blood' in human experience—a part at once destructive and, potentially, maturing—into relation with feelings which imply the understanding of a positive

1. Act IV, Scene vii.
2. Act IV, Scene iii.
3. Act V, Scene ii.

spiritual conception. If Leontes' behaviour at this stage leads to the reversal of that conception, and of the unity which derives from it, the perfection which he has repudiated stands out, firmly unshakeable, as a point of reference by which the surrounding action may be judged, in the constancy of his wife.

Only so can we read the poetry associated from the first with Hermione. Her earliest appearance is deliberately surrounded with religious associations and intimations of value. Polixenes addresses her during their opening exchange as 'most *sacred* lady', and backs the apostrophe with a further reference to 'your *precious* self'. Value and spiritual perfection are, indeed, closely associated in the queen's reply 'Grace to boot!' while the lines that follow, a comment on Polixenes' description of the childhood friendship that bound him to Leontes, set in their proper context of accepted constancy the ambivalent possibilities of passion:

> Of this make no conclusion, lest you say
> The queen and I are devils: yet go on;
> The offences we have made you do we'll answer,
> If you first sinn'd with us, and that with us
> You did continue fault, and that you slipp'd not
> With any but with us.

In fidelity to the family bond, indeed, lies the key to full, harmonious development of the spiritual faculties of the individual, and of that fidelity the 'gracious' queenliness of Hermione is the proper object. Before long, she is taking up once more, and more explicitly, the idea of 'grace':

> My last good deed was to entreat his stay:
> What was my first? it has an elder sister,
> Or I mistake you; O, would her name were Grace!

And when Leontes responds with his intense evocation of his courtship, already touched with a barely-defined sense of foreboding in 'crabbed' and 'sour', her comment is direct and decisive, ' 'Tis Grace, indeed!' In this unequivocal assertion of spiritual values, set against the disease and disintegration caused by her husband's suspicions, lies the key to Hermione's significance in the play.

I (b)

The full value of this assertion, however, is not apparent until it has been worked out, dramatically, speaking, in terms of Hermione's relationship to Leontes and to her child. This is the function of the following scene (ii. i), in which her husband's jealousy, brought into more direct contact with its object, stands revealed as much more than criminal short-sightedness. It is, indeed, a sensual repulsion of the uncontrolled 'blood' against a right sexual relationship, against natural fertility consecrated, given its proper spiritual context, in the bond of marriage. In his insults, Leontes stresses brutally the fact that his wife is with child:

> let her sport herself
> With that she's big with; for 'tis Polixenes
> Has made her swell thus.

His words re-echo, in the form of perverted brutality, the conversation between Hermione's ladies at the beginning of the scene, words which give a rich and natural quality to her state:

> I LADY: The queen your mother rounds apace: we shall
> Present our services to a fine new prince
> One of these days . . .
> 2 LADY: She is spread of late
> Into a goodly bulk: good time encounter her!

> (ii. i.)

The 'rounding' of the queen is here envisaged as part of a natural, beneficent process, 'goodly' and destined, in 'good time', to find its proper fulfilment in maternity. The unsoftened harshness of Leontes' use of 'big' and 'swell', with their implication of the grotesque and the deformed, appear, in the light of this contrast, as a deliberate inversion of nature which will produce its own fruit in the disruption of normal human relationships.

That disruption, indeed, follows logically from the nature of Leontes' sin, already indicated and now bearing fruit in action. His is more than a personal offence: it is against 'nature', and so against the 'grace' for which Hermione in her simplicity stands. The perverted keenness of his senses, at once sharpened and debased by the action of 'blood', have become a spiritual infection, like that which faced the Doctor in *Macbeth* when he said of his patient, 'More needs she the divine than the physician'. It is the essence of Leontes' tragedy that, having raised (by the process described in the previous scene) an irrational, and indeed unnatural impulse to the status of certain knowledge, he makes it the foundation of his whole being. Regarding his suspicion, with unconscious irony, as 'just censure' and a 'true opinion', he follows Othello in craving for 'lesser knowledge' and in regarding himself as less 'blest' than 'accursed' by what he believes he knows.[1] His knowledge, indeed, as it emerges through the powerful expression of his disillusionment, is 'infected'. It leads to abhorrence, to a sense of nausea which characterizes the whole of his utterance:

> There may be in the cup
> A spider steep'd, and one may drink, depart,
> And yet partake no venom; for his knowledge
> Is not infected: but if one present
> The abhorr'd ingredient to his eye, make known
> How he hath drunk, he cracks his gorge, his sides,
> With violent hefts. I have drunk, and seen the spider.
>
> (II. i.)

Like Othello, again, he rests the entire foundation of his

---

1. Compare Othello's despairing outburst to Iago:
> I had been happy if the general camp,
> Pioners and all, had tasted her sweet body,
> So I had nothing known. (III. iii.)

being upon the assertion of his error, in words which clearly imply the universal implications of his disorder:

> . . . if I mistake
> In those foundations which I build upon,
> The centre is not big enough to bear
> A school-boy's top.

The whole of Leontes' subsequent progress, from this moment to that in which he finally awakens to his folly, is contained in this image. Upon the central point of his illusory certainty his mind revolves in an ever-increasing rhythm of lunacy to the final collapse.

Hermione's reaction to the series of outrages to which she is exposed is, by contrast, simple, clear, and firmly-founded. In her suffering, the sense of spiritual acceptance is deliberately stressed—

> this action I now go on
> Is for my better grace—

and the note of purification formerly associated with Lear's sufferings is repeated with a more explicit sense of religious values. Unlike Lear, of course, Hermione does not develop, grow in moral insight; it is her function, not to be actively involved in a dramatic development, but to stand firm as a point of reference, a symbol of perfection achieved. The simplicity of her outlook, her confident anticipation of the moment when Leontes shall come to 'clearer knowledge', as distinct from the illusory, 'blood'-impelled 'certainty' which now drives him on in a frenzy of destructive action, contrasts not only with the reactions of her jealous husband, but even with that of those who surround him and are convinced of her innocence. Antigonus, for example, is driven by his indignation to repudiate Leontes' behaviour in terms that are themselves affected by a peculiar strain of bestiality, of excess:

> If it prove
> She's otherwise, I'll keep my stables where

I lodge my wife . . .
I have three daughters; the eldest is eleven;
The second and the third, nine, and some five;
If this prove true, they'll pay for't: by mine honour,
I'll geld them all; fourteen they shall not see,
To bring false generations: they are co-heirs:
And I had rather glib myself than they
Should not produce fair issue.   (II. i.)

This type of excess in imagery is familiar enough in some
kinds of Elizabethan writing.   The quality of the verse,
unusually flat and poorly realized for this play, should not
blind us, however, to the fact that Antigonus' reaction is
linked to the main conception.   The desire for 'fair issue' in
itself suggests this; and it is reasonable to derive from the
speech that Shakespeare is using this type of sensationalism
to extend the disorder produced by Leontes' conviction to a
wider sphere of infection.   From it, Hermione alone is
entirely free; and it is as 'the grain' of 'honesty' which
'sweetens' by its presence 'the dungy earth' (the image
recalls *Antony and Cleopatra*, not for the first time, and links
'grace' with a suggestion of natural, earthly fertility) that
she goes to prison, deprived of her son and awaiting the final
resolution.

The following scene (II. ii), introducing Paulina to
Hermione in prison, adds relatively little to the deeper meanings of the play.   Hermione herself continues to be presented
as a person naturally and spontaneously good, and her goodness is contrasted with the sombre nature of her surroundings; as the Gaoler puts it—

No court in Europe is too good for thee;
What does thou then in prison?

Paulina's passport to these surroundings is, in her own words,
her faith in Hermione's 'honesty and honour', a faith shared
by many of Leontes' courtiers but not to the point of
declaring it in the face of the royal power.   The most impor-

tant feature of the scene, however, is not this presentation of virtue but the birth, in prison and at the moment of her lowest fortunes, of Hermione's child. To the Gaoler who receives her, Paulina first puts the question, 'How fares our *gracious* lady?' thus contributing in passing to the atmosphere of 'grace' which we have learnt by now to associate with the queen. The reply is, of course, that Hermione has been delivered of 'a goodly babe', 'lusty and like to live', a baby born, indeed, in prison, but representing, as it were, the continuation of her mother's innocence. This babe Paulina undertakes to present to its father, in the hope that—

> The silence often of pure innocence
> Persuades when speaking fails;

a hope naïve indeed at this stage, in which the processes of passionate jealousy, only recently unloosed, have still to work out their full consequences in action, but one which will eventually be justified in terms of the complete design. Even now the comment of the lady-in-waiting, Emilia, brings innocence and natural fertility together. The 'honour' and 'goodness' of Paulina is such, she affirms, that her 'free undertaking' cannot miss a 'thriving issue'; and though her project will not, at this stage, lead to the success anticipated, the scene ends with Paulina replying to the Gaoler's misgivings with a statement that already points to the function of this child in the symbolic structure of the plot:

> You need not fear it, sir;
> This child was prisoner to the womb, and is
> By law and process of great nature thence
> Freed and enfranchised; not a party to
> The anger of the king, nor guilty of,
> If any be, the trespass of the queen.

Beneath the legal terminology in which this argument is stated, lies the first direct enunciation of one of the main themes of *The Winter's Tale*: the function of new-born innocence as a healing power in redressing the excesses that spring from the distortion of sexual feeling. Hermione's child is, like her mother, a 'prisoner', but only to 'the womb'. She is therefore essentially *free*, delivered by 'great nature' from whatever stain of original imperfection may have lurked in the passions of her parents, from which—real or imagined—she is entirely separated. Upon this conception, the whole of Perdita's reconciliatory function in the play is eventually based.

The meeting between Leontes and Paulina, who bears Hermione's child in her arms, follows immediately (ii. iii) upon this preparatory scene. It represents the next stage in Leontes' descending course. The scene opens with his assertion of his lack of rest, a lack which he shares with other great Shakespearean figures—and more especially Macbeth —who have proceeded against the use of nature. Like them, too, he is deluded enough to see in his sleeplessness no more than 'mere weakness', and to believe that surrender to the further action prompted by his jealousy can bring him the certainty, the sense of having carried out his just projects, which he lacks:

> . . . say that she were gone,
> Given to the fire, a moiety of my rest
> Might come to me again.

From this delusion he passes on, not without meaning, to a further source of unrest: the sickness of his son Mamillius. This sickness, however, Leontes characteristically misinterprets to fit in with his own obsession, seeing in it a sign of his son's instinctive 'nobleness', shocked by the 'dishonour' of his mother into a process which can only have death as its end:

> Conceiving the dishonour of his mother,
> He straight declined, droop'd, took it deeply,
> Fasten'd and fix'd the shame on't in himself,
> Threw off his spirit, his appetite, his sleep,
> And downright languish'd. (ii. iii.)

In point of fact, of course, the languishi.
above all an external manifestation of the ˅
his parents, of which death is, in terms ɔ
action, a logical conclusion; but of that dɛ
Hermione but Leontes in his folly that is the ɔ

The true sources of Leontes' feeling, in whɪ
unloosed finds expression in a mutually exacerbatiɪ
of frustration and sadism, emerges in his own biɪ
clusion:

> Camillo and Polixenes
> Laugh at me, make their pastime at my sorrow:
> They should not laugh if I could reach them, nor
> Shall she within my power.

The tendency to feel himself ridiculed, to regard his self-esteem as subject to affront, has been from the first a moving factor in Leontes' passion-driven behaviour. It expresses itself now in a baffled reaching out after his late friend and former counsellor, an impulse which, when frustrated by circumstances beyond his power to change, turns for compensation to the idea that Hermione is still available, still within his power. Leontes' motives at this stage combine something very similar to the jealousy of Othello with the fallacious search for peace undertaken by Macbeth. [1]

At this crucial moment, with Leontes half-aware of the baselessness of his proceedings but determined to cover his uneasiness with further passion-impelled action, Paulina makes her entry with the child. Her appearance is in itself a challenge to his whole state of mind, and not less so the fact that the infant she bears in her arms contrasts, in its new-born life and health, with the ominous decline of his son. Paulina's first words, addressed to the Lord who tries to refuse her entry, is in effect a denunciation of those who are

---

1. It is worth mentioning, perhaps, that the impotence felt by Leontes can be paralleled, to some degree, by Lear's:

> I will do such things,—
> What they are yet I know not, but they shall be
> The terrors of the earth. (ii. iv.)

issuaded from what they know to be the proper obligations of allegiance by the 'tyrannous passion' of their master; she follows this up with a defiant reference to Hermione as 'a gracious innocent soul', thus combining the idea of innocence with the central conception of 'grace' and stating the foundations of her own determination. She next proceeds, when informed of Leontes' lack of sleep, to touch on one of the most persistent Shakespearean symbols, that which sees rest as the cure for a divided soul, giving it a spiritual significance far beyond its plain physical effectiveness. 'I come to bring him sleep', she says, and proceeds to connect his lack of rest with the subservience of those around him, who 'creep like shadows by him', sighing 'at each his needless heavings', and thus contribute to his ignorance of his true state. She, by contrast, takes her stand upon the connection between true allegiance and a proper independence of judgement. By contrast with the flatterers who surround the monarch, she, both through her own words founded on the honest perception of true values, and through the burden she bears in her arms, has come to exercise a genuinely 'medicinal' function,

> to purge him of that humour
> That presses him from sleep.

It is scarcely necessary to point out that both the underlying conception at this point and the manner of its expression are very close to that of similar passages in *Macbeth*.

The following dialogue between Paulina and Leontes adds little to what is already clear. Leontes is, at bottom, frightened of Paulina, unwilling to let the light of common-sense play upon the dark corners of his intricate conscience. He calls her 'audacious lady', and charges Antigonus with her removal; she describes herself, in reply, as his 'loyal servant' —for loyalty to the royal authority is normally a proper part of virtue—his 'counsellor'—but, be it noted, 'obedient' in her discharge of this function—and, carrying on a line of thought anticipated above, the 'physician' of his spiritual ills. Having said so much, she proceeds to the heart of her mission, which consists in laying before him the daughter of his 'good queen' and in requesting his paternal blessing. The refusal of Leontes to respond to this appeal, added to the aggravated savagery which leads him to denounce his own child as 'bastard', thereby committing the supreme offence against his paternity and the unity of the family, at once thrusts aside the only possibility of reconciliation and intensifies the process of subjection to suffering with which the following action will be increasingly concerned. By the end of the scene, Leontes, having dismissed Paulina from his presence, has condemned his own new-born daughter to be exposed to the desert in exile from his dominions. The action, which represents in appearance the decisive victory of passion over normal human relationships, will none the less be seen to contain within itself the seeds of the final reconciliation.

The next scene (III. i), though apparently a mere decorative aside from the main development, is in fact an essential part of it. One of the clearest signs that Shakespeare, in *The Winter's Tale*, has passed beyond the period of experiment with his symbolic themes, is the greater organic unity he has succeeded in imposing upon the various stages of his plot. *Pericles*, as we have seen, seems to represent the grafting of Shakespearean material upon a story relatively crude in its conception. Although there are moments when it is difficult to separate the original matter, with its clear symbolic references, from the full development of the central theme, the general effect is clearly one of superimposition, of methods and a content barely fused into a single unity. In *Cymbeline*, too, a gap can be sensed between the sentimental conventionality of much of the main plot, and the highly individual poetic quality sometimes conferred upon it. In *The Winter's Tale*, the situation is different. That this is so is indicated by the fact that tragedy and reconciliation, death and rebirth do not merely exist side by side, forming an uneasy unity of sequence, but are closely bound together in a single process. That is why now, at the very moment when the consequences of Leontes' passionate impulses are becoming apparent, between his rejection of his child and the parody of judgement which, in his egoism, he is shortly to inflict upon his wife, the action shifts for a moment to an entirely different plane, indicates in passing the positive spiritual forces which are already, at this apparently unpropitious moment, in charge of the action. Such is the meaning of the dialogue, now interpolated, between Cleomenes and Dion on their return to Sicily with the god's vindication of Hermione's innocence. Placed at this particular moment, before the full tragedy has been unfolded, the peculiar quality of 'freshness' which invests Cleomenes' account of Delphos is doubly significant:

> The climate's delicate, the air most sweet,
> Fertile the isle, the temple much surpassing
> The common praise it bears. (III. i.)

We are immediately reminded of Banquo's description of Macbeth's castle,[1] which is similarly placed to point a contrast with the growing darkness of the surrounding action. There too the air was 'delicate', and the impression of holiness associated with the king's arrival—like that of Hermione, in whom, as we have suggested, the idea of the family receives its consecration in 'grace'—was reflected in images of fertility and the nimble sweetness of the senses. This is poetry, indeed, in which the delicacy of exquisite sensual refinement appears as the tangible manifestation of a hallowed state. Associated in Dion's reply with the 'celestial habits' and 'reverence' of the priests, and the spiritual quality, 'ceremonious, solemn, and unearthly', of the offering of the sacrifice, it becomes the prelude to a return journey which is 'rare, pleasant, speedy', filled to the brim with a pervading impression of the supernatural (an impression, however, which is itself conveyed through the continuous, intense operation of the senses), and leads finally to a taking-

1. Act I, Scene v

up of the keyword of the play in the final prayer *'gracious
be the issue'*.

The trial scene which follows (III. ii) is, as far as Leontes
himself is concerned, the turning-point in the whole action.
Leading him first to the depth of degradation, through the
public manifestation of his surrender to 'blood'-impelled
jealousy, it brings him finally to an understanding of his
error, and so to repentance and the establishment of at least
the preliminary conditions of reconciliation. From the very
first, indeed, Leontes' state of mind is more complex than
may appear in a cursory reading. If it is true that he is
proceeding to arraign Hermione in order that his own
action may find the public justification for which it craves—
for he himself announces that it is his purpose to be

clear'd
Of being tyrannous—

the depth of his sorrow is indicated in the keenly-sensed
phrase 'pushes 'gainst our heart', which at least suggests the
spirit later given full expression in his contrition. Leontes,
indeed, is already a man divided against himself. The
absolute self-centredness which he has shown from his first
appearance, and which suits the essentially unrealistic
nature of the whole development, justifying it in terms of
motive without overstepping into the field of realism, has
been the chief cause of his enslavement to his passions; but
the very manner of his proceeding shows that it is linked
in his mind with a doubt which he is anxious to exclude,
but which his very grief will eventually cause to develop.
The two sides of the character, mutually exclusive in the
long run, are balanced throughout this episode, and the
final revelation of the truth will bring about the destruction
of the original, precarious confidence which made their
union possible.

The exchange, which follows, between Leontes and
Hermione is clear enough. Her reply to his indictment sets
her 'integrity' squarely against the perversion which, being

131

itself false, will account her actions 'falsehood', and anticipates the finding of the oracle in so far as it expresses an
unequivocal consciousness of spiritual purpose:

> if powers divine,
> Behold our human actions, *as they do*,
> I doubt not then but innocence shall make
> False accusation blush, and tyranny
> Tremble at patience.   (III. ii.)

The assertion of the reality of supernatural purpose, common
to this play and to *The Tempest* (where it is carried further
to become the centre of the dramatic conception), needs to
be taken at its true value. It has, of course, to be completed,
saved from abstraction, by constant relation to an experience
assimilated and harmonized in poetic terms; but the poetry
itself, and the wealth of sensation which it expresses, calls
for the objective counterpart of belief as a necessary condition of its unification into an intelligible pattern. The
conflict between 'tyranny' and 'patience', between Leontes'
passion and Hermione's consciousness of 'grace', is, on any
reading, and filled out as it is by a universal interpretation
of experience, a main theme of the play. Having affirmed
her position, and defended her attitude to Polixenes as one
which it would have been both 'disobedience and ingrati-
tude' to swerve from, Hermione admits to Leontes that her
life is in his hands—

> My life stands in the level of your dreams—

and announces her readiness to lay it down. Before doing
so, however, and in defence of the honour she prizes more
than her life, she appeals to the sentence of the oracle.

The sentence, when uttered, naturally confirms Hermione
in her position. Leontes, for a moment, sweeps it aside as
'falsehood', but the answer to his rashness is brought to him
in a moment in the form of news that Mamillius is dead;
and, faced by this overwhelming blow, he utters his broken
confession of guilt:

Apollo's angry; and the heavens themselves
Do strike at my injustice.   (III. ii.)

This, like the rest of the scene, in which Paulina brings news
of Hermione's supposed 'death', is scarcely convincing in
any realistic sense.   In this play, however, the movement
of the fable, the relationship of its various stages in the
unfolding of an organic whole, has a value of its own, not
to be measured in terms of external credibility; it is as the
framework of a balanced conception, to which subsistent
life is given by the operation of the poetic intensities, that
we are to see it.   Judged in this way, the words just quoted
represent the birth of Leontes' repentance, stressed in the
interchange between Paulina and himself, at the same time
as it heaps upon his head the consequences of his folly.
Because of Leontes' sin against 'nature', and so against
'grace', Hermione has suffered and apparently died, the
natural relationship which bound him to Polixenes has been
rudely broken, the young prince Mamillius has died out of
the course of nature, and the winter of the god's displeasure
has rested on them all.   With the withdrawal and supposed
death of the queen, followed by Leontes' final gesture of
broken acceptance—

> Come and lead me
> To these sorrows—

the first stage of the play's development is complete.   The
rest is to show how 'grace' can be born out of the jarrings
and maladjustments produced by the unchecked operation
of 'blood', and the spring of right human relationship out
of the winter of disorder and penance.

II

The scene which follows (III. iii), though relatively short
and perhaps easily overlooked, is in fact the turning-point of
the whole play, of which it constitutes what we have agreed
to call the second 'movement'.   Centred on the symbolic

function of Perdita, it links the past and future action, looking back to the folly of Leontes at the same time as it anticipates the final resolution. The opening exchange between Antigonus and the Mariner serves, of course, to indicate the continuity between this new development and the events we have just witnessed. The disturbed skies and the angry seas which have so impressed the speakers bear a symbolic interpretation typical of the last plays. They carry on the impression of the divine displeasure which has so recently been visited on Leontes ('The heavens with what we have in hand are angry', as the Mariner puts it), and provide at the same time a background to the central content of the episode. The main speech of Antigonus, on the other hand, though it stresses once more in his account of his dream the note of holiness which has always been associated with Hermione—he saw her, he says, 'in pure white robes, like very sanctity'—is disappointingly slack in its impact; it is hard not to feel, in reading it, that the verse has about it a certain carelessness and lack of conviction, as though Shakespeare had been content for a moment to develop his plot, and even its 'symbolic' implications, without the degree of emotional assimilation required to give them full unity and power. It is one of the relatively rare occasions in *The Winter's Tale* where the poetic impulse seems to lag behind the external contrivance of the story.

The entry of the Shepherd and the Clown, however, brings us to the essential content of the scene. The first words of the Shepherd refer once more to the theme of developing maturity which plays so important a part in *The Winter's Tale*. 'I would there were no age between ten and three-and-twenty, or that youth would sleep out the rest: for there is nothing in the between but getting wenches with child, wronging the ancientry, stealing, fighting.' This reference to the interval of disturbed 'blood' between the innocence of youth (already evoked, it will be remembered, in Polixenes' early exchange with Hermione) and the fully controlled development of maturity, which it is the play's

purpose to re-create in the course of its complete 'symbolic'
integration, falls naturally into place at this stage in the
development of the fable. It is followed at once by a further
extension of content. With this indication of the maturing
function of 'blood'—here caught, as it were, in the intermediate condition of growth which finds its counterpart in
the state of the external action—is associated a contrast
between pastoral simplicity and the complexity of court life;
this contrast, in turn, is to become a secondary but persistent theme in the latter part of the play. The Shepherd,
whilst describing himself as 'not bookish', goes on to remark:
'I can read waiting-gentlewoman in the scape'. The whole
comment implies a criticism of the uncontrolled passions
concealed beneath the surface pretensions of court society,
at the same time as it gives due weight to the natural
impulses from which these passions derive. This it does by
balancing the note of stealth, of illicit secrecy, implied in
'stair-work', 'trunk-work', and 'behind-door-work' against
another, indicating the full, spontaneous state of living
health, reflected in the phrase 'they were warmer that got
this than the poor thing is here'. It would be wrong to
restrict the implications of 'warmer' here exclusively to the
protected, comfortable state of the child's supposed parents;
that sense, and the suggested contrast with poverty,
exposure to 'nature', certainly exists, but so does that of the
warmth of begetting as itself properly and normally human.
The operations of passion, in short, which Polixenes had
associated with evil ('the doctrine of ill-doing') and the
blighting of an innocence nostalgically, impossibly desired,
are here acquiring a warmth, a sense of life which contrasts
with the cold, exposed situation to which the new-born
Perdita has been submitted by her father's aberration.
All this, however, destined though it is to be taken up,
developed and integrated into the growing symbolic structure of *The Winter's Tale*, is secondary in importance to
the prose-dialogue which follows. Here, if anywhere, is the
point of balance upon which the whole action turns. The

singularly beautiful prose in which the storm and ship-wreck are evoked is of a kind that can be paralleled both in *Pericles* and in *The Tempest;* the parallels, indeed, and the author's evident desire to perfect this kind of description are proofs, if further evidence were needed, of the continuity of symbolic purpose behind these plays. The splendid power of the evocative imagery in this case—of which such a phrase as 'the ship boring the moon with her main-mast' is an indication—serves to create a background for the central remark of the whole scene: the Shepherd's simple, pregnant observation—'thou mettest with things dying, I with things new-born'. This scarcely needs the parallel from *Pericles*—

> . . . did you not name a tempest,
> A birth, and death? (v. iii)—

to give it point. The implication of the two phrases is indeed the same. Out of storm and tempest, themselves connected in the symbolic scheme with the results of human folly, is born a new life, which is destined to grow in the course of time into the harmony of 'grace' and to lead to final reconciliation. From this moment, Hermione's child is connected with the general theme of 'grace' and fertility born out of passion and jealousy. The child is the product of that mingling of 'bloods' which, misinterpreted in the light of his obsession, so repelled Leontes and jarred upon his peace; but it is also the outcome of that natural human fertility which is the soil of 'grace' itself, so that it looks not only back to the divisions of the past, but forward to the reconciliation of the future. The filling-out of this central intuition in terms of a rich particularity of experience is, indeed, the achievement of *The Winter's Tale.*

III (a)

The next decisive extension of the play's conception, which takes place in the great pastoral scene (IV. iv), is preceded by the successive taking up of a number of threads which contribute in different measure to the complete effect and indeed add something to its scope and inclusiveness. The first of these is the intervention of the Chorus (IV. i) which, from its suitable position at this, the point of balance of the plot, stresses the importance of the action of time. This, in so far as the temporal process contributes to the main plan, is worth noting; so too is the reference, made as it were in passing, to Perdita's growth in 'grace'. The following exchange between Polixenes and Camillo is mainly concerned with keeping the plot in motion, though it also contributes, in the form of passing phrases, to laying the principal themes before us. The dialogue, indeed, is couched in terms of age, sickness, and penitence, terms which suit the state of the speakers and correspond to their position, at this moment, in the general scheme. For Polixenes, it is a 'sickness' to deny anything to Camillo, and 'death' to part from him: whilst Camillo, in his reply, expresses himself as anxious to return to his country, not only to die ('to lay my bones there'), but also to 'allay' the sorrows of his 'penitent master'. In both of them, the state of winter, expressed through a combination of age and exile, predominates, although the connection with Leontes' penitence already looks forward to the future.

The last-mentioned idea, indeed, is also in the mind of Polixenes, and already associated with the idea of reconciliation; though his thoughts at this stage still turn mainly on the 'loss' of his former friend's 'most precious queen and children' rather than on the mutual estrangement of the kings themselves. He does, however, refer in a spirit akin to remorse ('Sicilia . . . whose very naming *punishes* me') to his own share in the events which brought that estrangement about. In the latter part of the scene, Polixenes' concern over the behaviour of his own son is itself seen in relation to the conception held by him of the royal dignity: 'Kings are no less unhappy, their issue not being gracious, than they are in losing them when they have approved their virtues'. The idea of 'grace' is here connected with the reference, a little below, to the 'princely exercises' which Florizel appears to be neglecting; it is part of the play's intention to stress that the reconciling love of the two royal children is a *princely* love, and that the virtues which they are called upon to embody in their situation are an essential part, properly understood, of the life of 'grace'. This will be further developed in the handling of the courtly theme, in its relation to pastoral convention, in the scene towards which all this part of the play is deliberately leading.

It is similarly as an anticipation of the pastoral episode that we are, in the main, to understand the introduction into the action of Autolycus, which immediately follows (IV. iii). Autolycus, indeed, has a part of his own to play in the complete conception. His comic function is that of one who is regarded as a little apart from the main structure, whose behaviour is in some sense irreducible to the social values of the play, calculated to throw upon the symbolic symmetry itself a touch of relativity, a sense of the incalculable individuality of the processes of life. Yet, although he is not identified, or indeed identifiable, with any neatly rounded scheme, there exists a relation between Autolycus and the complete conception; his vivacious spontaneity has something to contribute to the life-blood of the action, to the vitality without which it would be no more than an abstract play of empty symbols. This is indicated clearly in the song with which he makes his entry. If *The Winter's Tale* is built upon a pattern which reflects the movement of the seasons, from winter through the rebirth of spring to the full consummation of summer, it is clearly fitting at this point, as an introduction to the following Whitsun pastoral, that this song should indicate the restoration to life of the processes of nature after the prolonged recess of winter. Autolycus' song represents 'the sweet', the tender, reborn heart of the year; its concern is with the daffodil new-flowering and the impulse of the 'blood' that sets the 'pugging tooth' on edge, that finds its human counterpart, intensely alive and impatient of all social restraint, in the meeting with 'the doxy over the dale' and in 'tumbling in the hay'. In Autolycus the sense of freedom takes the form of an abandonment of all normal social forms and restraints, the positively valuable and the merely conventional alike. He tells us that he once served Prince Florizel but is now 'out of service'; his relation to the social world is in one sense that of an outcast, threatened with the terrors of 'beating and hanging', but in another that of a free man exercising a vitality which rests on the action of 'blood' and needs itself to be considered in relation to the complete experience offered by the play.

The key to Autolycus, and to his peculiar position in the action, can, indeed, be defined in the phrase from his own song that 'the red blood reigns in the winter's pale'. The reference to winter implies at once a contrast and a point of reference. It connects the episode now before us with the play's title, and establishes a relationship between the birth of spring in the heart of winter and the affirmation of the warm, living 'blood' of youth against the jealousy and care-laden envy of age, an affirmation shortly to be confirmed in the contrast between the young lovers and their elders. In Autolycus himself, of course, this outpouring of spontaneous life moves on the margin of social forms. It has indeed a predatory aspect comically expressed in his first action, the picking of the Clown's pocket; but this itself is, to some degree, a devaluation of his victim's new-found riches and the social pretensions which these have aroused in him. It represents, in any case, an element which will have in due course to be related, as far as may be, to the growing harmony. For the new and natural life expressed in the resurrection of spring is to be, once assumed into fully 'gracious' forms of living, a prelude to the final reconciliation; and the main significance of the pastoral which follows, thus stated in the form of an introductory theme, lies in its relation to the birth of spring out of winter, and life—even in the form of wayward, anarchic impulse—on the margin of social forms and conventions.

Thus introduced by this varied and tentative enunciation of its main themes, it is not difficult to see that the great pastoral scene (IV. iv) which constitutes the third 'movement' of *The Winter's Tale*, far from being simply, almost naïvely contrasted to the preceding bitterness, is an artistically logical development of the situation. The opening exchange between Florizel and Perdita, indeed, balances the sense of delicate, poetic beauty against a richer, more complex content. The theme of spring, of life reborn but not yet come to full maturity, is stressed from the first; it is explicit in Florizel's apostrophe to Perdita as—

> no shepherdess, but Flora
> Peering in April's front.

If this stood alone, the pastoral, decorative element might still be held to prevail, producing an effect of delicate make-believe which could then be regarded as implicit in the following comparison of the sheep-shearing to 'a meeting of the petty gods' of which Perdita, dressed out in the naïve finery her father has produced for her, would be no more than the 'queen'. Perdita's replies, however, both here and in the following dialogue, indicate that the true situation is more intricate. Behind the pastoral idyll lies the real world, with differences of social station of which she is throughout entirely conscious. Florizel's poetic expressions she sees as 'extremes', beneath which lie the fact that he has obscured his 'high self' as 'the gracious mark o' the land' at the same time as she, in her lowliness, has been 'prank'd up', raised to the imitation indeed of a goddess but in no sense endowed with any corresponding reality.

The introduction by Perdita of the vital conception of 'grace', now clearly associated with rank and courtliness, reminds us that it is no part of the purpose of the play to set up pastoral simplicity as a final, self-sufficient ideal. It is at best a condition associated with spring, an intermediate state which has much to offer to the courtly order, but which will need before the play is completed to be assimilated into that order if the effect to be achieved is to be something more than a pathetic illusion. Neither of the lovers, indeed, is destined to find fulfilment within the pastoral order. Meanwhile, the sense of happiness which Florizel finds in his love is from the first precarious, its validity doubtful in a way which anticipates the future development. When he blesses the accident which has brought him into contact with Perdita she, far from responding directly with emotions of the same kind, can only pray 'Now Jove afford you cause!' and add, in explanation of her misgivings:

> To me the difference forges dread; your greatness
> Hath not been used to fear.

In this exchange, as elsewhere, it is the stranger to pastoral life, the courtier and son of Polixenes, who expresses a naïve, romantic idealism, who is prepared to read into his passion a permanence which, although finally justified, is at least premature; whereas Perdita, supposedly a shepherd girl whose experience of the world is apparently limited by her status, is consistently realistic in her attitude. From Polixenes' point of view, as she knows, her external dignities as queen of the feast are no more than 'borrow'd flaunts', her attraction for Florizel no more than a sign that 'his work, so noble' has been in her 'vilely bound up'. The judgement so stated is not to be ignored; if, by the end of the action, it will have become irrelevant, it will yet be strong enough, during the course of this scene, to prevent the consummation of a union which would, in this context, still be premature.

A further indication of the presence of complexities that surpass mere idyllic feeling emerges from a careful reading of Florizel's effort to allay Perdita's misgivings.

> Apprehend
> Nothing but jollity,

he says, and goes on to argue that—

> The gods themselves,
> Humbling their deities to love, have taken
> The shapes of beasts upon them: Jupiter
> Became a bull, and bellow'd; the green Neptune
> A ram, and bleated; and the fire-robed god,
> Golden Apollo, a poor humble swain,
> As I seem now.

This cataloguing of divine misdeeds, based on Ovidian commonplaces familiar to the Elizabethan mind, reads oddly indeed in contrast to the effect of pastoral simplicity also indicated in the speech. The conception of love to which the gods humbled themselves, losing their divine nature to assume that of beasts, is neither simple nor idyllic; the passage stands for the introduction of 'blood' as an element in the poetic structure, associated indeed with the reborn greenness of spring—'*green* Neptune'—and even, by indirect implication, with the fire of Whitsun in the reference to Apollo, 'the *fire-robed* god', but also with the 'shapes of beasts' through which they achieved their purposes. At the end of the speech the rarity of Perdita's beauty is linked, in the speaker's mind, with the chastity of her love in a way that is far from simple or merely decorative: so much so, indeed, that the gods, originally quoted to justify Florizel's own behaviour, are implicitly rebuked for the inferior purity of their motives:

> Their transformations
> Were never for a piece of beauty rarer,
> Nor in a way so chaste, since my desires
> Run not before mine honour, nor my lusts
> Burn hotter than my faith. (IV. iv.)

It is natural to read this as an effort towards clarification, in which 'desires' are balanced against 'honour', and 'lusts'— strangely chosen word, one would have said, to use in a context of purely decorative pastoral—'burn', indeed, in accordance with their natural condition, but less hotly than the 'faith' which will eventually lead to their transformation.

In the light of this new indication of conflicting readings of the implications of 'blood', Perdita's characteristically realistic comment—'Your resolution cannot hold'—and her sense of the irresistible 'power of the king' lead her logically to conclude that the kind of relationship imagined by Florizel is not, and cannot in the nature of things be, final; either he will have to bow to the will of Polixenes, thus breaking their union in order to return to the social world, or she will have to change her own state, thus raising their relationship to a level not definable in strictly pastoral terms:

> One of these two must be necessities,
> Which then will speak, that you must change this purpose,
> Or I my life.

To Florizel, still unaware of the true complexities into which he is entering, these forebodings are no more than 'forced thoughts', and he begs her accordingly to

> Strangle such thoughts as these with anything
> That you behold the while.

In support of this advice, he asserts his own constancy in the face of destiny, announces—

> I'll be thine, my fair,
> Or not my father's,

and affirms, more profoundly,

> I cannot be
> Mine own, nor anything to any, if
> I am not thine.

The last statement is emphatically true, and upon this truth their union will in due course be built and exercise its healing function; but before this can take place, it will have to be related to depths of experience of which the speaker, at least, is still unaware. When this has been achieved, and the pressure of external events already foreseen by Perdita has taken its course, the time will be ripe for a 'nuptial' of which this pastoral scene is no more than an anticipation.

The following episode, after Perdita has taken upon herself 'the hostess-ship o' the day' is, in turn, a great deal more than the beautiful piece of decoration which we might be inclined to see in it. The distribution of the flowers to the assembled guests has, indeed, an essential place in the development of the symbolic motives of the play; the fact that these motives are superbly realized in poetry adds to the force of their impact, but in no way changes their true nature. To her two elderly guests, Polixenes and Camillo, Perdita gives 'rosemary and rue', both flowers, as Polixenes himself points out, 'of winter', and therefore at once recalling the tragedy through which this pair has already passed and anticipating the part they (or at least the king) are shortly to play in breaking up the spring-like mood of consecrated love; but, as she is careful to point out, these are also flowers associated with 'remembrance', and therefore ultimately with the penitence—the choice of 'rue' is, in this respect, significant—which will in due course be a prelude to the restoration of 'grace'. It is this suggestion of a possible redeeming quality that gives force to Perdita's observation that these are flowers which keep—

Seeming and savour all the winter long,

implying thus the presence of the sap of life beneath the apparent death of the season.

This, however, is no more than a prelude to the main part of the flower-episode, which takes up and develops themes already foreshadowed in Polixenes' earlier account of his youthful friendship with Leontes. Its purpose, in fact, is to give the particular situation there outlined a setting in the universal processes of nature, and the pastoral convention is never used to more subtle effect than in Perdita's reply to Polixenes—

> Sir, the year growing ancient,
> Not yet on summer's death, nor on the birth
> Of trembling winter, the fairest flowers o' the season
> Are our carnations and streak'd gillyvors,
> Which some call nature's bastards: of that kind
> Our rustic garden's barren; and I care not
> To get slips of them. (IV. iv.)

A reader aware of the possibilities of Shakespearean language will not pass by as mere poetic decoration the beautiful linking of summer and winter, birth and death, into continuity. 'Death' is joined to summer, and 'birth' and 'trembling' are given to winter, so as to suggest that the passage of the seasons is only part of one inseparable process; and, since we know already that the relations of birth and death are central to the play, we now realize that the various developments of *The Winter's Tale* are, like the cycle of the year, a necessary and connected whole. The contrast of the two seasons has, moreover, a further meaning. Summer is coupled with the flowering of youth into the love of Florizel and Perdita, whilst 'winter' reminds us that the age of their parents, just recalled by Perdita through her gift of flowers, will before the end of this same scene once more affect their children's relationship. It is, indeed, a winter of lust and egotism, a winter which implies the vanity and barrenness of jealous, impotent age, in contrast to the summer of youth in which it fails to see its own natural, normal fulfilment by succession. The coming brutality of Polixenes in separating the lovers is an exact complement to Leontes' earlier sin; it proceeds from the same impotence of aged blood, as we are shown by the continual emphasis upon age and bitterness. By the time Camillo has brought his two masters together, both will have had cause to regret the importunities of passion. At present, however, the play has only reached a stage midway between the winter of disordered passion and the full summer of 'grace'. Perdita, in the second part of her speech, goes on to make this clear. Between the terminal seasons, so to call them, of winter and summer, unregenerate 'nature' and the fullness of 'grace', there are flowers which have a certain beauty of their own, but a beauty imperfect and, as it were, alloyed, like that of human passion unconsummated by 'grace'. These flowers are '*carn*ations' (the root has a clear connection with the flesh) and 'streak'd gillyvors', 'bastards' between crude nature and the realm of 'grace'.

It is important to catch these associations; but more striking still is the discussion with Polixenes which arises from Perdita's attitude to the flowers she herself has mentioned. To her refusal to 'get slips of them', Polixenes replies by asking her to explain the motive which has led her to reject them, and receives an answer which is in effect a statement of Perdita's position in the play as Hermione's daughter, and so as a manifestation of the pure, undiluted essence of 'grace':

> I have heard it said
> There is an art which in their piedness shares
> With great creating nature.

For Perdita, in her simple integrity, 'piedness', the creation of 'art', or artifice, is contrary to the creative simplicity of 'nature'; the ambiguous and the artificial are rejected by her, in flowers as in human beings, and her conception of life is one which admits of no possible addition to, or 'sharing' with, natural perfection. This is, however, one conception of 'nature', and Polixenes greatly extends the scope of the discussion when he points out that the 'streak'd' process is after all engrained in nature herself; in the same way, the action of 'blood', though capable of producing—as it has produced in the earlier scenes—the disruption of harmony and natural relationship, is essential to a full growth into maturity:

> Say there be;
> Yet nature is made better by no mean,
> But nature makes that mean: so, over that art

146

Which you say adds to nature, is an art
That nature makes. You see, sweet maid, we marry
A gentler scion to the wildest stock,
And make conceive a bark of baser kind
By bud of nobler race: this is an art
Which doth mend nature, change it rather, but
The art itself is nature. (IV. iv.)

The expression of this argument is worth the most careful attention, because it brings us very close to the central meanings of the play. To Perdita's conception of 'art' as an addition to 'nature', and therefore, from the standpoint of her absolute simplicity, as a deformation of it, Polixenes opposes another of 'art' as completing 'nature', based on it, indeed, but as its crown and perfection. The conception is clearly one which is capable of expression in human and social terms, and Polixenes, in what follows, proceeds to make this relation explicit. After describing Perdita as 'sweet maid'—the reference to virginity is capable, for all its beauty, of indicating an incompleteness which will shortly be taken up more openly—he goes on to discuss the process of grafting in terms of marriage, the union, in this case, of 'the wildest stock' (in other words, 'nature', or, in human terms, 'blood', unregenerate humanity) to 'a gentler scion', the product of civilized urbanity, of 'nature' in its complete, fulfilled sense, which is 'grace'. In this sense, the process of grafting, far from being, as Perdita fears, a perversion of natural virtue, is itself natural, merely the unfolding in man of the full possibilities of 'nature', which require a civilized soil and a spiritual end for their complete flowering. The 'bark of *baser* kind'—the adjective is now clearly indicative of the lack of the civilized graces—is made to 'conceive' by 'a bud of *nobler* race': the idea of birth following on marriage thus acquires a new and wider meaning, becomes a completion, itself natural, of 'nature', an assumption by normal humanity of the crowning qualities, social and spiritual, of 'grace'.

Perdita's reply, however, shows that the achievement of this union is still premature. To Polixenes' attempt, on the strength of this argument, to dissuade her from excluding these flowers, she turns away with an extreme repulsion which is most significant:

> I'll not put
> The dibble in earth to set one slip of them;
> No more than were I painted I would wish
> This youth should say 'twere well, and only therefore
> Desire to breed by me.

The introduction of the familiar Elizabethan horror of being 'painted', together with the force of 'breed', which once more stresses the relevance of consummation in marriage, shatters pretty thoroughly any suggestion that this scene is exclusively concerned with the maintenance of a state of idyllic make-believe. Clearly, the innocent poetry so far given to Florizel and Perdita—itself, as we have seen, full of half-suspected undercurrents—is no sufficient resolution of the great disunities developed in the early part of the play, and the brief moment of pastoral felicity is, in fact, shortly to be broken by the open intervention of Polixenes. Only when the action has been decisively raised from the pastoral level will a final integration become conceivable.

The further list of flowers now presented by Perdita to Polixenes indeed confirms this. It indicates at once her sense of the connection that she feels to exist between his person and the operations of 'blood', and her repudiation of the latter. '*Hot* lavender', by the significant choice of adjective, stresses the importunity of passion, and the marigold,

> that goes to bed wi' the sun
> And with him rises, weeping,

indicates the disillusion that follows on the self-sufficient pursuit of desire. Perdita, in short, is at once repudiating excess, which her innocence rightly finds incompatible with the development of the 'gracious' life, and showing that this same innocence is still unprepared to come to terms with certain necessary aspects of mature experience. Her youth rejects an attitude that is essentially that of 'men of middle age', and indeed her own marriage will eventually and naturally be with youth, from which the stresses and egoisms present in Polixenes will be excluded; but it also, at this stage, suggests an exclusion of passion, 'blood', which is itself incompatible with maturity.

The impression conveyed in this exchange is confirmed by the presence of a certain pathetic weakness, a kind of wilting from life, in the great list of flowers presented to Florizel which immediately follows. The emphasis on 'virgin branches' and 'maidenheads' is full of meaning in the light of the intense reaction against passion which preceded it; still more so is the contrast with 'hot lavender', already referred to, and the other flowers given to men of middle age. Above all, there is the feeling behind such lines as—

> . . . pale primroses,
> That die unmarried, ere they can behold
> Bright Phoebus in his strength, a malady
> Most incident to maids.

The beauty of these lines is devoid of strength, even clings pathetically to its own lack of vigour. The final reconciliation will be far less precarious. The spring-like beauty of this episode will have to be intensified by being joined, in due course, to the deep note of penitence in Leontes. Only thus can the idyllic pastoral be given sufficient substance to balance the harshness of the early scenes; and only so can a feeling for innocent beauty be raised to the level of Shakespeare's unique sensation of the fertility and maturity of 'grace'.

Meanwhile the vitality which, in spite of what we have said about her flower speech, underlies Perdita's love for Florizel is indicated by the reference to the royal flowers— 'bold oxlips' and 'the crown imperial'—with which she

rounds off her apostrophe, and by the intense feeling for life
which emerges from her final turning to her lover:

PERDITA: O, these I lack,
            To make you garlands of; and my sweet friend,
            To strew him o'er and o'er.
FLORIZEL: What, like a corse?
PERDITA: No, like a bank for love to lie and play on;
            Not like a corse; or if, not to be buried,
            But quick and in mine arms.

The previous references to 'maladies' and unconsummated
fading find their natural climax in Florizel's pathetically
romantic evocation of the idea of death; but equally natural,
equally a part of the beautifully balanced effect, is the
spontaneous warmth of Perdita's reply. The consummation
of their mutual love is *not* to lie in death, but in a reaction
towards life. Florizel is not to be 'buried' by the flowers
which she will bestow on him, but these are to be a sign of
the vitality which is to deliver him 'quick' into her arms.
The powerful strength of Perdita's youthful emotion has
already, at this moment, laid the foundations for the final
consummation, and the reference, which follows, to 'Whitsun
pastorals' is far more than a piece of decorative folk-lore.
It introduces, deliberately and at this most fitting moment,
the theme of the Holy Spirit to stress the note of 'grace'
(for Whitsun is, in the Christian cycle which conditions,
however indirectly, the deeper purposes of *The Winter's
Tale*, the feast of the descent of the Holy Spirit, harbinger
of grace) as a crown to that of spring and love with which
this scene is concerned.

These utterances of Perdita are balanced, immediately
below, by the quality of Florizel's reply, which can be said
to gather up in a most immediate form the basic sensation
of the play:

                What you do
Still betters what is done. When you speak, sweet,

I'ld have you do it ever: when you sing,
I'ld have you buy and sell so, so give alms.
Pray so; and for the ordering your affairs,
To sing them too: when you do dance, I wish you
A wave o' the sea, that you might ever do
Nothing but that; move still, still so,
And own no other function; each your doing,
So singular in each particular,
Crowns what you are doing in the present deeds,
That all your acts are queens.   (IV. iv.)

The most striking quality of this passage is the sensation it
conveys of balance, of a continual relationship between
motion and stillness. The verse is carefully constructed to
reproduce this sensation, this balance, in terms of the rise
and fall of the speaking voice. Consider the effect of the
double 'so' in the fourth line, the first bringing the movement of the speech to its height and the second deliberately
leading from that height, whilst a third 'so' in the next line
binds the central idea to those which follow; a little further
on, there is still another 'so', again associated with two
balanced phrases, bringing out still further the relationship
of motion to stillness, the unity of experience to the inces-
sant flow of its material. The same effect is obtained by the
choice of echoing sounds in 'singular' and 'particular'. Still
more important is the final association of *present* deeds'
with *all* your acts'; every act of Perdita's involves all her
perfections and is a complete expression of her natural
queenliness. And this, in turn, connects her with the central
image of the whole speech—that of the wave which is
always in motion, and yet is ever the same. This image,
like the speech of which it forms a part, is, of course, much
more than a beautiful piece of decorative poetry. It is
rather the particular expression of a vital theme of the play,
and indeed of all Shakespeare's mature plays—the relation
between the values of human life which postulate timelessness, and the impersonal 'devouring' action of time which

wears these values ceaselessly away. The wave image conveys perfectly the necessary relation between the mutability of life and the infinite value of human experience which it conditions, but which is finally incommensurate with it. When this intuition, and that of Perdita in the expression of her love, has been gathered up into the wider symbolic framework of penitence and reconciliation the full scope of *The Winter's Tale* will be finally clear.

The following exchanges, leading up to the pastoral dance, have their own significance in relation to what has gone before. Perdita replies to Florizel's celebration of her perfections by contrasting them with the empty conventions and flattery that are characteristic of court life, as seen from the standpoint of the simplicities of the pastoral state; were it not clear to her that her 'Doricles' is an *'unstain'd* shepherd' (the adjective, with its suggestion of a contrasted corruption is emphatic enough to stand out against the appearance of conventionality), she would have good reason to fear that he wooed her 'the false way'. The fact, of course, that Florizel is indeed a false shepherd, that he proceeds from the court life of which Perdita is so critical, lends force to this observation. Florizel replies with an assertion of their mutual sincerity that finds its outward symbol, pastoral-wise, in the dance—

> . . . so turtles pair,
> That never mean to part—

and in Perdita's forthright confirmation of this symbol of plighted faith: 'I'll swear for 'em'. Beneath the conventional surface of this exchange, and of the comments with which it is surrounded, the imagery continues to indicate motives of deeper complexity. The presence of 'blood', of the force of physical passion, is conveyed, with varying degrees of directness, in Perdita's reference to the 'true blood' which 'peeps fairly' through Florizel's youth, and in Camillo's observation to Polixenes:

He tells her something
That makes her blood look out.

The implications of 'blood', beyond the obvious indication
of the blush of modesty, need careful consideration here.
On the one hand, as we have suggested, it evokes the physical
basis of emotion that underlies the surface of pastoral
simplicity; on the other, it indicates the theme of genuine
nobility, at once distinct from court corruption and its
'stain' and from the artificial simplicity of 'curds and cream'.
The true nobility of the lovers pierces through their
pastoral disguise, is expressed in the lasting and serious
quality of their mutual devotion, in the light of which
Perdita's perfections acquire a significance greater than her
apparent status:

> . . . nothing she does or seems
> But smacks of something greater than herself,
> Too noble for this place,

and by comparison with which Florizel's royal origins are
merely of secondary importance. The pattern woven out
of the various connotations of 'blood', its expression of
natural simplicity, its consummation in passionate dedication, and its relation to the two worlds, aristocratic and
pastoral, which meet at the sheep-shearing, is an essential
part of the full meaning of this scene.

With the exchange between Florizel and Perdita thus
complete, the rest of this episode is concerned with the
introduction of themes previously touched on but still
capable of development. The dance of shepherds and shepherdesses, indeed, is followed by an exchange which reminds
us of the presence, masked and rather ominously apart, of
Polixenes and Camillo, who will shortly break with disruptive effect into the action. For the moment, Polixenes
merely approaches the Shepherd, to obtain from him an
account of his own son. He receives, in reply to his question,
an affirmation of Florizel's truthfulness ('He looks like

sooth'), which cuts across his own resentful opinion, and a further contribution to the poetic evocation of his love for Perdita:

> He says he loves my daughter:
> I think so too; for never gazed the moon
> Upon the water, as he'll stand and read
> As 'twere my daughter's eyes; and, to be plain,
> I think there is not half a kiss to choose
> Who loves another best.

This kind of imagery is clearly a suitable continuation of the 'wave'-image recently evoked by Florizel; it carries on the same impression of a competition between equals, a passion that calls forth its like in the object of its contemplation. Polixenes' further comment 'She dances featly' prompts the Shepherd to reply 'So does she anything', which is even more directly an echo of Florizel's recent apostrophe; whilst his obscure sense that Polixenes' disguised son is more than he appears, has 'a worthy feeding', is balanced by the conviction that Perdita's own virtues are correspondingly beyond those that could be expected of her supposed pastoral condition:

> if young Doricles
> Do light upon her, she shall bring him that
> Which he not dreams of.

The purpose of this short interlude, scarcely more than glanced at in a brief exchange between persons unaware of their true situation in respect of one another, is partly to carry on the spirit of the preceding declarations of love and partly to stress the enormity of Polixenes' behaviour in breaking up this singularly beautiful and promising relationship. The break-up, when it comes, will be a necessary part of the complete development with which the play is concerned. It is none the less monstrous, an aberration from right human feeling which bears upon it the mark of tragedy.

III (b)

The break-up, however, is not immediately brought to a head. The development of the action towards it, which from now on takes precedence over the expression and analysis of youthful love, is interrupted by the entry, first of the Servant and then of Autolycus with his ballads, which break the growing tension and add to the spirit of pastoral innocence a note of wayward humanity which will also have to be related eventually to the complete pattern. It cannot be said that this entry, and the comic-pastoral exchanges to which it leads, immediately extend the scope of the conception. At best, they balance the rarified idealism with which we have been so far concerned with a more human note, and in particular with a more direct evocation of the flesh. Such remarks as that of Autolycus describing one of his ballads 'against the hard hearts of maids':—

. . . it was thought she was a woman, and was turned into a cold fish for she would not exchange flesh with one that loved her—

remind us in spirit of certain exchanges in *The Tempest* between Stephano and Trinculo. Neither are, in themselves, of the first order, but both represent a feeling characteristic of Shakespeare at this late stage in his dramatic career. We might call it, perhaps, the desire to balance so much spiritual symbolism, so much intensity of poetic refinement, with a broader human quality. The 'flesh' still has its claims in this remote world of pastoral and youthful nostalgia: claims perhaps not felt with sufficient intensity to be placed in the foreground, or to be developed with full conviction, but necessary to the complete effect. In any case, since the essence of Autolycus lies, as we have said, in his waywardness, it seems only logical that his utterances should not, especially at this stage when the development of the play's pattern as a whole is manifestly incomplete, be susceptible of full integration. Stephano and Trinculo will be, in turn, left by Prospero on the island which he himself abandons to return to the fullness of civilized life; it is part of the conception of Autolycus that he too should be independent, free in his mixture of calculation and impulse, from the imposition of clear symbolic significance.

The episode has, meanwhile, served to give the scene as a whole a decisive new twist, which confirms the fact that it is rounded off by a dance of 'twelve satyrs'. Since the previous dance, at the end of the exchange between Perdita and her lover, was one of 'shepherds and shepherdesses', this implies that the spirit of the action is about to undergo an important change. That change is heralded by the return to the main development of Polixenes as an active figure. 'Is it not too far gone? 'Tis time to part them': the aside to Camillo is nothing less than a sign that the pastoral idyll is to be interrupted, that Perdita's previous references to 'winter' were more than poetic decoration, that human passion in its less attractive form is to make its bitter entry as a determining feature of the action. The full disclosure is finally brought about by Florizel's declaration of his love, which is first given universal value by the speaker calling as witnesses to it, not merely Polixenes and Camillo, but—

> more
> Than he, and men, the earth, the heavens, and all,

and then deliberately raised to a level of absolute dedication:

> . . . were I crown'd the most imperial monarch,
> Thereof most worthy, were I the fairest youth
> That ever made eye swerve, had force and knowledge
> More than was ever man's, I would not prize them
> Without her love; for her employ them all;
> Commend them and condemn them to her service
> Or to their own perdition.

With Perdita's straightforward but all-embracing confirmation—

156

By the pattern of mine own thoughts I cut out
The purity of his,

the way is finally open for the two lovers to take hands and
prepare to plight their troth before Perdita's 'father' and
with the two unknown strangers to witness.

At this moment Polixenes finally intervenes. In consider-
ing the meaning of his intervention, we need to bear certain
distinctions clearly in mind. His first question to Florizel,
'Have you a father?' and its sequel, 'Knows he of this?' is
in itself entirely reasonable, fits in completely with the
spirit of the play. Paternity, in Shakespeare's last plays, is
the keystone of the family pattern, and no marriage can be
held complete which does not request, and receive, the
father's blessing. When Florizel replies emphatically, 'He
neither does nor shall', he is in fact expressing readiness to
accept a relationship essentially incomplete, and so incapable
of achieving full consummation. The spirit in which
Polixenes develops his protest, however, places the situation
in a new light. That a father—

Is at the nuptial of his son a guest
That best becomes the table.

is beyond question; but the peculiar bitterness with which
this father stresses his anger, his sense of exclusion, introduces a new element into the situation:

Is not your father grown incapable
Of reasonable affairs? is he not stupid
With age and altering rheums? can he speak? hear?
Know man from man? dispute his own estate?
Lies he not bed-rid? and again does nothing
But what he did being childish?

We need not go so far as to suppose that, in thus invoking
in ironic terms a hypothetical old age, Polixenes is describing
his own state. Indeed, Florizel's reply, his affirmation of his
father's 'health and ampler strength', indicates that this is

not so; but the peculiar intensity of his utterance suggests at least that the shadow of age is present in his mind, that it is in a mood of tragic bitterness not unmixed with resentment against the active spontaneity of youth that he now discloses himself. If Florizel is wrong in refusing his father's plea, which the Shepherd—incidentally—backs, it is hard not to feel that Polixenes, in the spirit suggested by his reference to the father—

> all whose joy is nothing else
> But fair posterity,

is clinging in effect to the nearest available experience that recalls his own lost youth.

If this reading should not strike us, by itself, as being inevitable, the following imposition of 'divorce' upon the lovers is conclusive. The argument that repudiates the wedding of 'a sceptre's heir' to a 'sheep-hook' is less respectable, given the point of view of pastoral convention, than that based on the natural rights of paternity; though not without force to an Elizabethan mind, it has already, in effect, been destroyed in this particular instance by Perdita's clear-sighted affirmation of the rights of herself and her lover. And when Polixenes turns on the Shepherd, who so recently backed him in his appeal to his son, and condemns him to be hanged, it is clear that he has fallen into a course of passionate error scarcely less disastrous, in its way, than that which has already destroyed Leontes' peace. The two cases are, indeed, parallel. Polixenes' intervention brings into the pastoral action the winter of lust and sin, a condition which springs from the vanity and barrenness of jealous, impotent age, in contrast to the summer of youth. His brutality in separating the lovers, and more especially his ferocious attack upon Perdita's beauty (the spirit of bitter repudiation behind 'hoop his body' indicates clearly the source of his indignation, and explains the singularly gratuitous cruelty of 'I'll have thy beauty scratched with briars'), form an exact complement to Leontes' earlier behaviour; they proceed from the same impotence of aged blood, as we are shown by the continual emphasis, already considered, upon age and bitterness. By the time Camillo has brought his two masters together, *both* will have had cause to regret, in different ways, the importunities of the 'blood'. Meanwhile, the shattering of the pastoral idyll could hardly be more thoroughly accomplished.

Already, however, and during the course of the same scene, the foundations of recovery are being laid. This is first implied in the firmness of Perdita, her declared fearlessness and her blunt assertion of an equality that the claims of false dignity cannot affect:

> I was about to speak and tell him plainly,
> The self-same sun that shines upon his court
> Hides not his visage from our cottage, but
> Looks on alike.

In itself, of course, this assertion of the equality of 'court' and 'cottage' is a commonplace of pastoral, the expression of a convention rather than the reflection of any deep reality. In Perdita, however, it is distinguished by being consistent with everything else in her character. From the first, she has asserted her love for Florizel with forthright simplicity; her values, founded on this feeling for her lover, are simply, unshakeably consistent, and the contrast between her integrity and the false conceptions of a society which has divorced place from personal worth is essential to the complete conception. Having awoken from her 'dream', and honestly admitted her grief, she is ready to return to her former life, without either vain illusion or regrets that are ultimately self-deceiving:

> I told you what would come of this: beseech you,
> Of your own state take care: this dream of mine,—
> Being now awake, I'll queen it no inch further,
> But milk my ewes and weep.

Something deeper than mere pastoral convention speaks here. Perdita's words possess a human quality, a moral integrity, that raises them out of the category of commonplace and makes a positive contribution to the development of the complete symbolic pattern. To this attitude, the corresponding firmness of Florizel—

> I am but sorry, not afeard; delay'd,
> But nothing alter'd: what I was, I am—

is indeed a fitting response. His love for Perdita is a manifestation of natural attraction capable of being considered in terms more universal than itself:

> It cannot fail but by
> The violation of my faith; and then
> Let nature crush the sides o' the earth together
> And mar the seeds within!

The true love of youth, contrasted at this stage with the envious impotence of age, is connected with the normal processes of fertility: as such, its ultimate validity is assured.

It is natural, after this assertion of mutual integrity, that the concluding exchanges of the scene should set the action on the road to recovery. The first sign of this, in symbolic terms, is Florizel's determination to 'put to sea'; for no reading of Shakespeare's last plays can ignore the frequency with which those who have met misfortunes on land turn to the sea, and find safety after exposure to adventure. Perdita herself was formerly exposed to the perils of a storm which did not, however, finally destroy her; now Florizel, in his hour of trial, turns to the waters to seek compensation for what he appears to have lost on shore. His 'irremoveable' decision, in turn, affords an opportunity for Camillo to re-enter the action with a clear vision already in his mind of the full and final reconciliation for which he is working. Camillo now has no place in the tyrannous behaviour of Polixenes, just as, in the early action, he repudiated the excesses of Leontes; having thus shared, but without blame, the vicissitudes of both his royal masters, he is a fitting

instrument for the final harmony to which he already looks
forward. Beyond the saving from danger of Florizel, which
is his immediate aim, he sees the possibility of obtaining
once more the 'sight' of 'dear Sicilia'—

> And that unhappy king, my master, whom
> I so much thirst to see.

To Florizel, still affected by the blow he has so recently
suffered, Camillo's purpose seems 'almost a miracle'; the
phrase, indicating that there is about Camillo himself at this
stage 'something more than man', suggests the presence of
the divine working behind his project, a purpose of which
Camillo himself is from this time forth and in increasing
measure the instrument.

The development of the symbolic theme is clearly
expressed in the terms by which Camillo now urges upon
Florizel the necessity of flying to the court of Leontes. He
and Perdita are to arrive there as man and bride, for she is
to be 'habited'

> as it becomes
> The partner of your bed;

already, the idea of fulfilment in marriage is stressed, and
seen as prelude to a further line of development:

> Methinks I see
> Leontes opening his free arms and weeping
> His welcomes forth; asks thee the son forgiveness,
> As 'twere i' the father's person; kisses the hands
> Of your fresh princess; o'er and o'er divides him
> 'Twixt his unkindness and his kindness; the one
> He chides to hell and bids the other grow
> Faster than thought or time. (IV. iv.)

The expression here, fully in the late symbolic manner, is
worth consideration in certain detail. The gesture anticipated from Leontes is conveyed in terms of liberality, the
opening of his '*free* arms' to the refugees from the wrath of
Polixenes; but his welcome is also associated, in its emotional

fullness, with grief for his past acts, the 'weeping' prompted in him by a consideration of his own responsibility. This attitude in turn leads to an affirmation of the central symbolic situation, the conditions through which alone reconciliation is possible; the request for 'forgiveness' through the son for the wrong formerly inflicted on the father leads to an emotional revaluation of Perdita, Florizel's '*fresh* princess' (the adjective is full of the suggestion of life spontaneously reborn), herself the instrument of a reconciliation even deeper and more intimate than the speaker yet knows. Finally, the state of Leontes is envisaged by Camillo as one divided between memories of the past ('his unkindness') and present regeneration ('his kindness'); the one is confined to the 'hell' which we may associate with the depth of his past sufferings, and the other is ready to 'grow', to flower in the freshness of 'gracious' reconciliation.

To this assertion of reviving hope, Florizel replies, with an image characteristically drawn from natural processes, by his 'there is some sap in this'; against which again Camillo, in his following speech, sets the contrast between the reconciliation which he anticipates and the state of tragic exposure to circumstance which otherwise seems to emerge from Florizel's proposed flight. In the absence of the re-integration into the sacred unities of the family and of friendship which is now being planned, life can be no more than an exposure to suffering in which the most that can be achieved is not to drift into deeper misfortune—

> Nothing so certain as your anchors, who
> Do their best office, if they can but stay you
> Where you'll be loath to be—

and where even love appears, in the bitterness of mature experience, to be subject to degeneration:

> besides you know
> Prosperity's the very bond of love,
> Whose fresh complexion and whose heart together
> Affliction alters.

Such open statements of realistic pessimism as these remove the play decisively from the sphere of pastoral make-believe. Perdita, with her usual integrity, denies the full implications of Camillo's sober phrases, distinguishing between the force of outer circumstances, to which she gives full weight, and the changeless quality which she feels in her own emotion:

> One of these is true;
> I think affliction may subdue the cheek,
> But not take in the mind.

At this stage, most typically, neither statement is complete without the other. Camillo's experienced bitterness, born of his past connection with events which seem amply to confirm it, is balanced against the new, the *fresh* intuition (to echo the adjective recently applied to Perdita) in a way that cannot, at this stage, be finally resolved. It is, indeed, this resolution, in terms of the symbolic development of plot and image, that will be the central purpose of the final episodes of the play. Florizel's concluding apostrophe to Camillo—'Preserver of my father, now of me'—corresponds to the spirit of this purpose; it binds together the past action and the new indications of the present, giving each its due place in a single harmonious line of development.

The end of the pastoral scene, besides winding up the exchange between Camillo and Florizel, is mainly devoted to the independent vision of Autolycus and to his relations with the Shepherd and the Clown. The purpose, as we have suggested, is to introduce a note of relativity into the action, a sense that even the most serious of the novelties we have just witnessed are not to be regarded as final in their validity. The recent outburst of Polixenes, apparently so tragic in its consequences for the lovers, is reduced by Autolycus to the 'old man's . . . whoo-bub against his daughter and the king's son'; what seemed so recently a matter of vital consequence becomes from this new point of view a distraction which deflects the speaker from his main purpose, itself followed with a compelling vitality. Autolycus' joy in his 'art' is reflected in the exuberance of his 'no hearing, no feeling, but my sir's song and admiring the nothing of it': though, of course, the self-evaluation implied in 'the *nothing* of it' reduces even this airy manifestation of energy to its proper place. The spirit of Autolycus, though clearly not all, or even a principal element in the play, is a necessary background to the main theme. Evidently, it is not a true reflection of the spirit of *The Winter's Tale* that honesty is a 'fool' and 'Trust, his sworn brother, a very simple gentleman'; but the energy with which this point of view is stated, always within the limits of 'nothingness', lends a touch of relativity, of human irreducibility which is itself part of the complete effect.

The conversation between Autolycus and the Shepherds, which brings the scene to a close, is equally relevant in a similar, subsidiary sense. It is, primarily, yet another manifestation of his delight in the superiority of his natural endowments, and the spirit of it emerges already from his opening phrase:

> . . . to have an open ear, a quick eye, and a nimble hand, is necessary for a cut-purse; a good nose is requisite also, to smell out work for the other senses.

The limitations of this outlook, however, are not less evident than its qualities, for the speaker's conclusion that 'this is the time that the unjust man doth thrive' is clearly no part of the prevailing spirit of the play. Autolycus, in fact, moves throughout on the margin of the action. He is a reminder that the complexity of life is not readily to be reduced to any symbolic scheme, however generous and inclusive; and, in the process of exercising his function, he conveys a criticism of social forms and pretensions which has its place in Shakespeare's handling of the pastoral conventions. This criticism is conveyed, of course, in familiar terms by Autolycus' assumption of a courtly disguise ('receives not thy nose court-odour from me? reflect I not on thy baseness court-contempt?'), and—by implication—

in his offer to intervene before the king. To this the Shepherd and the Clown respond with a characteristic mixture of naïvety and their own reading, simply and undisguisedly cynical, of the way of the world. 'Though authority be a stubborn bear, yet he is oft led by the nose with gold': though this observation does not respond to the spirit of the 'gracious' conclusion to which the play is moving, it does in part corroborate Autolycus' own attitude, and needs therefore to be considered as one more device in a consistent attempt to give life to the pastoral convention, to make it acceptable as a reflection, symbolical indeed but none the less true to experience, of the variety of human motives and feelings.

IV (a)

The return to Leontes, which follows immediately on the conclusion of the pastoral scene, brings us to the last, the reconciliatory movement of the play. Leontes is introduced, through the words of Cleomenes, at the moment in which the 'saint-like sorrow' which has prevailed in him since the revelation of Hermione's innocence is ready to be crowned by reconciliation with the divine powers he has offended. The years which have passed since his last appearance, far from being an example of careless dramatic construction, correspond to a pause, a break necessary to the whole conception. They have been passed in a sorrow that is in no sense merely nostalgic, a despairing regret for the results of his folly. To Cleomenes, indeed, it appears as a prelude to sanctity. His faults have been 'redeem'd', his trespass balanced by a corresponding penitence, and the time has now come when he can be called upon, without undue levity, to 'forget' his past, to accept by reassuming his full royal functions the forgiveness which the 'heavens' are now ready to grant him. The steeping of the action in a supernatural atmosphere, although anticipated from the first, only now becomes fully explicit, emerges to play its part in the resolution of the action. It follows, not by chance, on the scene which introduced the fresh spirit of spring-like pastoral, temporarily broken by its lack of power to resist the bitter enmity of 'blood', but now ready to be reinforced by the deeper experience of the 'grace'-smitten Leontes.

Leontes, however, cannot immediately accept the invitation of his courtiers. The play at this point, as always, aims at a development, not a contrast; the past is not forgotten, but taken up, assumed into the present, transformed by a healing action of 'grace' which only the passage of time has brought to maturity. For Leontes, if not for those around him, the consequences of his sin are still alive, and their memory makes it impossible for him to act as a free man. His reply to Cleomenes, therefore, is a refusal, but one which, whilst affirming the continuous presence of the past, in fact transforms it, takes it up into his own deepened understanding:

> Whilst I remember
> Her and her virtues, I cannot forget
> My blemishes in them; and so still think of
> The wrong I did myself: which was so much,
> That heirless it hath made my kingdom; and
> Destroy'd the sweet'st companion that e'er man
> Bred his hopes out of. (v. i.)

The beautiful rhythmic movement of these lines, so characteristic of Shakespeare's late verse in its combination of freedom with a close subjection to the underlying development of meaning, is perfectly contrived to relate the situation of Leontes to the main symbolic threads of the play. They are broken, in fact, into two parts at the words 'the wrong I did myself'; what precedes leads up to this, the intimate recognition of a deep, self-inflicted wound, whilst what follows at once accepts the consequences of his own act and prepares the way for an extension beyond the merely personal and self-accusing, indicating the response of the speaker to a new stage in the unfolding of the temporal pattern. The temporal process, indeed, acquires in these perfectly constructed lines a deep moral value of its own. The memory ('I remember') of Hermione and her 'virtues' is still alive in Leontes, makes it impossible for him to over-look his own 'blemishes in them', which it would be both sinful and insensitive, even after sixteen years and in spite of the arguments of Cleomenes, to forget; but the same passage of time which has been powerless to efface the past has taught him that the 'wrong' which so lives in his mind has been done less to Hermione, whose gracious virtue has long since emerged unaffected from her trial, than to him-self. This change, not from remorse to forgetfulness, but from despair to a more inclusive moral perspective, prepares the way for the final reconciliation.

The development of the speech as a whole, indeed, con-firms this interpretation. Once more, the rhythmic con-struction is of vital importance. Within the main division already referred to, the verse is characterized by the barely perceptible pauses at the end of the freely flowing lines, pauses deliberately indicated by the necessities of speech and preparing the way, step by step, for the stressed enuncia-tion of its most important aspects. In the first part, as we have seen, the weight of memory in Leontes leads him to recall the perfections of Hermione and to weigh them against the magnitude of his faults. These have been so great ('so much': the poignancy of the apparently simple expression is stressed by its place at the end of a rhythmic unit) that, in the later lines, they are referred to as affecting not only his own happiness, but the whole of the society for whose health and proper functioning he is, as king, peculiarly responsible. They have left his kingdom 'heirless' and 'destroy'd' (once again the break after the inconclusive 'and' in the preceding line adds power to a word itself loaded with tragic meaning) the 'sweet'st companion'—

> that e'er man
> Bred his hopes out of.

The sharp bitterness of 'destroy'd' is balanced by the intense pathos of 'sweet'st' and leads up to the final evocation, in 'bred', of fertility as the tangible expression of the deepest 'hopes' of paternity. The speech, in fact, is calculated to bring out, and relate intimately, the two characteristics which at this moment predominate in Leontes, and which give new depth to the preliminary utterance of Cleomenes, which they extend without, however, contradicting. The first of these is his 'saint-like sorrow', a repentance for past sins kept alive in him by the unfailing memory of Hermione, and the second is his desire for an heir to be the fulfilment, as king and father alike, of which his sin has deprived him. It is here, however, that the past more especially lives on in the present as a limiting, restraining influence. A new son for Leontes can only be born from Hermione, whom he believes to be dead: can only therefore be the daughter whom, in his past folly, he condemned to die.

The exchange which follows between Leontes and his two contrasted advisers, Paulina and Dion, stresses the positions that are now awaiting resolution through the action of time. For Paulina, Hermione is unique, 'unparallel'd', and the fact that Leontes 'kill'd' her (the word strikes him with a bitterness from which he recoils, but which he recognizes as just) needs to be atoned for as an irreparable loss; for Dion, Leontes is king as well as husband and his duty to the state justifies a line of conduct which, as an individual, he would not necessarily be required to follow. His speech, indeed, set against Paulina's call to keep faith, has a meaning far beyond its value in developing the argument:

> What were more holy
> Than to rejoice the former queen is well?
> What holier than, for royalty's repair,
> For present comfort and for future good,
> To bless the bed of majesty again
> With a sweet fellow to't? (v. i.)

The desire for an heir which, considered by Leontes in

purely personal terms, prompted him to a keen sense of his loss, is now taken out of the purely individual sphere, acquires a fresh universality in relation to the traditional conception of royalty in its social function. Dion's words, moreover, add the essential note of sanctity ('holy . . . holier') to the emphasis on human fertility which preceded it, thus extending decisively the scope of an emotion which, on the purely personal plane, could hardly compensate the preceding tragedy. We now begin to see how the pattern of the play is to be completed. Penitence and devotion, kept alive in Leontes by his memory and by Paulina's stressing of his responsibility for his loss, can be raised to the level of sanctity, on a plane in which the personal and royal motives become one continuous reality, and the functions of 'blood', no longer the cause of jealousies and divisions which have exhausted their tragic consequences with the passage of time, are seen as a source of life to the unified and gracious personality.

The necessary prelude to reconciliation, meanwhile, is a further projection of the past into the present, a poignant deepening of Leontes' love for Hermione. This is apparent when he says of her:

I might have look'd upon my queen's full eyes;
Have taken treasure from her lips,

and when Paulina takes up and emphasizes the sensation of spiritual wealth in her reply—

And left them
More rich for what they yielded;

the lover's gift of himself in emotional fullness becomes, typically, a cause of deeper enrichment. Here, indeed, as in so many of the later plays, fullness and riches are typical attributes of the Shakespearean state of grace. Again, when Leontes abjures all other loves as he remembers the eyes of his former queen—

> Stars, stars,
> And all eyes else dead coals!—

the intensity of his emotion suggests how the typically Shakespearean sense of the constant pressure of 'devouring time' is in the process of being overcome. The answer, of course, is not that of the philosopher, but of the artist. It consists in opposing to the action of time, sensibly apprehended, the value of Leontes' experience, intensifying it as a sensation of boundless wealth, until time itself is felt to be only a necessary element in the creation of this rich intuition. Time, as at certain moments of *Antony and Cleopatra*, has become irrelevant; in *The Winter's Tale*, it has simply served to shape the fullness of grace. Only, whereas in *Antony* the achievement of transcendent, vital justification is purely personal, balanced against aspects of corruption and egoism which threaten it continually with collapse, Leontes' love for Hermione, here recalled, kept alive in a spirit of penitence and growing self-understanding, exists in a symbolic framework more ample than itself, which gives it meaning and universality of context. Hermione lives in Leontes' mind as a 'sainted spirit', and his state is still that of an 'offender', 'soul-vex'd', exposed to the alternatives personified in Paulina and Dion, awaiting a resolution which cannot be merely that suggested by personal feeling. When Leontes, in a spirit of religious dedication ('so be blest my spirit!'), accepts Paulina's request that he should not marry again without her consent, and when she deliberately makes him face the full implications of this—

> That
> Shall be when your first queen's again in breath;
> Never till then—

we realize that we are moving in a world essentially different from that of *Antony and Cleopatra*, less limited to the merely personal, more universal and symbolic in its implications. The restored fulfilment of Leontes' love is to take place against a background more ample than anything in that love itself. The past, far from being forgotten, will need to live again in the present as a formative influence, the feeling of the individual will find its proper context in the social obligations of the king, and both will be subject together to a common dedication to the ends of 'grace'. There could be no better indication of the essential novelty of Shakespeare's purpose in these, the last plays of his full maturity.

The situation of Leontes having been thus clarified, the action proceeds by stages to prepare the way for the final resolution. The first step is the entry of the Gentleman announcing the approach of Florizel with his 'princess'. His evocation of—

> . . . the most peerless piece of earth, I think,
> That e'er the sun shone bright on,

both contributes to the effect of 'value' which is essential to Perdita's symbolic function, and calls forth from Paulina, watchful as ever for the rights of Hermione, a reproof steeped in the sense of tragic mutability:

> O Hermione,
> As every present time doth boast itself
> Above a better gone, so must thy grave
> Give way to what's seen now!

The inexorable passage of time is here stated once more as a persistent background to the main action. Not finally valid, not even—we may say—at this stage a main theme of the play, it is none the less present as a persistent base, a reality which gives humanity and pathos to the symbolic situation and is clearly associated with Hermione's sixteen years' concealment, still to be revealed. The Gentleman's admission—'the one I have almost forgot'—points in the same direction. Hermione as a mere memory cannot live, affirm her being against fresh realities, except in the fixed, absolute devotion of Paulina, which itself imposes upon Leontes an abstraction from the current world that will be, in the long run, impossible to maintain; only her final 'resurrection', and the fact that her youthful perfection lives, spiritually and physically, in the person of her daughter, will make the final triumph over mutability possible. Meanwhile, the stress is already laid upon Perdita's perfection conceived in terms of a call to spiritual devotion:

> This is a creature,
> Would she begin a sect, might quench the zeal
> Of all professors else;

and we are told of her that—

> Women will love her, that she is a woman
> More worth than any man; men, that she is
> The rarest of all women.

'Worth', 'rarity'; these are words which exercise a familiar attraction in the last plays, from *Pericles* onward. They call forth from the regenerate Leontes a response of gracious tenderness which finds issue, even before he has seen Florizel and his companion, in a summons to his 'embracement'.

Before the actual entry of the newcomers, Paulina is given another opportunity, brief but intensely used, to relate the past to the present and to foreshadow their association in a spirit of all-embracing richness. In so doing, she brings the sorrowful past, still alive in her afflicted master, more closely into contact with the germinating growth of the future. Mamillius, 'jewel of children', would have been, had he lived, of the same age as the prince now about to enter. The fact, and the manner of stating it, at once associates the idea of treasure once more with that of youth, and comes home to Leontes with a pain not less intense for the temporal remoteness of its cause:

> Prithee, no more; cease; thou know'st
> He dies to me again when talk'd of.

Sorrow and reconciliation, life and death are being bound together, firmly and tenderly, in the expanding content of the play.

The actual entry of the fugitives brings us finally to the first great episode in the pattern of reconciliation which we are now engaged in tracing through its successive stages. Leontes' speech, welcoming them, is worthy, in its rich, symbolic beauty, of the occasion:

> Your mother was most true to wedlock, prince;
> For she did print your royal father off,
> Conceiving you: were I but twenty one,
> Your father's image is so hit in you,
> His very air, that I should call you brother,
> As I did him, and speak of something wildly
> By us perform'd before. Most dearly welcome!
> And your fair princess,—goddess!—O, alas!
> I lost a couple, that 'twixt heaven and earth
> Might thus have stood begetting wonder, as
> You, gracious couple, do! and then I lost,
> All mine own folly, the society,
> Amity, too, of your brave father, whom,
> Though bearing misery, I desire my life
> Once more to look on him. (v. i.)

The opening words, raising once more the theme of 'wedlock' and fidelity—and was not Leontes' sin against Hermione in the first place a revelation of the lack of such faith? —go on to stress the 'royalty' both of Polixenes and his son, thus reaffirming the special dignity which is part of the complete effect; the emphasis upon conception, birth, we have seen already to presage the growth of renewed life. The thought, however, raises in the speaker memories of his own past. Seeing before him the 'image' of Polixenes reflected in his son, he is reminded of the times when his former friend was his 'brother', joined to him by a union the youthful intimacy of which was broken through actions by themselves 'wildly . . . perform'd before'. Leontes' past

173

experience, in fact, though not forgotten, is falling, as it were, into perspective, completed by the present which is dominated by what is at once an image of the past repeating itself and a new birth.

In its double nature as reflection of the past revived and the present newly born, this vision of Florizel is as welcome to Leontes as the 'fair princess' whose true identity is still unknown to him, but whose perfect beauty, symbol of an inner state of perfection, leads him to address her as nothing less than 'goddess'. In the light of this vision of a new generation of lovers, Hermione and Perdita appear in turn as memories of superhuman rarity:

> I lost a couple, that 'twixt heaven and earth
> Might thus have stood begetting wonder, as
> You, gracious couple, do.

This imaginative transfiguration of humanity reminds us once more, in its intensity, of *Antony and Cleopatra*, though here—as we have suggested before—it stands no more as a mere expression of personal sentiment, subject to a process of change and disillusionment which its intensity can only in part, and precariously, ignore, but is rather incorporated into a symbolic vision that transcends the purely personal; the fact that the couple now before him are seen as 'gracious' reinforces the effect with the most inclusive conception of the whole play. Unlike Cleopatra, moreover, Leontes is not content to isolate himself from his own past. On the contrary, his sense of this harmonious, transcendent vision gains its force by being set against his memory of the passion-driven act that originally destroyed its forerunner. Against the rebirth still unachieved in his mind is set a sense of loss, proceeding from his own 'folly' and implying the breaking of the link, essentially *social* (the word 'society' is not used accidentally), of 'amity' that bound him to the father whose features are now so hauntingly repeated in his son. Thus poised between past and present, aware of age and anticipating a certain rebirth, Leontes' is the state of

one who, although 'bearing misery' in the shape of sorrow
for acts still felt to be beyond repair, desires life in so far as
it may bring him to reconciliation. To the spirit of this
speech, Florizel's reply, with its mention of an 'infirmity'
in Polixenes which is felt to be the natural consequence of
'worn times' and to correspond to Leontes' own age, is an
affirmation of continued relationship. The attitude of the
speaker's father to his former friend is still one of loving
devotion:

> . . . whom he loves,
> He bade me say so, more than all the sceptres
> And those that bear them living.

If the idea of royalty is an important element in the symbolic conception of *The Winter's Tale*, it is still secondary
to the depth of human feeling. It is, indeed, the latter,
incarnate in the figures of their respective children, that confers true poetic validity upon the final reconciliation.

To this expression of emotion, Leontes replies with a
spontaneous overflow of feeling. Polixenes is his 'brother',
related to him by a tie that is felt to be even stronger than
that of friendship, that implies a unity of blood; in a play
in which the most intimate relationships of the family play
so great a part, this insistence upon fraternity, repeated
from the speech previously quoted, is not an accident. The
traditional conception of brotherhood in royalty is bound,
in fact, to a deeper, more intimate relationship which is
close to the heart of the play. Prompted by this resurgence
of emotion, the memory of his past behaviour stirs anew in
Leontes, like the new birth which it indeed is—

> . . . the wrongs I have done thee stir
> Afresh within me—

and the salutations of Florizel, so '*rarely* kind' (the choice of
adverb again has something to contribute to the total
effect), prompts his 'behind-hand slackness' to a response.
This competition in generosity of emotion, feeling vieing

with feeling in an effect of cumulative harmony, recalls the
spirit of the exchanges between Duncan and the loyal
Banquo in the early scenes of *Macbeth*.[1] The response, in
turn, is associated with the rebirth of the seasons with which
so much in the spirit of the play has been conceived:

> Welcome hither,
> As is the spring to the earth.

The fresh kindling of positive emotion in Leontes is in this
way related to the natural movement of the seasons, and the
link that binds developed understanding to this renewed
access of feeling is further stressed just below in the reference
to the 'ungentle' storms and 'fearful usage' through which
Perdita, 'this paragon', has passed to make this moment
possible; to it corresponds properly the speaker's own admission that he is still, at least in his own eyes, 'a man not
worth her pains'.

The following exchange between Florizel and Leontes,
after a reference to the 'prosperous south-wind friendly'
which has brought the fugitives to Bohemia and which
contrasts, in its own passing fashion, with earlier references
to the elements in tempest, leads up to a direct expression
of welcome, in which once more the unmistakable note of
poetic symbolism is present:

> The blessed gods
> Purge all infection from our air whilst you
> Do climate here! You have a holy father,
> A graceful gentleman; against whose person,
> So sacred as it is, I have done sin:
> For which the heavens, taking angry note,

---

1. See *Macbeth*, I. iv:

> DUNCAN: I have begun to plant thee, and will labour
> To make thee full of growing. . . .
> BANQUO: There if I grow,
> The harvest, is your own.
> DUNCAN: My plentuous joys,
> Wanton in fullness, seek to hide themselves
> In drops of sorrow.

Have left me issueless; and your father's blest,
As he from heaven merits it, with you
Worthy his goodness. What might I have been,
Might I a son and daughter now have look'd on,
Such goodly things as you.   (v. i.)

Practically every expression in this speech can be paralleled
in Shakespeare's later writing, of which it is in some sense a
kind of condensed fulfilment. The reference to the 'blessed
gods', taking up the providential note that has been present
in the play at least since the intervention of the oracle,[1]
leads up to a prayer that the air may be 'purged' of 'all
infection' during the visitor's stay; we are reminded again
of the spirit of Banquo's description of Macbeth's castle at
Inverness,[2] and the unusual choice of the verb 'climate', for
'sojourn', weds the elements more closely to the spiritual
state that is being conveyed. The 'infection', of course, has
connections with the passion that destroyed Leontes' peace
at the outset; it recalls Polixenes' reference[3] to the 'infected
jelly' into which his 'best blood' should have been transformed, had Leontes' suspicion been true.   From this
opening welcome, it is natural for Leontes to look back from
Florizel before him to his father, the friend of his youth,
in whom he sees holiness and a suggestion of 'grace'—he
calls him 'holy' father and 'graceful gentleman'—combined;
and against the memory of this 'sacred' person there rises in
his mind the sense of the wrong inflicted upon him, now
given its full moral weight as an offence against the right
ordering of life, as 'sin'. The movement of the imagery,
first connecting pure 'air' with the action of the 'gods', and
then leading up through the idea of purification implied in
'purge all infection' to that of sin, which is moral disease
calling—as in the case of the Doctors in *Macbeth* and *Lear*
who ministered less to the ills of the flesh than to the infirmi-

---

1. Act III, Scene i.
2. *Macbeth*, Act I, Scene vi.
3. Act I, Scene ii.

ties of the spirit—for its appropriate purgation, is characteristic; so is the counter-process which links 'holy' and
'graceful', culminating in the direct assertion of the religious
value of just kingship:

> . . . against whose person,
> So *sacred* as it is, I have done sin.

The state of Leontes preparatory to the final reconciliation,
combining the memory of wrong inflicted in the past with
a present depth of penitence for the 'sin' the full enormity
of which he has now come to understand, receives here its
full expression.

The complete content of the speech, however, has still to
be completed in its later lines. The idea of sin leads naturally
to that of the divine displeasure which has lain so heavily
for sixteen years upon the speaker, and which has accompanied him from maturity to old age:

> For which the heavens, taking angry note,
> Have left me issueless.

The anger of the heavens, indeed, implies something more
than a mere figurative reference to the divine displeasure,
more closely knit into the play's symbolic structure and more
directly related to its human vicissitudes. It bears, in
'angry', a clear sense of threatening storm-clouds, and thus
connects the speech with the symbolic theme of tempest
through which, in all the late plays, sin has to be led,
through atonement in accepted suffering, to final reconciliation; the very rhythm of the lines is one which seems at this
time to have been significant to Shakespeare, who repeated
it, or something very similar, in the lines from Ariel's great
speech in *The Tempest*:

> . . . for which foul deed
> The powers, delaying, not forgetting, have
> Incensed the seas and shores, yea, all the creatures
> Against your peace.[1]

1. *The Tempest*, Act III, Scene iii. This passage is discussed on pp. 248–252.

'Sin' for 'foul deed', the 'heavens' for 'the powers', 'taking angry note' for 'delaying, not forgetting': the movement of the thought as conveyed by poetic rhythm deliberately devised to lay stress upon the presence of weighty and inevitable judgement is surely similar enough to point to a significant unity of conception, and the similarity is furthered by the fact that, as Leontes has been left 'issueless', so Alonso was 'bereft' of his son. To deprive the offender, at least in his own belief, of natural fulfilment in the shape of issue is, indeed, the normal reaction of the 'heavens' in these plays to sin, the unbridled action of passion breaking down the limits of sweet reason; and it is no accident that Leontes, thus left childless, as he still believes, through his own action, sees Florizel's father, his lost companion, as 'blest', in response to his merits, by the 'heavens' with an heir 'worthy his goodness'. The speech ends on a note of nostalgia for what the speaker has lost, in terms which themselves look forward to the final effect.

The moment of reconciliation, however, is not yet due for development. Progress towards it is interrupted, not for the first time, by an unwelcome entry; as always, the achievement of final unity has to be gained, not in passivity, but in a series of reactions, of which this is the last and the most inclusive, against the continued pressure of the forces making for disruption. A Lord enters with the news, well-nigh incredible to those addressed, that Polixenes is at hand in chase of his son, who has cast off his princely 'dignity' and filial 'duty' alike to attach himself to 'a shepherd's daughter'. The accusation, though not, of course, finally valid, needs, given the symbolic formulations on which the action rests, to be taken seriously enough to amount to a new turn in the development of the play. Once more, as formerly in the pastoral scene, the entry of Polixenes is associated with the bitterness of age and frustrated mortality; he is said to be threatening the shepherds with 'diverse deaths in death', and the re-entry of the tragic note is given universal meaning in the momentary bitterness of Perdita's phrase, 'the heaven sets spies upon us'. It seems, indeed, that the same heaven which Leontes has recently invoked as the key to loving reconciliation has now set itself against the celebration of her contract to Florizel. The changed position of Leontes, however, is the key to the next stage in the unfolding of the complete story. Accepting what is, indeed, an essential part of the play's conception, for which royalty is sacred and the bonds that bind child to father in duty necessary to lasting reconciliation, he expresses his sorrow that Florizel seems to have broken a relationship to which he was 'tied in duty', and that the object of his choice seems not to be so *rich* (the very choice of the word carries its own weight) in moral 'worth' and princely standing as in the beauty which she so undeniably possesses. Beauty, however, is by now an external attribute of merit, and Florizel is able to set against the thought of affliction a counter-assertion of the value of his love:

> Though Fortune, visible an enemy,
> Should chase us with my father, power no jot
> Has she to change our loves.

'Fortune', as always, is in herself blind, the enemy of personal bonds that reach out after timelessness; but the relationship itself which feels this enmity is already, in the last resort, beyond her power. In asserting this, Florizel appeals to Leontes' own memory of his lost youth—

> Remember since you owed no more to time
> Than I do now—

and the appeal, joined to the sight of a 'precious mistress' in whom Leontes, though still unaware of the truth, obscurely senses the continuation of his own youth, is strong enough to coincide with the understanding born of experience and moral maturity and leads him to take up the task of mediation. Paulina's protest that his eye, in admiring Perdita, 'hath too much youth in't', is countered by his assertion that, in praising her, it is of his lost wife that he is thinking—

> I thought of her,
> Even in these looks I made.

Florizel's 'desires' appear to him, in the light of this, as in no sense contrary to 'honour', and the friendship which binds him to father and son alike is such that he, who was formerly the cause of division and tragedy, can now become the instrument of restored harmony. With that end in mind, he proceeds to his meeting with Polixenes.

The following scene (v. ii) is one of those episodes, characteristic of Shakespeare's later manner, in which incidents apparently trivial, even seemingly marginal to the main story, are woven by the conscious elaboration of style into a developing symbolic fabric. Its grave and involved prose is seen, in fact, on closer reading, not to be mere decoration, but to belong to the spirit of the play, in forming which it plays its own distinctive part. It opens, of course, with the Gentleman's account of the finding, sixteen years ago, of the child Perdita, as related by the Shepherd; and the manner of the telling, far from being an excursion into literary artifice, is admirably calculated both to maintain the necessary 'legendary' quality of the episode, the sense of remoteness in time, and to further the symbolic unity of the whole conception. The Gentleman's first speech insists on the idea of finding ('the manner how he found it': 'I heard the shepherd say, he found the child'), and introduces the sense of 'amazedness', of having been present at the birth of high issues as yet most imperfectly understood; his second utterance introduces us fully into the emotional atmosphere of this finding, which is one of miracle and spiritual significance:

> . . . they seemed almost, with staring on one another, to tear the cases of their eyes; there was speech in their dumbness, language in their very gesture; they looked as they had heard of a world ransomed, or one destroy'd: a notable passion of wonder appeared in them; but the wisest beholder, that knew no more but seeing, could not

say if the importance were joy or sorrow; but in the extremity of the one, it must be. (v. ii.)

The resemblance of the phrase 'to tear the cases of their eyes' with certain repeated images from *King Lear*[1] is perhaps too tenuous to be insisted on, but it is just worth noting that the two aspects of sight, physical and spiritual, are closely related in that play, and that here too the Gentleman feels himself to be present at events whose meaning is more than material, events of whose significance he has barely more than a glimpse. The element of wonder, essential to the whole episode, is implicit in the speechlessness that itself, translated into gesture, became charged with half-revealed significance in the eyes of the bystander; those present at this finding, and in a position to appreciate its full meaning, were rapt into contemplation, stricken with a silence beyond the possibilities of speech. The basis of their wonder, fundamentally religious, is indicated in the following reference to 'a world *ransomed*', with its gravely Christian implications, and in the contrast implied by 'destroyed'; the 'passion of wonder' which overcame the central figures, as recorded by this minor observer, is allied to their sense of the spiritual qualities involved in this miraculous rebirth of a dead past. The likeness of joy to sorrow, especially evident here to those who have no key to the full meaning of the action to which they are witnesses, is, of course, familiar in Shakespeare's late plays; and so is the sense of the 'extremity' which must accompany either emotion, a feeling of being poised on the edge of an experience which may be related either in terms of life or death, but which is unquestionably near the limits of human understanding. The confirmation, brought by the second Gentleman, that 'the oracle is fulfilled', itself takes us back sixteen years and recalls the entry into the action of an explicitly religious sanction; the result now is a 'wonder' which, though not

1. Compare, for example, Gloucester's reply to Lear's command that he should 'read': 'What, with the case of eyes?' (*King Lear*, IV. vi).

incompatible with a certain gentle scepticism ('ballad-makers cannot be able to express it'), is a proper prelude to the final resolution.

The entry of the Third Gentleman, the first direct eye-witness of the scene, builds up still further the symbolic effect. The prose, at once carefully elaborated and finely evocative, is, once more, a factor of primary importance. Even such a phrase as 'if ever truth were pregnant by circumstance' has its further function in contributing to the general sense of fertility, of significant birth set in the process of time; and the terms of the description of the child which immediately follows are related less to anything immediately seen than to the communication of an underlying content:

> . . . the majesty of the creature in resemblance of the mother, the affection of nobleness which nature shows above her breeding, and many other evidences proclaim her with all certainty to be the king's daughter.

The 'majesty' of Perdita, conceived as a reflection of that of Hermione, is evidently related to one of the main concepts of the play. 'Nobleness', too, exercises a function in associating the civilized, courtly graces with the universal simplicities of life as their crown and goal. The 'nobleness' of Perdita is bestowed upon her by 'nature', and stands out in contrast to her supposed humble 'breeding'. One of the main results of the final integration will be to bridge the gap between pastoral simplicity and the civilized graces, bringing them together in a harmonious unity.

The description thus conveyed leads up to the meeting between the two kings, and with it to the healing of the first of the great breaches which the effects of passion had introduced into the early action. Once again, the words of the Gentleman are charged with symbolic undertones:

There might you have beheld one joy crown another,

183

. . . that it seemed sorrow wept to take leave of them, for their joy waded in tears.

Once more, the apparently contrary emotions of joy and sorrow have become fused, so that the one, far from undoing its opposite, reinforces it, becomes an element in its full expression. Each new joy is the 'crown' of its predecessor, so that emotion itself is related to the inclusive effect of 'majesty'; at the same time, this joy expresses itself in tears, in a sorrow which 'wept to take leave of them' in the moment of being replaced by the joy of new discovery. In Leontes, 'the joy of his found daughter' is balanced against the 'loss', still present in his memory, of her mother; and the happiness of his reunion with Polixenes expresses itself immediately, in the typical manner of these plays, in a request for 'forgiveness' in respect of his earlier sin. The wrapping of this description in carefully elaborated forms of expression, coupled with the stressing of its similarity to an old 'tale', contributes to removing the action from common modes of feeling, and thus to the creation of the necessary symbolic atmosphere.

The reconciliation having been thus described, the Gentleman proceeds to recall once more the tempest from which Perdita was saved by the shepherd; the 'instruments' which 'aided to expose' her 'were even then lost when it was found'. This new variation upon the theme of loss and finding reflects once more what is now in effect the prevailing rhythm of the action; and Paulina, too, at the moment of 'locking' the princess to her heart in embrace, clings to her with a depth of emotion which is intensified by her having learnt in the same moment of her husband's end, and, above all, by the 'danger of losing' which gives a fresh keenness to the positive emotions of the play. By so doing, she concludes an act 'worth the audience of kings and princes' in its dignity; 'for by such'—not accidentally—'it was acted'.

The following account of Perdita's grief for Hermione's

supposed death—expressed in prose in which, for once, the artificiality of elaboration seems to be insufficiently integrated into a true artistic effect[1]—leads up to the first mention of the 'statue' in Paulina's keeping, and so anticipates the last stage in the final resolution. The statue, be it noted, is celebrated as a work of art which could 'beguile nature', had it only the attribute of eternity which would enable it to create 'breath'. In point of fact, the statue will, of course, come to life, raising the imitation of 'art' to the life of nature, in much the same way as the pastoral simplicities have been perfected in their courtly setting. The conversation finishes by referring explicitly to the birth of 'some new grace', an anticipation at once of the final reconciliation and a contribution to its emotional completeness. The whole has been an admirable example of the manner in which the artificiality of conventional Elizabethan prose has been turned to a purpose which transcends its apparent limitations. The action, having been transferred to the court, requires a courtly style to set against the pastoral simplicities which preceded its final stages; but this style needs to be rich without being artificial, to secure an exploration of emotion that is not merely conventional, approaching it from a vast number of viewpoints and bringing these together in implied comparisons whose complexity is more than conventional. For the operation of artistic intuition, gathering up dissimilarities and fusing them into a superior unity which is, in this case, the entry into a new, richer life, this peculiar prose is a most suitable instrument.

The last part of the scene, having thus created its effect of harmony, returns by way of contrast to the unassimilated simplicities of life. In this way, the effect of excessive simplification is once more avoided, and common vitality given a place of its own in the complete pattern. Autolycus, significantly, refers immediately after the departure of the

---

1. Note, for example, such a phrase as 'one of the *prettiest* touches of all and that which *angled for mine eyes, caught the water though not the fish* . . .', where the decorative purpose clearly prevails.

courtiers to 'the dash of my former life in me'; he, at least, is not ready to be assimilated to any symbolic scheme, however noble and compelling in its vision, and the contrast between the 'dash' of unregenerate humanity and the theme of 'grace' is clearly deliberate. The following mention of the sea-sickness of the shepherd's daughter contributes similarly to this sense of contrast. His exchange with the Shepherd and the Clown, who now appear for the last time, introduces in turn a comment, gently pointed with irony, upon the claims to the civilized graces implied in the aristocratic conception behind the word 'gentleman'. The Clown, indeed, takes up a familiar Shakespearean theme when he associates the aristocratic ideal with that of external appearance: 'See you those clothes? say you see them not, and think me still no gentleman born: you were best say these robes are not gentleman born'. The spirit of the play is very different, of course, from that which inspired in *King Lear* the crucial confronting of the pride implied in rich raiment with the reality of 'unaccommodated man', but it comes still from the same experience. The contrast is now between inherent aristocracy, a true graciousness born, in the last analysis, of nature, but perfected by 'grace', and the superficial assumption of the external features of rank. The naïvety with which the Clown is ready to equate the two serves at once as a contrast and a criticism, bringing out the true value of the main conception and qualifying it with a saving irony.

A similar effect is produced, just below, by the telling association of simple pretension with true, and equally simple grief, implied in 'so we wept, and there was the first gentleman-like tears that ever we shed'. The note of relativity is maintained in the Clown's following question to Autolycus: 'Thou wilt amend thy life?' to which the latter gives an off-hand consent which not even the Shepherd accepts as other than it is: 'You may say it'—that Autolycus is now as 'honest a true fellow as any is in Bohemia'—'but not swear it'. Most telling of all comes, at the end of the scene, the Clown's farewell to Autolycus, with which the latter, enigmatic to the last, leaves the action:

> If it be ne'er so false, a true gentleman may swear it in the behalf of his friend: and I'll swear to the prince thou art a tall fellow of thy hands and that thou wilt not be drunk; but I know thou art no tall fellow of thy hands and that thou wilt be drunk: but I'll swear it, and I would thou wouldst be a tall fellow of thy hands. (v. ii.)

The Clown's desire stands out, in a contrast at once comic and pathetic, against a reality that cannot be assimilated completely into any symbolic design, however gracious and inclusive. As he swears on behalf of Autolycus, he knows that his oath is in fact unfounded, that its object will continue to exist on the margin of the new life, enhancing its beauty by contrast but giving it also a sense of relativity, of pathos, which not even its splendid realization in terms of poetic integration can entirely overcome; his realistic knowledge is balanced against his desire that things should be otherwise than they are, and the episode concludes on a note, between comic and resigned, that has its part in the complete conception. Seeing 'the kings and the princes' as 'our kindred', with a pretentiousness that is absurd, comic, but not entirely devoid of pathos, his attitude stands out alike against the spirit of the main court action and against the comment implied in the constant scepticism of Autolycus.

iv (b)

The transformation towards which the whole action has been pointing is completed, given visible dramatic expression, in the final scene (v. iii). In it, the Shakespearean experience, different in kind and quality from anything else in English poetry, reaches a complete integration. The fetters of the plot are dissolved; or rather, the plot itself, conceived as an extension of the poetic development which we have traced through the course of the play, is at last finally assimilated to the interplay of imagery. The words of the reconciled parties at the foot of Hermione's 'statue' are as significant in their sequence as in their thematic content and plain sense; they proceed by an antiphonal building-up towards the final, inclusive harmony. This sequence is given continuity, external projection by the various successive stages of the plot, by the process of Leontes' slow awakening to the fact that Hermione herself is before him, and by the almost imperceptible stages of her coming to life, which itself corresponds to the definitive birth of the new 'grace' out of the long winter of his penance. In this final scene, plot finally assumes its full status as the crown of an intricate development of poetic resources. Technique becomes the free and adequate instrument of experience, and the development of imagery which we have traced through the pattern of this play is given an adequate external consummation, seen as logically complete.

Compared with this general impression, irresistibly conveyed by the very movement of the action towards its conclusion, the analysis of detail becomes of secondary importance, almost unnecessary in view of the degree of clarity finally achieved. The distinctive Shakespearean use of imagery, however, although more closely identified than ever before with the flow of dramatic incident, is still pervasively present. The opening exchange between Leontes and Paulina echoes, this time on a level of full mutual sincerity, the relationship between royal bounty and devoted service which characterizes the early scenes of *Macbeth*. To Leontes' salutation of the 'grave and good' Paulina and to his thanks for the 'great comfort' he has received from her in his past trials, she replies with a simple rejoinder:

> All my services
> You have paid home;

and goes on to describe as 'a surplus of your grace', impossible to repay in like measure, his royal condescension in visiting her house.[1] The introduction is brought to a close, just before Paulina unveils the niche to reveal Hermione, with the statement that the queen's 'dead likeness', like her 'peerless life', has a unique quality:

> Excels whatever yet you look'd upon
> Or hand of man hath done.

For this reason, as a work of art which yet excels art, Paulina has kept her treasure 'lonely, apart', a 'lively' mocking of life, as close to its original as sleep is to death.

Leontes' first reaction to the revelation of the motionless 'statue' is one of 'silence' and 'wonder'. His first words, recalling his past treatment of Hermione, are a request that she should 'chide' him; his second utterance contrasts his sense of sin explicitly with the perfection he remembers and associates his memory of that perfection significantly with a new birth:

> . . . for she was as tender
> As infancy and grace.

It is, indeed, a rebirth whose successive stages we are now witnessing, a rebirth the impression of which is strengthened in Leontes by his acute sense of the passage of time; for the Hermione he sees is 'wrinkled' as the wife of his memories never was, and Paulina has to explain that this is due to the artist's skill in taking into account the years which have passed since her 'death'. The relation of the time-theme to those of rebirth and reconciliation is thus retained to the last as a necessary part of the complete effect.

1. For the conception, though not of course for the spirit, compare the following from *Macbeth*:

> All our service
> In every point twice done, and then done double,
> Were poor and single business to contend
> Against those honours deep and broad wherewith
> Your majesty loads our house. (I. vi.)

Leontes' final comment, 'We honour you with trouble', can also be paralleled in Duncan's:

> The love that follows us sometimes is our trouble,
> Which still we thank as love.

The first reaction of Leontes to the restored image of his 'dead' wife is, significantly, one of profound disquiet. The sight is now as 'piercing' to his soul, as full of memories of the follies he has committed, as her life, by himself destroyed, might have been to his 'good comfort'. In Perdita, on the other hand, the vision produces the first move towards reconciliation. She kneels and, like all the children of these plays in like situation, implores her parent's 'blessing'. Her prayer, moreover, is addressed to her 'that ended when I but begun', binding together—as in *Pericles*—mother and daughter in the single process of re-created life which this play aims at conveying. It is, in fact, the triumph of this continuity, a triumph as natural and inevitable as life itself, that we are witnessing. When Leontes is 'transported' by the contrary emotions which assail him, when, in spite of the grief which the sight of the 'statue' has roused in him, he begs that the deceptive life-likeness, as he still considers it, may not be taken from him:

Make me to think so twenty years together,

and echoes the idea so emphatically, a little later, in his exclamation 'No, not these twenty years', he is once more suggesting that time can stand still as he contemplates his love. This can only be justified by the power of the poetic process, which shows that this conception of love is one of life and value, incommensurate with time, which has now become only a condition of it. It is not an accident that Hermione's slow re-awakening—slow both to ease the intolerable shock to Leontes' own senses and to reflect the successive stages of his own full awakening to reality—is from now on surrounded by symbols explicitly religious. The 'statue' itself is said to be placed in a 'chapel', and the war between Leontes' contradictory feelings is envisaged as one in which good and evil spirits are at odds for possession of his soul. Above all, and most explicitly, Paulina stresses that, as a prelude to Hermione's 'descending'—

It is required
You do awake your faith;

the solemnity of the expression, and the subsequent calling
upon music, here as ever the indication of harmony, forces
us to give due weight to the underlying sense of the action.
Without 'faith', indeed, the awakening of the 'statue' will
appear a mere prodigy, an external marvel, not the logical
crown of a long and rich spiritual process that it in fact is.

Paulina's final call to Hermione removes any doubt as to
the true scope of the 'resurrection' we are about to witness:

> 'Tis time, descend; be stone no more; approach;
> Strike all that look upon with marvel. Come,
> I'll fill your grave up; stir, nay, come away,
> Bequeath to death your numbness, for from him
> Dear life redeems you.   (v. iii.)

The first line, broken into short phrases, intense, insistent,
is as much the evocation to a descending spirit as a call to
Hermione to leave her pedestal. Her restoration to Leontes
is to be hailed as a 'marvel' of more than physical content,
as the miracle of life spiritually re-born. The sense of
temporal impermanence overcome is indeed present in the
reference to the filling up of the grave, the returning of
former 'numbness' to death, and—most plainly of all—in
the assertion of the *redemption* by 'dear life' from the bonds
of mortality. Finally, and to dissipate the remaining fears
of those around her, Paulina insists that such 'spells' as she
has exercised are 'lawful', and the actions of Hermione herself consistently 'holy'; the adjective confirms, if further
confirmation were needed at this stage, the essentially
religious nature of the action we are witnessing.

With Leontes and Hermione finally embraced, to the
wonder of those who surround them, it only remains for the
play to be rounded off by the gesture, also typical of these
comedies, by which the family unity is finally restored, and
in which the father bestows his blessing. First Paulina

restores Perdita to her mother, confirming the daughter's own instinct and laying emphasis on the symbolic meaning carried by her name:—

> Kneel
> And pray your mother's blessing. Turn, good lady;
> Our Perdita is found;

and secondly, Hermione, in terms barely less familiar, makes it her first act in her new state to beseech the gods to 'look down' and pour their 'graces' upon her daughter's head. With the marrying of Paulina to Camillo, ratified by 'us, a pair of kings', Leontes and Polixenes newly rejoined in amity, the pattern of reconciliation is finally complete. It would be hard to find, even in Shakespeare, a more profound purpose more consistently carried out to its proper artistic conclusion.

V

THE TEMPEST

WHETHER *The Tempest*, which we may assume to have been written almost immediately after *The Winter's Tale*, is or is not a more satisfactory play is a question about which opinions may reasonably differ. What seems certain is that it represents a further and logical development in the 'symbolic' technique evolved in the series of Shakespeare's last comedies. We might define this development by saying that, whereas *The Winter's Tale* is still concerned with the evolution of experience towards its completely adequate symbolic representation, *The Tempest* assumes that this consummation has already been achieved, so that the various characters and situations exist from the first entirely in terms of a definite 'symbolic' function. The sense of motion and development which is so prominent in the earlier comedy, and which F. R. Leavis possibly had in mind when he referred some years ago to its 'organic' character,[1] is no longer a primary feature of *The Tempest*. Its absence, although we may agree that it makes the play poorer in a certain human content, was the inevitable consequence of a great artist's inability to repeat himself; for *The Tempest* is, whether we prefer it or not, the logical conclusion of the integrating process that produced *The Winter's Tale*, and consequently of Shakespeare's art.

The main outline of the 'symbolic' pattern of the play

1. *Scrutiny*, April, 1942, p. 345.

follows familiar lines. We should never forget, in this respect, that it is called *The Tempest*, and that it opens in a storm at sea. As in *The Winter's Tale*, the storm and the calm which follows it are related respectively to the tragedy caused by human passion and the reconciliation which, after a period of trial to which the actors are exposed in order to determine their respective responsibilities and access to redemption, follows upon repentance in its aftermath. At the centre of the action, formerly victim of the storm raised by the unleashed forces of egoism, but now as much the master of events as he is in control of the physical tempest he has raised to bring his enemies to the stage upon which their destinies are to be decided, stands the enigmatic figure of Prospero. At once the victim and the master of circumstances—and it is perhaps this double aspect of his nature which has proved, for many readers, the stumbling-block in the way of a full acceptance of the play—Prospero emerges increasingly, as the plot takes shape, as the instrument of judgement. Through his actions, and those of Ariel acting at his behest, the different motives which prevail in his former enemies are brought to the surface, evaluated and finally judged. In the process of judgement, the meeting of Prospero's daughter with the son of Alonso provides a symbolic ground for reconciliation in the familiar Shakespearean manner. Only after the final restoration of harmony, and the judgement that precedes it, have taken place on the island does Prospero, with his restored associates, return to resume his place in the human society from which envy and ambition had originally driven him.

I

The opening scene of *The Tempest*, though not in itself of outstanding quality, has often been indicated as an example, in its placing, of the superior structural coherence of the play when compared with *The Winter's Tale*. In point of fact, and if our account of the earlier comedy is accepted, it indicates rather an essential change of purpose. The storm scene in *The Winter's Tale* had occupied a central position in the plot, variously related both to the clash of motives and passions which led to the exposure of Leontes' child and to the reconciliation to which this most unnatural act would eventually, and in its own despite, lead. In *The Tempest*, on the other hand, it has become a point of departure, present indeed throughout the later action in the minds of those initially exposed to it, but present rather as a memory, a prelude to further development, than as an incident related both to the past and the future unfolding of events. More than a device making for dramatic compactness, the change is a sign that the new play is to start, in a very real sense, where its predecessor left off, that the sense of organic development *in time*, which gave *The Winter's Tale* its marvellous sense of related variety, is to be replaced by a judgement which will be timeless and, as far as may be, permanent in its implications. Compared with the significance of this changed position, the chief features of the scene—the vigorous handling of action, and the contrast between the direct, tense expression of the mariners and the various degrees of helplessness and cynicism revealed by the court personalities exposed to the unfamiliar dangers of the elements—are of secondary importance.

With Prospero's opening exposition to Miranda (I. ii) the symbolic design of the play begins to take shape. A certain monotony in the dramatic presentation—for the long episode is little more than a monologue—contrasts with the more varied movement, the greater interplay of character and motive in *The Winter's Tale*, and once more reflects the essential difference of purpose foreshadowed in the introduction. Just as the tempest was there pushed back from the central position it had occupied in the earlier play to become a mere point of departure, so now the past history of Prospero and Miranda, their origins and the events which have brought them to the island, are reconstructed in their successive stages by an exposition which looks backward from the present, recalling the various steps which have led to the decisive choice which now confronts them. Yet, referring though it does to the past, and so deliberately abstracted from any immediate reflection in external dramatic action, Prospero's exposition has a logic of its own, which is given its counterpart in the successive stages of Miranda's awakening response. His aim is to bring her, by recalling her forgotten past, to an understanding of her present situation, not only as an exile on the island, but as a human being on the threshold of her moral maturity. Our awareness of this, since it follows the various steps in her own awakening, is necessarily gradual. Its gradualness, indeed, is essential to the effect of development, of growth towards full comprehension, at which the episode aims; for it confers a sense of motion, of purposeful change leading up to a decisive climax, upon the otherwise static quality of the dialogue. To accept this sense without seeking to impose upon this exposition a dramatic content foreign to its conception, is to take an important step in understanding the play.

Although this understanding comes to us, in the nature of things, gradually, the tone and phrasing of Prospero's first speech is itself significant:

> There's no harm done . . .
>   No harm.
> I have done nothing but in care of thee,
> Of thee, my dear one, thee my daughter, who
> Art ignorant of what thou art, naught knowing
> Of whence I am; nor that I am more better
> Than Prospero, master of a full poor cell,
> And thy no greater father. (I. ii.)

Prospero's confidence, which stands out in the reiterated 'No harm done . . . No harm' as though he wished from the first to stress his perfect mastery of the situation, contrasts with the compassionate fear which is Miranda's instinctive emotion. Miranda, responding to the promptings of her 'piteous heart', is full of fear. Her fear, natural, attractive, human as it is, springs from her ignorance. It is a product of the same inexperience which has just led her, in the opening speech of the scene, to imagine 'some noble creature' upon Alonso's ship and to live throughout with visions of a 'brave new world' and of the ennobled humanity that is to live in it. In these visions, simplicity and the birth of a genuine spiritual need are strangely intertwined. For Miranda, precisely because she has seen nothing of the world and its inhabitants, the ship which she has just seen has a visionary quality, is 'a brave vessel', a 'good ship', whilst those aboard it who are exposed to the elements are, by a touch of spiritual feeling which will find its full meaning in the later action, 'fraughting souls', waiting for some dim divine intervention to save them from the storm which threatens them with destruction. That the vision is inadequate, that it does not correspond to the facts, will be apparent as soon as Alonso and his companions reach the safety of Prospero's island; that it is based on a true instinct, a sense of human potentialities which is to be carried into full civilized life, will finally emerge from the scenes of reconciliation in which Miranda herself is, in due course, to play a central part.

Prospero, even at this stage, does not disapprove of these visions, or of 'the virtue of compassion' which his own deliberate action has roused to expression in his daughter. Eventually, he will endorse her feelings, give them their proper place in his own comprehensive view of spiritual reality; but, before this can be done, they need to be reconciled to a fuller experience of the possibilities of human nature. It is the story of Florizel and Perdita over again. As their full happiness involved, as a preliminary condition, the breaking-up of the rustic paradise in which they first met, so must Miranda leave behind her the 'ignorance' of her own nature, come to know 'what she is' in a way that can never be achieved in the isolation of her life on the island. As a first step, she will have to learn that life has not been entirely bounded for her by the relations of a father and a daughter happily contained within the limits of 'a full poor cell'. This 'cell' of retirement has been forced upon her father by her enemies, and the time has come for Miranda, in the process of awakening to her own past, to know this and so to deepen her instinctive compassion by exposure to experience:

'Tis time
I should inform thee farther.

Miranda, in her compassionate helplessness, has wished herself 'a god of power' to pluck her still imaginary hero from danger; but Prospero—who is a 'god of power', at least in so far as fullness of understanding and the sanction which Destiny has conferred upon his actions can make him one—has deliberately willed a storm which is itself symbolically bound to the previous action and which will bring his daughter, along with suspense and the shadow of suffering, a realization of what mature experience really means. That is why he is able from the first to tell her 'I have done nothing but in care of thee', and that is why, in spite of the loss that the tempest seems to have brought about, there has been 'no harm done'. No harm, indeed, but—for those capable of responding adequately to the new situation—the necessary prelude to a fuller and more complete life.

In the telling of the story which follows Miranda is, as it were, awakened gradually into maturity. As he pierces the dream which has been so far her innocent life on the island, Prospero introduces her to the wider prospects which lie before her. More properly speaking, by penetrating the veil which shrouds for her 'the dark backward and abysm of time' (and surely, in the charged mysteriousness of the phrase, we sense as much a reference to the universal human situation as to Miranda's peculiar position) he makes her aware, in terms of her own past, of the knot of mingled motives which constitute the behaviour of man in society. In the course of this exposition, her state is closely and variously related to the main conception; for the successive stages by which her mature judgement emerges from the dream in which it has so far been enveloped correspond to the development which, by bringing together Prospero and his former enemies, is to restore both to a full participation in civilized life. Dream and reality, sentimental idealization and mature judgement are in fact integrated by participation in the successive stages, different but related, of a single action.

The first thing Miranda has to learn, after so many years passed in the idyllic simplicity of Prospero's refuge, is her connection with another and more complex mode of life. As soon as she has been induced to recall that such a life has indeed been hers, her question immediately raises a moral issue:

> O, the heavens,
> What foul play had we, that we came from thence?
> Or blessed was't we did?

In this way, Miranda brings out, at least by implication, a problem that could never have occurred to her in the undisturbed state of simplicity which has so far been hers, a problem, moreover, which lies at the heart of the play's conception. What explanation can be put forward, within the providential philosophy so confidently announced by Prospero, for 'foul play' of the kind which has by his own account deprived them of their civilized inheritance? Prospero is ready with an answer which will require the unfolding of the full pattern of the action to give it force and content, but which already indicates the foundations of his confidence:

> Both, both, my girl.
> By foul play (as thou say'st) were we heav'd thence,
> But blessedly holp hither.

From the assertion that the fugitives were protected by providential action during their journey to the island it is only a step to affirm that their exile itself was, spiritually speaking, a privilege. Evil, apparently inconceivable on the island—for Caliban's instincts are still safely under control—has to be taken into account in human affairs as part of the necessary price of maturity. The reason, so far as we can see it—and Prospero's answer barely suggests the source of his confidence—lies in the opportunity it offers for the working out of a final state of 'grace'. We are not asked to accept this, so long before the end of the play; indeed, it would be wrong to suppose that Shakespeare expects us to see, in the use of the word 'blessedly', taken up by Prospero from Miranda's own question, anything more than a thread of conviction round which some kind of order may eventually gather. For the moment, his attention is primarily fixed upon expounding, still as a necessary step in his daughter's education, the nature of evil as revealed in the behaviour of his enemies.

In accordance with this aim, Miranda's awakening is next connected with the wider social themes with which the play deals. Remembering previous works of Shakespeare, it is not surprising to find as we follow the story of Prospero's expulsion from Milan that evil in *The Tempest* has two aspects—personal and social—which stand in the closest relation one to another. Throughout the tragedies the first consequence of evil is anarchy and its starting-point the overthrow of 'degree', of natural order in its various forms, by the dominating force of passion. 'Degree', in turn, is associated in ever-increasing measure with the human institutions, the family and the body politic, in which personal 'value' receives, as it were, an external projection, a sanction in the objective order of things. These two institutions, the family and the state, are based, in the widest sense of the word, upon reason and are in turn the foundations of a civilized, moral way of living; and it is only when passion in the individual overcomes reason and aims at their destruction that evil enters society. Seen from this standpoint, *The Tempest* is a full-fledged symbolic treatment of themes more directly, personally indicated in earlier plays.

In the story of Prospero's expulsion evil strikes both at the roots of human stability—for as head of the state he was the guarantor of that 'degree' by which alone societies can prosper—and at the unity of the family to overthrow the natural order of things. In casting Prospero with his daughter on to the open sea Antonio transgressed both against the Duke of Milan and his own brother.

His first crime in the social, political order—so to call it— is deliberately related to the character of his victim. The account given by Prospero of his dukedom reminds us of the story of Vincenzo in *Measure for Measure*. Like that mysterious personage Prospero lived 'retired', withdrawn from the world and devoted entirely to contemplation and the 'liberal' arts:

> I, thus neglecting worldly ends, all dedicated
> To closeness, and the bettering of my mind
> With that which, but by being so retired,
> O'er prized all popular rate;

and, like him again, he delegated the whole of his power to another. In so doing, both opened the way for the entry of evil into their respective dominions. Prospero is quite explicit about this when he tells Miranda that his own 'closeness', his 'neglect' (and the choice of words clearly indicates a critical intention) of the ends of government—

> in my false brother
> Awak'd an evil nature, and my trust,
> Like a good parent, did beget of him
> A falsehood in its contrary, as great
> As my trust was, which had indeed no limit,
> A confidence sans bound.

The similarity between Prospero and the Duke of Vienna, two characters separated by several years of Shakespeare's most intense creative activity, is some indication of the continuity of spirit in which the plays were conceived. Both appear increasingly, as their stories are unfolded, to be in control of the events which their own actions originally precipitated. Both, indeed, eventually attain a certain omniscience, even a reflection of divinity, which enables them finally to pass judgement upon those whose behaviour they have been observing throughout the play; but in each case, this omniscience, this capacity to judge, is based on an understanding which has first been deepened by contact with reality. Prospero, of course, is more secure than the Duke in his mastery. It follows naturally from the shifting forward to its latest stages of the temporal action of the play, that his apprenticeship to experience has already been served before *The Tempest* opens, so that we hear of it now only as something in the past, whereas the Duke, conceived by Shakespeare before the process of deepening insight shadowed in the great tragedies had taken place, is still involved in his own search for clarification.[1] But the position of both is, at bottom, similar. Both begin by dedicating themselves to an ideal of purely personal perfection, and both in so doing neglect not only the social duties of their position, but also an instrument, when properly considered, for the attainment of that perfection itself. The position of Prospero is complicated, however, by a further factor which once more points to the presence behind the play of the full tragic experience. Not only is his rule overthrown by that of a self-seeking usurper for whom the sacred guarantees of 'degree' mean nothing, but the corruption which brings him suffering and loss springs from his own family.

At this point the political is re-enforced by the presentation of the family theme. Prospero's brother Antonio, who should have been his chief supporter by the most intimate personal ties, becomes in Milan—

> The ivy which had hid my princely trunk,
> And suck'd my verdure out on't.

1. We are told of Vincenzo that he has always been 'one that, above all other strifes, contended specially to know himself' (*Measure for Measure*, III. ii).

Perhaps only the very intimacy of the ties which bind a man to his brother enable Antonio to assume a part so completely contrary to Prospero's own; the man of the world is, as it were, the enemy of the contemplative precisely because of the unity of blood that joins them in unwilling intimacy. To Antonio's crime against the state, against the sacred intangibility of 'degree', is added at all events a crime against the bond of unity in the family which Prospero feels even more deeply:

> I prithee, mark me, that a brother should
> Be so perfidious!

The two crimes are, in fact, one, a common subversion of the natural order of things, a descent into anarchy prompted by personal selfishness which is, in the Shakespearean outlook of the great plays, the supreme cause of tragedy. But Prospero's past retirement has helped unwittingly to bring these crimes about; and so only now, after helpless exposure to the tempestuous seas and years of confinement to a 'poor cell' on a 'most desolate isle'—desolate, in spite of all the graces with which his wisdom has endowed it, because deprived of human society—is he in a position to assume with authority his vocation of judgement.

In the account, which follows, of Prospero's expulsion from Milan and of his arrival with Miranda on the island, the two main themes of this opening part of the play—his past history and her introduction, through the telling of it, to the maturity which awaits her—are brought together, revealed as mutually illuminating aspects of a dramatic conception that embraces them in an ample symbolic design. Prospero's recreation of events combines a charged economy of phrase with a wealth of undertones which contribute, each within its own concreteness, to the total effect. The expulsion itself is described as having been consummated on a midnight 'fated to the purpose', singularly appropriate to the unnatural motives of those who inspired it. In 'the dead of darkness' beneath which here, as always, evil seeks to conceal its perversity from the revealing light of day,[1] Prospero and his helpless daughter ('thy crying self') were 'hurried' in secrecy to the 'rotten carcass' destined for them, exposed to the pressure (implacable and yet, by comparison with human cruelty, compassionate) of the sea:

> . . . there they hoist us,
> To cry to the seas that roar'd to us; to sigh
> To the winds, whose pity, sighing back again,
> Did us but loving wrong.

Beneath the action of the storm, which appears to reflect in its apparent pitilessness the inhumanity of man, there lies a sense of spiritual fitness, a correspondence with the situation, tragic indeed but not beyond redemption, of its human victims. The roaring waves answer their cries, and to their sighs the sea, 'sighing back again', responds with an action which, though merciless, is finally 'loving', open to compassion. The double nature of Shakespeare's tragic symbolism, at once implacable and in its human associations redeeming, is once more indicated.[2]

These first indications are immediately supported by a number of factors more directly related to the personal action. The first of these, as Prospero now recalls it, is the effect upon him of his daughter's infant presence in the storm:

> MIRANDA: Alack, what trouble
> Was I then to you!
> PROSPERO: O, a cherubin
> Thou wast that did preserve me.

From the very first, long before her attainment of the moral consciousness which he is now awakening in her, the presence of Miranda has been a source of sustainment to Prospero. 'Infused with a fortitude from heaven', she

---

1. The parallels with *Macbeth*, in this use of contrasted images of light and darkness, are too familiar to need quotation.

2. Compare Ferdinand's 'though the seas threaten, they are merciful' (v. i), and other passages referred to in our study of this play.

represented, in the moment of her father's betrayal, a positive guarantee of continuity, of spiritual sustainment, which gave him the power to resist. She, in his own words,

> raised in me
> An undergoing stomach, to bear up
> Against what should ensue.

In the light of this memory, the later part of Prospero's account once more affirms, and with full explicitness, the presence of a saving design behind their vicissitudes. 'How came we ashore?' asks Miranda, living through her father's words, for the first time and on the threshold of a decisive broadening of her own experience, these incidents from her past life; and Prospero's reply 'By Providence divine' is supported by a number of details which possess, beyond their immediate concreteness, a cumulative effect of refreshment and regeneration. The food and 'fresh water' which enabled the outcasts to live through their ordeal had been provided through the 'charity', the natural human feeling of the 'noble Neapolitan', Gonzalo; to his 'gentleness', again, the pair owed 'rich garments', 'stuffs and necessaries' and, above all, the volumes that Prospero prized above his dukedom and upon his possession of which his present power rests.

Thus supported by his own contemplative resources, strengthened by the compassionate innocence of his daughter and confirmed by the fellow-feeling which, even in the midst of court corruption and intrigue, stands out as an attribute of true nobility, Prospero has been able on his island to transform 'sea-sorrow' into a step in the attainment of fuller understanding. The end of his exposition shows him aware of a decisive moment in his fortunes:

> By accident most strange, bountiful Fortune,
> Now my dear lady, hath mine enemies
> Brought to this shore; and by my prescience
> I find my zenith doth depend upon

> A most auspicious star, whose influence
> If now I court not, but omit, my fortunes
> Will ever after droop.

From the victim of adverse circumstances, Prospero has become the recipient of the favours of 'bountiful fortune' and even, in a sense, a collaborator in her purposes; for if the bringing of his former enemies into his reach was the result originally of events beyond his control, of 'accident most strange', their arrival on the island has been the result of his deliberate, controlling action. In exercising his power he has come, as the play opens, to the moment of decisive choice which will determine whether he, together with Miranda and those of his former enemies who are capable of redemption, will be restored in due course to their full stature as civilized beings.

For beyond the judgement which he has now to exercise, Prospero has another purpose, even more familiar in the pattern of these symbolic comedies, to achieve: that of reconciliation. The old order, broken by the disruptive entry of passion into what had been the closest of natural relationships, needs to be restored on the foundations of a wider, enriched experience. It is here that the process of Miranda's education, incorporated into the action now about to open on the island, illuminates the main symbolic theme. The instrument of reconciliation, as in *The Winter's Tale*, is to be the love spontaneously born in the children of the fathers whose natural union passion had destroyed; Ferdinand and Miranda, like Florizel and Perdita before them, can restore the happiness of their parents just because they have had no share, no responsibility, in the sin which had led them to tragedy. Accordingly, at the very beginning of the action—not, as in *The Winter's Tale*, in the middle, for *The Tempest* concentrates our attention almost entirely upon the last, the reconciling stage in the symbolic process— Miranda, having been initiated by her father into the secret of her own past, sees Ferdinand. Moved still by innocence, she greets him at once as something supernatural, the representative of a humanity exalted above the normal condition of man. To the deliberate poetic remoteness of Prospero's awakening phrase, 'The fringed curtains of thine eyes advance', which anticipates in its own way the transformation of common reality through Ariel's magic music into 'something rich and strange', she responds with the question:

> What is't? a spirit?
> Lord, how it looks about! Believe me, sir,
> It carries a brave form. But 'tis a spirit;

and when Prospero has explained that she is indeed looking at a man, she continues with an even more direct reference to divinity:

> I might call him
> *A thing divine*, for nothing natural
> I ever saw so noble.

The first sight of Ferdinand's *'brave* form' (the adjective, of course, will occur again to express the quality of Miranda's rapture) is here given a definite supernatural note which is in no sense foreign to the main conception. The idea of *nobility* exalted to something like a state of divinity is essential to Shakespeare's purpose. It is, indeed, the conclusion to which Prospero himself is moving; but the moment for asserting it has not yet come, and so, after recognizing that events are following the course laid down in his design ('As my soul prompts it'), he interrupts his daughter's ecstasy, breaks off the developing love, to which Ferdinand has immediately responded, with what seems unnecessary brutality.

Prospero's own explanation, in his aside, of the course he has so unexpectedly chosen—

> . . . this swift business
> I must uneasy make, lest too light winning
> Make the prize light—

is indeed most perfunctory. No doubt Shakespeare thought it sufficient to allow events to explain themselves. The enriched poetic content of the final scenes of reconciliation will be sufficient, when the time comes, to show that Ferdinand's love for Miranda has grown in depth, in maturity of content, by the test to which it has been subjected. For the fact is that the idealization, *divinization* of Ferdinand apparent in this first meeting, based though it is on instincts that will ultimately prove to be sound, is premature. Miranda's sentiments reflect a tenderness and compassion which are still insufficiently mature, still unsupported by an adequate depth of spiritual insight; that Ferdinand, at this moment, is concerned to find her a 'maid', virgin in body and spirit alike, is at once proper and an indication that further possibilities lie before her.[1] She now greets Ferdinand as a god simply because nothing like him has so far entered her experience; for, as Prospero himself is quick to remind her, she has seen no other creature with human attributes than himself and Caliban. Her enthusiasm argues from a naïve belief that nothing wicked can inhabit so fair a form:

> There's nothing ill can dwell in such a temple;
> If the ill spirit have so fair a house,
> Good things will strive to dwell with it.

The religious associations of 'temple' and 'spirit' are relevant, and will eventually be taken up to form part of the final harmony; but they need first to be substantiated, confirmed by contact with human realities. When Prospero reproves his daughter for seeing finality in her lack of experience:—

> Thou thinkst there are no more such shapes as he,
> Having seen but him and Caliban—

his words, harsh as they are, stand for a truth. Miranda herself suggests, unwittingly, that these realities may be

1. The spirit of Perdita's flower-speeches in *The Winter's Tale*, discussed above (p. 149), is not dissimilar in intention.

dangerous. Their outward form, even though it conceals true evil ('ill'), may be so 'fair' that even 'good' things will be carried away and 'strive to dwell with it'. The behaviour of the men who have been cast ashore on the island by Prospero's action—many of them presumably not so much less 'god-like' (at least in potentiality) than Ferdinand to Miranda's inexperienced eyes—will soon show how dangerous her simple assumptions can be. Their conduct calls for consideration in the main body of the action before Prospero's reconciling purpose can take shape, or before the devotion of the lovers can fairly be established as more than surrender to a romantic dream. Only after his former enemies have done their worst and been, in turn, dominated by the superior power and insight of the man upon whose wronging their temporal good-fortune has so far depended will he be able to unite his daughter convincingly to Ferdinand in terms that are little short of god-like. But the divinity—such as it is—will then be founded upon a true reading of human nature and will express a spiritual reality, not merely a sentimental intuition; and this insight will have been obtained in the process of passing judgement on all the characters in the play.

II

It is to pass judgement, indeed, as a prelude to reconciliation that Prospero has caused all those concerned in his former banishment to be cast ashore on the island. From their first appearance there (II. i), in a state poised between dream and reality and so favourable to the release of motives and desires so far held in check, covered by the mask imposed by adaptation to their respective social conditions, he subjects them to what is, in effect, an analysis of their relative guilts. Having brought them together and in his power, he proceeds to differentiate carefully between them; for some will turn out to be capable of redemption and others, in spite of his efforts, not. Their capacity is tested by their reactions to the ordeal to which they are now exposed. Their arrival shatters the idyllic seclusion which had formerly prevailed on the island, a seclusion which was, in some sense, a continuation of that abstraction from the world which had cost Prospero his dukedom. It replaces one dream, coherent, idyllic, tranquil, by a number of others, fragments of diverse experiences, contradictory and shot through with motives reflected from external reality and here at once isolated and presented in their true nature. By so doing, it both shatters the dream and makes possible the awakening into a more mature, a more inclusive experience; and, in the course of this development, it completes the education of Miranda, already initiated by her father, and expands decisively the context in which her idealism finds, in due course, its fulfilment.

Of all the newcomers, Alonso, the King of Naples and—it is important to remember—the character who believes himself to have lost most in the wreck, comes best out of the test. [1] Having lost, as he thinks, his son, and feeling that his journey to Tunis has been the cause of the disaster in which he and his companions have been involved, he refuses from the first to be comforted. His only reply to Gonzalo's loquacious consolation is 'Prithee, peace'; and when Sebastian reproaches him with having brought so much needless suffering upon those around him he makes no attempt to deny this, but merely points out that, though his be the greater part of the blame (if blame it is), he also bears the brunt of the suffering:

SEBASTIAN: The fault's your own.
ALONSO: So is the dear'st of the loss.

In the intensity of 'dear'st' we can sense the emotional quality peculiar to Shakespeare's later symbolism. It is just through the 'dearness' of Alonso's loss—'dear', because at once great and potentially precious—that the possibility of

---

1. Excluding, of course, Gonzalo, who cannot be said to develop in the course of the action.

his redemption lies. In his refusal to be comforted, he recalls the Leontes of the last scenes of *The Winter's Tale*. To throw off sorrow in such a situation is to be insensible, and insensibility is perhaps in Shakespeare's mind at the time of writing these plays the greatest obstacle to redemption. Alonso, of course, is a slighter, a dimmer personage than Leontes. Unlike the latter, he does not really understand the reason for which this trial has been imposed upon him; and the suppression of the earlier stages of the story, part of the changed purpose of the later play, takes from him the possibility of development, and so of depth of moral perspective. He has forgotten, so it seems, his treatment of Prospero, but meanwhile the very inconsolable quality of his sorrow shows that he is capable of repentance; and Shakespeare no doubt intends to emphasize this when he makes him capable of receiving the restoring visitation of sleep. Sleep, which deserted Macbeth after the murder of Duncan and which preceded the last stage of Lear's entry into self-knowledge, temporary happiness, and the recovery of his reason, preserves in *The Tempest* the healing significance which we have learned to associate with it; and Prospero himself, acting through Ariel, bestows it upon those whose spiritual state is such that they can accept it. Alonso can do so because, as we have said, he is morally sensitive; and so his response to Ariel's music is a positive one:

> I wish mine eyes
> Would, with themselves, shut up my thoughts. I find
> They are inclined to do so.

Sebastian's comments, in turn, insincerely offered though they are, are in themselves profoundly true to the Shakespearean intuition:

> Please you, sir,
> Do not omit the heavy offer of it:
> It seldom visits sorrow; when it doth,
> It is a comforter.

So Alonso sleeps in response to the invitation of the music, and his sleep is a sign that he will, when the time comes for his understanding to be completed, find his place in the final reconciliation.

The next stage in the analysis, more active and variously concrete in its implications, concerns Antonio and Sebastian. Their first appearance marks them out, in the repartee to which they subject Gonzalo's efforts to cheer Alonso, as courtly cynics of the familiar Shakespearean type, their intelligence applied exclusively to purposes of destruction. When Adrian, otherwise insignificant, and Gonzalo speak of the island in terms that directly recall Banquo's account of Macbeth's castle at the moment of Duncan's arrival before it,[1] their reaction is, to those who appreciate Shakespeare's handling of details of this kind, full of meaning:

ADRIAN: It [the island] must needs be of subtle, tender, and delicate temperance. . . . The air breathes upon us here most sweetly.

SEBASTIAN: As if it had lungs, and rotten ones.

ANTONIO: Or as 'twere perfumed by a fen.

GONZALO: Here is everything advantageous to life.

ANTONIO: True, save means to live. . . .

GONZALO: But the rarity of it is, which is indeed almost beyond credit. . . that our garments, being, as they were, drenched in the sea, hold notwithstanding their freshness and glosses, being rather new-dyed than stain'd with salt water.

ANTONIO: If but one of his pockets could speak, would it not say he lies?

The fresh sweetness of the air, the 'tender and delicate temperance' of the island, are images of the kind generally associated, in the later plays, with the presence of 'grace'; whilst the fact, insisted upon more than once by Gonzalo, that immersion in the tempest-driven waters has left the garments of Alonso and his fellows even fresher than they

1. Act I, Scene vi.

had been before, is perhaps more directly, symbolical.
However that may be, 'grace' in Shakespeare always has its
enemy in the cynic, the destructive critic who belittles its
intimations in terms of his own sensuality and reduces its
value to worthlessness. In so doing he becomes the vehicle
of the profound emotional disturbance which, taken together
with the positive reaction against its implications, produced
the great tragedies. Sebastian and Antonio, indeed, are the
natural successors to Iago. The grossness of their utterances,
the evocation of 'rotten lungs' and the 'perfume' of the fen,
are typical inversions of the 'grace'-images of Adrian and
Alonso, and the reference, coarsely physical, to Gonzalo's
pockets is part of the same attitude. With no conception of
value, divorced from that free reverence for the natural
order upon which any tolerable civilized life must, according
to the basic symbolism of these plays, be founded, the part
played by these two in *The Tempest* is necessarily destructive,
anarchic. That is why they, unlike Alonso, remain finally
beyond the limits of Prospero's reconciling action.

Taken in itself, the cynicism shown by Sebastian and
Antonio does not seem of great moment. It soon appears,
however, as the prelude to graver crimes. The moral
anarchy fostered by the destructive intelligence does not
confine itself to conceits and witticisms. As soon as Alonso,
succumbing to the inspired harmony of Ariel, surrenders to
the sleep which foreshadows forgiveness and the healing of his
sorrows, they turn to plot against order and humanity itself.
Shakespeare, indeed, stresses their wakefulness, their inability
to receive or understand spiritual refreshment, in the wonder
with which they comment on Alonso's drowsiness:

SEBASTIAN: What a strange drowsiness possesses them!
ANTONIO: It is the quality of the climate.
SEBASTIAN: Why
          Doth it not then our eyelids sink? I find not
          Myself dispos'd to sleep.
ANTONIO: Nor I, my spirits are nimble.

The rejection of sleep, the cynic's refusal to accept assimilation into the dream which has been cast as its distinctive quality upon the island, is a step to more inhuman decisions. Operating through the 'nimbleness' of the critical faculty, the vivacity which reflects no more than its own subsistent anarchy, it leads logically to a conception of crime. Prospero's enemy, who has already conspired to eject him from his rightful position, feels himself once more dominated by the desire for power. And yet, even in this stressed wakefulness—such is the all-embracing power of Ariel's spell—there is a quality of sleep, of the suspension of the normal exercise of control. Antonio's design comes to Sebastian as through a haze, piercing his self-ignorance and waking him, indeed, but into a strange suspension of his normal faculties. 'What, art thou waking?' he asks, and receives Antonio's incisive reply, 'Dost thou hear me speak?' For Sebastian, it is 'a sleepy language' that he hears, one still wrapped in a persistent cloudiness of purpose:

> It is a sleepy language, and thou speak'st
> Out of thy sleep. What is it thou didst say?
> This is a strange repose, to be asleep
> With eyes wide open; standing, speaking, moving,
> And yet so fast asleep.

It is as though the sleep induced by Ariel through his music—a sleep which leads to that abstraction from normal life which is part of Prospero's intention—has affected the various courtiers in different ways, according to the disposition of their normal, waking selves. To Gonzalo, instinctively rather than reflectively loyal, it has brought simple repose, to Alonso an anticipation of repentance through the contemplation of his own past acts and the tragedy to which these have now led him. For Sebastian, harbouring an ambition of which he is still imperfectly conscious, it has meant a suspension of the will, a sleep in waking which will give Antonio the chance to act upon him. To each, in fact, it has come as a pause, an abstraction from their normal selves in which their true natures are revealed, seen in relation to the ends anticipated by Prospero when he brought them to the island. In this respect at least, symbolic devices foreshadowed in earlier plays find in *The Tempest* a more ample dramatic expression.

Within the climate thus pervasively established, Antonio's words, as he turns to Sebastian, indicate the birth of his new design:

> . . . methinks I see it in thy face,
> What thou should'st be: the occasion speaks thee, and
> My strong imagination sees a crown
> Dropping upon thy head.

This strikes a note familiar in earlier plays. Antonio is not the first Shakespearean character whose 'strong imagination', looking forward to a crime not yet apparent to an accomplice of weaker will, sees that accomplice crowned in anticipation of the future. Lady Macbeth, after crowning her husband in her thoughts, played in the death of Duncan very much the part played by Antonio in the plan to dispose of Alonso. In Antonio's case, however, the part played by passion is replaced by the 'rational' conviction that the moral sanctions of 'nature' have no power to restrain the ruthless following of self-interest, and the result is a character more abstractedly, less dramatically sustained. Antonio, in short, represents the motives of Iago and Edmund deprived in part of the autonomy which gave them tragic force and subdued to the requirements of the prevailing symbolic scheme. His motive power, however, derives, like theirs, from a peculiarly self-sufficient conception of fortune:

> Noble Sebastian,
> Thou lettst thy fortune sleep—die, rather, wink'st
> Whiles thou art waking.

The new twist thus given to the prevailing sleep-image is deeply characteristic of the speaker. To act is to be awake, to seize the chance for self-assertion which fortune has offered; to hesitate, on the other hand, is to 'wink', to sleep beneath the appearance of watchfulness. This is the 'philosophy' which, carried to its logical conclusion, formerly led Antonio to play the chief part in his brother's banishment and which now, energetically communicated to Sebastian, leads his weaker associate to contemplate a similar betrayal of Alonso.

In accordance with this general conception of the relationship between them, the two plotters are carefully distinguished in their attitude. The difference between them is well put in the course of their own dialogue:

SEBASTIAN: Well, I am standing water.
ANTONIO: I'll teach you how to flow.
SEBASTIAN: Do so: to ebb
          Hereditary sloth instructs me.

Against Alonso, as previously against Prospero, Antonio is the arch-criminal. It is he who provides the energy of the plot, who shows the active desire to destroy all that stands in the way of his advancement, who—in short—moves the relatively languid Sebastian to act. His favourite theme is, characteristically, the conviction that the gap, interposed by scruple or mere indecision, between the desire of the heart and the will to achieve it through action is a contemptible weakness, logically inconceivable:

O,
If you but knew how you the purpose cherish
Whiles thus you mock it! how, in stripping it,
You more invest it! Ebbing men, indeed,
Most often do so near the bottom run
By their own fear or sloth. [1]

In the world of court intrigue, where there is no alternative but to advance or be rejected, where ebb and flow belong

1. It seems scarcely necessary to quote, for a parallel line of thought, Lady Macbeth's remarks on her husband's indecision:
                    . . . thoud'st have, great Glamis,
          That which rather thou dost fear to do
          Than wishest, should be undone. (*Macbeth*, I. v.)

to the nature of things and the difference between them is measured by the ruthless determination to achieve power, clarity of purpose and freedom from scruple are the keys to success. Antonio, by exposing the contradiction between Sebastian's surface scruples and the desires which lie at the bottom of his mind, becomes the inspiration of the plot. He is, indeed, a force, a moving principle, and, as such, Prospero's declared enemy. The speed with which his mind habitually moves is conveyed in the motion of his speech. When Sebastian doubtfully brings up the name of Claribel as Alonso's heiress, we can feel the intensity of his thought in motion to dispose of this obstacle to his plans:

> She that is queen of Tunis; she that dwells
> Ten leagues beyond man's life; she that from Naples
> Can have no note, unless the sun were post,—
> The man in the moon's too slow,—till new-born chins
> Be rough and razorable.

The quick passage from idea to idea, the easy recourse to far-fetched, even grotesque comparisons ('Ten leagues beyond man's life', 'the man in the moon', 'unless the sun were post'), the interpolation of the phrase about the moon as an afterthought in the middle of another which itself leaps from the sun to 'new-born chins'—all this is thoroughly typical. The destructive energy of Iago, the same sense of keen intelligence at the service of anarchic forces, has descended to Antonio. In his mind at least, the present opportunity is all. When he speaks to Sebastian of Claribel, it is to thrust aside the past as irrelevant, except in so far as it has led up to the decisive choice which is the true interest of the present:

> . . . she that from whom
> We were all sea-swallowed, though some cast again,
> And by that destiny, to perform an act
> Whereof what's past is prologue; what to come,
> In yours and my discharge.

It is no accident that Antonio at this point echoes, in his own way, some of the leading principles of Prospero's thought. He too has his own view, perfectly logical and consistent, of what is implied by the conception of 'destiny'. 'Destiny', indeed, in so far as it has meaning for him, lies in the performance of his own will. Delivered by an act of fortune after having been 'sea-swallowed', 'cast again' upon the island on which he and his fellows now find themselves, their salvation is not for him, as for Alonso, an occasion for reflection and ultimately for repentance, but merely a 'prologue' to the action already conceived, willed, and at last in his power to discharge. The past, which dominates Alonso's thought as a continual presence, interests Antonio only in so far as it has led to the opportunity offered by the present moment; the future, 'what's to come', is in his power and in that of his accomplice, 'in yours and my discharge'. That is why it is he, already the prime mover in Prospero's banishment, who now, by inciting Sebastian to a similar crime against his brother, becomes his chief antagonist in the conflict of good and evil, natural harmony and distorted 'reason', which is the real theme of *The Tempest*.

The resemblance with Iago is carried a step further in a most interesting passage from the same dialogue. Sebastian is slow to be convinced, almost as slow—and for much the same reasons of timidity and sheer incapacity to think clearly—as Roderigo in *Othello*. Somewhere at the back of his slow mind, a doubt, an obscure formulation of conscience, is slowly working its way to the light. It expresses itself finally in reply to Antonio's eager pressing of him to seize the unique occasion which has offered itself:

> And how does your content
> Tender your own good fortune?

For Antonio the occasion capriciously offered by blind fortune is everything: that, and—as we have seen—the capacity to seize it by a decisive act of the will, so as to make one's 'content' fit with what chance has offered. More cynically, because more clearly, intellectually convinced of the sense-less nature of the fluctuations of fortune, Antonio repeats the advice given by Lady Macbeth to her husband; still more significantly—and for similar reasons, to be traced ultimately to a pessimistic interpretation of the value of human actions—his advice is substantially that given by Machiavelli to his Prince. Success depends on the seizing of occasions, and in practical affairs to succeed is the nearest approach to a categorical necessity. Only Machiavelli, beneath his appearance of detachment, is not a cynic and his Prince is intended to have a purpose—that of saving Florence, and perhaps through Florence Italy, from the recurrent misery and degradation of foreign invasion; whereas Antonio has no aim, can conceive indeed of none, beyond personal advancement.

But Sebastian, slow as he is and—what is more—willing to be convinced, still does not reply directly. His uncertainty finally expresses itself in an observation of whose profound meaning he is doubtless not completely aware:

> I remember
> You did supplant your brother Prospero.

Properly interpreted, this remark is something very like a warning. Antonio, who is now moving him to supplant Alonso, once acted himself against Prospero. Shakespeare does not, at this moment in which Sebastian is being led to make his decisive choice, wish this fact to be forgotten. This is partly because we are to bear in mind always that it is Antonio, Prospero's brother, who is the moving spirit in the evil of this play, the real conflict being between him and his original victim; but there is also another reason. For what Sebastian is really trying to say is this: once the accepted bonds of conscience and kingship have been broken by an act of usurpation, once the moral foundations of 'degree' have been undermined both in the individual and in the relations of society, what is to prevent Antonio, should it serve his purposes, from turning upon the creation of his will? Once he has given his consent Sebastian is as likely as Alonso to be in danger. As in the case of Macbeth, one crime will tend to become the stepping-stone to another; there is no logical stopping-place between the first over-throw of 'degree', of natural relationship in its various forms, and the complete abandonment of the restraints imposed by conscience upon which all such 'degree', and with it the possibility of ordered human existence, is founded.

Antonio replies simply by pointing to his own success as a sufficient justification for his actions:

> True;
> And look how well my garments sit upon me,
> Much feater than before; my brother's servants
> Were then my fellows, now they are my men.

The curiously personal twist given to the 'fresh garments' symbol elsewhere present in the play is thoroughly consistent with the rest of Antonio's thought. Substantially allied to the argument of Iago and still more of Edmund in his dis-missal of 'legitimacy' as an irrelevant prejudice, it introduces once more into the play that sense of the uncertainty, the precariousness, of court life which has already been developed as an important theme in *Cymbeline* and *The Winter's Tale* and which represents the realistic obverse of the pastoral convention also used in these plays. It ends by convincing Sebastian that the action which seems to offer him most hope of profit, of advancement, is thereby justified. But first he expresses his doubt a little more directly: 'But for your conscience?' The cynical energy of Antonio's reply reminds us still more immediately of Iago. The very word, as indicating any reality outside that consistent with his own will, is meaningless to him:

> Ay, sir, where lies that? if it were a kibe,
> 'Twould put me to my slipper: but I feel not
> This deity in my bosom: twenty consciences,
> That stand 'twixt me and Milan, candied be they,
> And melt ere they molest!

The opening image, with its reduction of conscience to a 'kibe', that is, to a purely physical inconvenience of the kind which alone Antonio can conceive, is pure Iago. So is the sneering reference to 'deity', a word which can mean nothing to him but a sentimental illusion intervening between a man and the furthering of those selfish ends in the attainment of which alone he fulfils his manhood. The sense of sentimental unreality is driven home by the references, common in Shakespeare and everywhere expressive of loathing, to 'candied' and 'melt'; the stomach of the consistent, practical man of action revolts against these finicky attempts to restrict his progress. The speech continues, still reflecting the vivacity of the speaker in its rhythm and expression:

> Here lies your brother,
> No better than the earth he lies upon,
> If he were that which now he's like (that's dead)
> Whom I, with this obedient steel, three inches of it,
> Can lay to bed for ever; whiles you, doing thus,
> To the perpetual wink for aye might put
> This ancient morsel, this Sir Prudence, who
> Should not upbraid our course. For all the rest,
> They'll take suggestion as a cat laps milk;
> They'll tell the clock to any business that
> We say befits the hour.

No one can deny Antonio's brilliance in persuasion. His words reflect the intense destructive energy of the man, energy to which his intelligence is bound in faithful service. They have vigour enough, and more, to move the sluggish Sebastian to his purposes. Behind them lies a deep-seated pessimism, the conviction that a dead man is 'no better than the earth he lies upon' and that only three inches of steel, 'obedient' to a will firmly determined to carry out its own selfish purposes, lie between his victim and extinction. If this be so, if conscience be a mere 'kibe', an inconvenient 'deity' which a moment's reasoning can put securely to sleep, then the murder of a man who stands between himself and power is the most natural thing in the world; so natural that he can discuss that man's death in terms of putting him 'to bed for ever'. As for Gonzalo and those who, like him, still feel conscience as a living thing, they are brushed aside in the contemptuous 'ancient morsel', 'Sir Prudence', and in the brilliant, scornful comparison implied in 'They'll take suggestion as a cat laps milk'. The whole thing, given the will, the determination to act in freedom from all scruple, is simplicity itself.

Sebastian has nothing positive to oppose to this conviction of anarchy. He yields at once, and as he yields, Shakespeare is careful to remind us once more of Antonio's other crime:

> Thy case, dear friend,
> Shall be my precedent; as thou gott'st Milan,
> I'll come by Naples. Draw thy sword; one stroke
> Shall free thee from the tribute which thou payest,
> And I the king shall love thee.

The last words show how fully Sebastian has succumbed to the spirit of Antonio. 'One stroke', one simple decisive action is sufficient to cut through all the obstacles which antiquated ties of conscience and custom put in the way of the plotters; and in a world in which only the blow really counts, the decisive stroke backed by the will resolved to achieve its personally dictated ends, everything is simple. The blow when struck, moreover, is to free Antonio from 'tribute', from the material pledge of that natural allegiance on which all order really depends. It is all simple, so simple that it leads fatally to destruction: a destruction logically implied in the act itself even before it is condemned by Prospero and judged by the standards of the moral law which upholds him and which he, within his limited sphere, in turn upholds.

III

In the presentation, during the same scene, of the social situation (so to call it) created on the island mainly by

Prospero's devisings, the development of the principal conception is carried a step further. We have seen already, in *Cymbeline* and *The Winter's Tale*, that the relationship between natural simplicity and the civilized life is a constant theme of the last plays. It is not, as we have also had occasion to see, presented in the form of a simple contrast. The state of nature, as each of these plays conceives it, safeguards virtues which need to be taken into account in any balanced view of life, virtues, moreover, which are deliberately contrasted to the corruption, emptiness, and insecurity which the surface polish of court life so imperfectly conceals; but these virtues, left to themselves, abstracted from their full human context, languish and reveal their essential incompleteness. They need, in other words, to be assumed into a complete scale of civilized values, and this necessity is at once social and, as far as the individual is concerned, maturing. In this way, the theme of 'nature' and its relation to the full civilized state, is related to the time-theme which is also prominent in these plays. The passage of time involves, in human terms, the problem of maturity, a problem inherent in the development of life and in no way to be evaded. To seek to escape it, to perpetuate an idyllic state of innocence, is, in the long run, impossible; overtaken by the maturity which the passage of time imposes upon them, Guiderius and Arviragus break out from the state of simplicity in which their foster-father has sought to maintain them, Florizel and Perdita find their pastoral idyll interrupted by the hostile entry of Polixenes, bringing with him the 'sneaping wind' of ageing envy that first forces them to face the possibility of tragedy and finally, by bringing them to the court of Leontes, prepares the way for a full, civilized consummation of the implications, both personal and social, of marriage.

In *The Tempest* a similar conception is developed in a more openly allegorical form. By bringing to the island the various persons who in some way have affected his own past, Prospero isolates them, forces them to see themselves as they really are and so to come to terms with their respective responsibilities. For the island is in part, but only in part, abstracted from real life; and beneath the dream-like quality which pervades it exists a connection, maintained on the symbolic level, with external reality. If life imposes, in some sense, the need to balance body and spirit, instinct and 'reason', 'nature' and 'grace', these aspects are present there in Caliban and Ariel, reduced to their essential expression in poetry and held together, maintained each in its proper sphere, by Prospero's controlling action. The appearance of Alonso and Gonzalo, Antonio and Sebastian at once shatters this harmony and opens the way to a more inclusive unity; for if their behaviour on the island confirms, by the end of the play, the need for a return to the external, the waking world, the conditions of that return, and indeed the very possibility of it, are determined by their own behaviour during the dream.

The transition to this new stage in the play, less individual, more explicitly 'social' in its derivations, is provided by a speech in which Gonzalo is made the mouthpiece for a statement, apparently drawn from Montaigne, of those nostalgic speculations about primeval simplicity which seem to have so greatly attracted the sophisticated court societies of the sixteenth century and to which the discovery of the New World had given a fresh, though far from unambiguous meaning. In landing upon the island Alonso and his followers are placed in the possession of what they consider to be virgin soil. Here, according to Gonzalo, is their opportunity to organize a community untainted by competition or the shadow of ambition, an arcadian anarchy founded upon the permission given to each of its members to follow his own instincts. His remarks, with the accompanying comments of Antonio and Sebastian, are full of interest:

GONZALO: Had I plantation of this isle, my lord,—
ANTONIO: He'd sow it with nettle-seed.
SEBASTIAN: Or docks or mallows.

GONZALO: And were the king on't, what would I do?
SEBASTIAN: 'Scape being drunk for want of wine.
GONZALO: I' the commonwealth I would by contraries
Execute all things; for no kind of traffic
Would I admit; no name of magistrate;
Letters should not be known; riches, poverty,
And use of service, none. . . .
No occupation, all men idle, all;
And women too, but innocent and pure;
No sovereignty;—
SEBASTIAN: Yet he would be king on't.
ANTONIO: The latter end of his commonwealth forgets
the beginning.

The dispassionate, academic catalogue in which Gonzalo expresses himself reflects perfectly the unreality of the whole dream. He is at this stage, and indeed on repeated occasions through the play, a personage satirically conceived, whose loyalty—although it will make him in the final scenes, as we shall see, a mouthpiece, for some of its deepest positive content, and although it always contrasts with the sophisticated treachery in evidence around him—should not blind us to the pedantry, the notable abstraction which is also part of his view of life. Once more, we are in the presence of commonplace literary themes of the age, which Shakespeare is turning to his own ends. The nostalgia for an arcadian simplicity which produced, among other things, the pastoral convention of the sixteenth century was an international development which a writer like Cervantes, in Don Quixote's discourse on the Golden Age, [1] could raise to true intensity of feeling. No doubt it was a half-realized reaction against the sense of confusion and moral pessimism which dominated so much of the court life of the time. Yet it was not Shakespeare's purpose here to express any nostalgia of this kind, but rather at once to set its idyllic content in opposition to the court corruption we have already seen in

1. *Don Quixote*, Part I, Ch. xi.

Q

action and to use its inherent weakness as a foil to bring out certain conceptions, in no sense conventional, of his own.

This double purpose accounts for the peculiar spirit of the argument thus developed in terms basically derivative, but for ends fundamentally personal. The causes of strife and inequality among men are indeed to be excluded, in accordance with Gonzalo's dream, from the ideal commonwealth, but with them, as soon appears, most of the distinctive qualities of a fully human life. Gonzalo's words, immediately after the exchange with Sebastian and Antonio already quoted, clearly reveal the connection with the earlier plays. They show by the manner of their expression that the state of innocence is also necessarily the state of inexperience:

> All things in common nature should produce
> Without sweat or endeavour: treason, felony,
> Sword, pike, knife, gun, or need of any engine
> Would I not have; but nature should bring forth
> Of its own kind, all foison, all abundance,
> To feed my innocent people.

All this is to come about, according to Gonzalo's dream, 'without sweat or endeavour'; but also—we have to add— without the salutary experience of effort from which is born, often slowly and painfully, the capacity to distinguish between good and evil which is the foundation of the moral life. For knowledge of good implies awareness of the evil from which it is distinguished; and this awareness is acquired through a process, difficult but redeeming, of procreation and maturity. The relation of the sexual theme to the temporal process, so insisted upon in these plays, is once more stressed in the words of Gonzalo's critics; and, cynics though they are, their attitude is none the less relevant, part of the complete picture. The insufficiency of Gonzalo's simplicity, already implied in the flat, abstract tone of his own speech, is directly revealed by the comments of Antonio and Sebastian:

SEBASTIAN: No marrying 'mong his subjects?
ANTONIO: None, man, all idle; whores and knaves.

Gonzalo's commonwealth is founded, in despite of the essential loyalty of his own nature, upon an amorality which leaves place for the 'nettle-seed', 'docks', and 'mallows' mentioned by his critics to take possession of the soil. The fact that men like Antonio and Sebastian exist proves in itself that some kind of cultivation of the human terrain is necessary. This cultivation, as they point out, is admitted by Gonzalo himself when he imagines that he is king of the island; for the 'latter', the anarchic end of his common-wealth, has forgotten that its beginning was founded upon kingship, accepted authority, 'degree'. The substance of the passage, as we have already indicated, is closely paralleled in the conception which underlies the treatment of the pastoral scene in *The Winter's Tale*. The state of nature is one which man must, in the nature of things, outgrow as his experience develops. The crucial problem is whether this development will be towards 'good', in the acceptance of some adequate moral standard spontaneously accepted as a condition of maturity (a standard sanctioned, in this play, by the Destiny which upholds Prospero) or towards the anarchy of unlimited desires.

At this point, and with the problem of the state of nature thus before us, it is time to consider Caliban. For Caliban, half man and half beast, represents the real state of nature far more truly than any of Gonzalo's courtly theorizings, and in his relations with Prospero the connection between 'nature' and the 'social', civilized state is incorporated into the dream, the reflected reality, of life on the island. The poetic strain which, it has been generally agreed, Caliban possesses, corresponds in him to the positive aspect of the real state of nature. Unlike the men with whom he comes into contact and who corrupt him, Caliban has the advan-tage of being in touch with natural simplicity. His poetry turns invariably upon his knowledge of and appreciation for

the natural forces which surround him. When Trinculo and
Stephano meet him (II. ii) he offers, in language that contrasts vividly and surely of set intention with their coarseness, to show them 'the best springs' and 'berries', where the
jay's nest is to be found, and how to 'snare the nimble
marmoset'. All this is attractive, so attractive that we are
sometimes apt to find Prospero's harshness to him in a
preceding scene—'Thou poisonous slave, got by the devil
himself' (I. ii)—excessive and unsympathetic. Yet, if we
consider further, the harshness is a necessary part of the
complete conception. For Caliban, with his natural simplicity, is indissolubly bound to Prospero. Prospero himself
admits this to Miranda when he tells her:

> We cannot miss him: he does make our fire,
> Fetch in our wood, and serves in offices
> That profit us. (I. ii.)

The kind of life that Prospero has established in his retreat
assumes, in fact, the submission of Caliban as a necessary
condition. That this submission requires an effort, implies
a continual strain, indicates once more that the island is a
reflection of the outer world.

Its state previous to Prospero's arrival is, as he himself
describes it (I. ii), significant in this respect. Prospero has
not been the first to establish his control upon the state of
nature. His arrival was preceded by that of Sycorax, the
'foul', 'damned' witch—

> who with age and envy
> Was grown into a hoop.

Exiled, like Prospero himself, though for reasons clearly
contrary, from civilized society in 'Argier', and possessed of
a magic opposed to his in that it bore fruit in—

> mischiefs manifold, and sorceries terrible
> To enter human hearing,

the rule she established on the island can be considered the
reverse of his own. It exercised itself, indeed, over the same

elements as he himself still controls: on the one hand, Ariel
—symbol, if the word may pass to describe so intangible, so
essentially poetic a creation, of the imaginative power, the
fancy which now finds liberty and integration in Prospero's
own spiritual vision—and, on the other, her own offspring,
Caliban. Only, of course, being what she was, the effects of
her rule were exactly contrary to his. Where Ariel, in the
service of Prospero, is working towards the freedom which
has been promised him, Sycorax reduced him to servitude,
enslaved him to matter, walled him into a 'cloven pine',
expressing her resentment at his refusal to obey her by sub-
duing him to her own material nature. Ariel, indeed, is
expressly described by Prospero as a 'spirit too *delicate*' (the
adjective is frequently used in the last plays, and always
bears, in its sense of the refinement of the material, a
spiritual connotation) to carry out the '*earthy* and abhorred
commands' imposed upon him. The result, as Prospero
recalls it, was a torment conveyed through a sense of intolerable subjection to material confinement, to deformity, and
one, moreover, which Sycorax herself, whose power, being
evil, was limited to the material, was unable to undo. From
this situation, Prospero, who controls matter from the
standpoint of a superior spirituality, was able to save him;
and, though he exacts from Ariel service for as long as the
situation on the island has to be directed to its conclusion,
it is a service which is recognized to be the prelude to
freedom.

The position of Caliban is, as near as may be, the exact
reversal of this. As the offspring of the witch and during
the period of her domination, he was free when Ariel was
imprisoned; and now that, unlike Ariel, he is in captivity,
his subjection is the consequence of his own nature and of
his relation to the new order represented by his master.
For Caliban, besides being necessary to Prospero, is at least
in part his own creation. Finding him on the island and
needing him, Prospero tried from the first to incorporate
him into the new civilized order of moral realities; and

Caliban himself in his reply at once admits this and turns it into a most formidable indictment of the whole civilizing process which began by flattering him and finally turned into his tyrant:

> When thou camest first,
> Thou strók'st me, and madest much of me; wouldst give me
> Water with berries in it; and teach me how
> To name the bigger light, and how the less,
> That burn by day and night; and then I lov'd thee,
> And show'd thee all the qualities o' the isle,
> The fresh springs, brine-pits, barren place and fertile;
> Curs'd be I that did so! All the charms
> Of Sycorax, toads, beetles, bats, light on you!
> For I am all the subjects that you have,
> Which first was mine own king. (I. ii.)

From this we may learn more than one thing fundamental to the play. In the first place, the poetry which we admire in Caliban was given to him, at least in part, by Prospero; the instinctive appreciation was, if we like, his own, a natural endowment, but the gift of expression, essentially a social, a civilizing gift, came to him from Prospero. The natural and the civilized orders are, in other words, inextricably mixed, and the problem with which Prospero is wrestling is simply that the natural, animal man tends obstinately to anarchy. For the burden of Caliban's grievance is that Prospero has deprived him of his freedom, subjected his individuality to the pre-eminence of spiritual rule:

> For I am all the subjects that you have,
> Which first was mine own king;

and he goes on to accuse Prospero of keeping him in prison who had originally been master of the whole island. Prospero's answer once more shows the problem in all its complexity:

> I have used thee,
> Filth as thou art, with human care, and lodg'd thee
> In mine own cell, till thou didst seek to violate
> The honour of my child.

Caliban, who is necessary to Prospero, whose animal instincts are a true part of human nature, is yet, by virtue of his very qualities, recalcitrant to all restraint, to every claim of moral discipline. Regarding himself as the true owner of the island ('This island's mine by Sycorax my mother'), he associates himself with it in its 'state of nature', its condition before the hated measure of 'cultivation' imposed upon himself and it alike by the arrival of Prospero. In point of fact, however, the 'state of nature' is less an idyllic simplicity, of the kind already evoked by Gonzalo, than a void, waiting to be filled in accordance with a purpose stronger, more potent for either good or evil, than itself. The rule of Prospero is an alternative, not to natural spontaneity, but to the power of Sycorax. In Caliban, as in his mother, it is the evil impulse, actively opposed to the civilized graces and even to the possibility of social intercourse, which ultimately triumphs; and so he, in his own way, echoes Antonio by asserting his right to enjoy whatever appeals to his passions as desirable. When Prospero gave him liberty and the use of his own cell, he used this freedom to attack his master's dearest possession in the person of his daughter.

The conflict of flesh and spirit, a reflection of that between civilized values and the state of nature, is not at this point within sight of resolution. The animal instincts which man inherits from his natural origins can neither be ignored, for they are a necessary part of his being, nor integrated in the new spiritual order at which Prospero aims; and so they are in bondage to the master who came to give them significance but who has in fact destroyed their original spontaneity:

> PROSPERO: Abhorred slave,
> Which any print of goodness will not take,
> Being capable of all ill! I pitied thee,

Took pains to make thee speak, taught thee
    each hour
One thing or other: when thou did'st not,
    savage,
Know thy own meaning, but wouldst gabble,
    like
A thing most brutish, I endow'd thy purposes
With words that made them known. But thy
    vile race,
Though thou didst learn, had that in't which
    good natures
Could not abide to be with: therefore wast
    thou
Deservedly confined into this rock, who had'st
Deserved more than a prison.

CALIBAN: You taught me language, and my profit on't
    Is, I know how to curse.

Denunciation and reply are each, from their own point of
view, unanswerable. Set against Prospero's purpose of
spiritualizing the island, pervading its life with his own
moral awareness, the kind of 'nature' represented by Caliban
is not simply amoral, empty of definite social form and
content, but positively evil; born as he is of the witch who
herself by her arrival filled a void on the island, he is at
once recalcitrant to any 'print of goodness', such as that
which his master has sought to impose upon him through
education, and—in the absence of such a 'print'—'capable
of all ill'. From Caliban's point of view, on the other hand,
island born and claiming possession by length of tenure,
Prospero is an intruder whose arrival has upset a balance,
a harmony that formerly existed, a state in which 'freedom',
as he conceives it, was a tangible possession. The first result
of this incompatibility of views is that the educative process
itself, the attempt to absorb 'nature' into a distinctively
civilized order, not only fails, but is the cause of a dangerous
extension of the capacity for ill. The 'purposes' which

Caliban has learned, through Prospero, to express in words, 'to make known', are those which follow from his birth; his 'vile race', though capable of assimilating the knowledge offered to it, remains what it has always been, something which—

good natures
Could not abide to be with.

The imprisonment of Caliban—amply 'deserved' from Prospero's point of view—is a necessary measure of self-preservation; but to the creature thus enslaved it is rather a corruption of 'natural' simplicity, the negation of an original state of freedom. How to harmonize these points of view, how to reconcile the claims of instinct with those of reasonable spirituality, is something that Prospero himself does not yet appear to see. Not until the events precipitated on the island by the advent of strangers have taken their course and Ariel has spoken with the voice of judgement, is there any sign of clarification.

The deficiencies of Caliban's natural anarchism, already suggested by Prospero, are further illustrated by his meeting with Stephano and Trinculo. Once more the theme is one which was being worked out in the New World before the eyes of Shakespeare's contemporaries. The arrival on the island of men from the outer world of 'civilization' is fatal to the natural creature, who escapes from the bondage of Prospero only to fall into that, infinitely more degrading, of the basest camp-followers of a supposedly civilized society. Caliban is, of course, greatly superior to Stephano and Trinculo. The poetry of his simplicity is enough to ensure that; but, divorced as he is from spiritual judgement and seeking only the anarchic freedom of his desires, he falls into a slavery which the superiority of his expression, being so incongruous, serves only to make still more grotesque. Seduced by the 'celestial liquor' which Stephano gives him, he offers to serve him as a god:

I prithee be my god.

That's a brave god and bears celestial liquors;
I'll kneel to him.

I'll kiss thy foot and swear myself thy subject.   (II. ii.)

His aim in doing so is above all to free himself from service—
'I'll bear him no more sticks, but follow thee'—but, in
following the freedom thus offered him by his fallacious instincts in a situation which these no longer serve him to
interpret, he goes out drunk, crying 'Freedom, hey-day!' indeed, but reduced in reality to a slavery far more degrading
than any to which he had been subjected before.

The depth of his degradation, and that of his new masters,
is fully brought out when they next appear.   It is, on a
lower level, the equivalent of the spirit which inspired
Sebastian and Antonio to plot against Alonso.   By this time,
the subjection of 'nature', as shown in Caliban—it is no
accident that he is more than once referred to as a 'natural',
with its double meaning of savage and mentally deficient—
has produced its logical result.   Stephano has become, in his
own estimation, the master, the parody of a king, on the
island; he sees Caliban as his 'lieutenant', and answers his
servile devotion with a patronage that ministers, above all,
to his self-esteem.   Trinculo is at once less active and more
critical.   He retains, with a lesser degree of vanity, some
understanding of the true position, as is proved when he
remarks:

. . . the folly of this island! They say there's but five
upon this isle: we are three of them; if the other two be
brained like us, the state totters (III. ii),

and again, when Caliban salutes Stephano as his lord:

'Lord', quoth he! That a monster should be such a natural,

to which Stephano, with a caricature of dignity, replies:
'Trinculo, keep a good tongue in your head; if you prove a
mutineer—the next tree!' The reference to contemporary
events, the exposure of the reality behind the pretensions of

the superior race to fulfil its civilizing mission, is equally implied in the following remark: 'The poor monster's my subject, and he shall not suffer indignity'. To an empty benevolence born of equally baseless self-estimation, Caliban replies by abasing himself in a caricature of the court suitor making his supplication; 'Wilt thou be pleased to hearken once again to the suit I made to thee?', receiving Stephano's reply in a gesture at once empty and finally absurd: 'Marry will I; kneel and repeat it; I will stand, and so shall Trinculo.' It is part of the quality of the island to reflect, in its dream-world, exterior reality; each of the shipwrecked characters reverts, under the new conditions, to his own nature, and the result is a cross-section of society related at every point to the greater world without.

Completely enslaved as he now is in his ignorance, Caliban is still capable of imposing upon his new masters a purpose which they would otherwise lack. He begins to inspire the drunken sailors to plot against Prospero; animality, faced with what seems to be a void and rushing in to fill it, takes charge of human nature and debases it to new levels of evil. For Caliban, ridiculous though he has become in his worship of Stephano and Trinculo, is far more dangerous than the other two. In the brutal savagery of his proposals something breaks out that has been held in check so far, albeit uneasily, by the domination of Prospero. That something finds expression in the unrestrained physical cruelty of the speeches in which he outlines his plot. Prospero is to be brained in his sleep, to have his skull battered in with a log, to be 'paunched' with a stake, to have his throat cut; most brutally of all, perhaps—

> I'll yield thee him asleep
> Where thou mayst knock a nail into his head.   (III. ii.)

First, however, and above all, he must be deprived of the sources of his power:

> Remember
> First to possess his books; for without them

He's but a sot as I am, nor hath not
One spirit to command: they all do hate him
As rootedly as I.

In ascribing his own hatred to the other servants of Prospero,
Caliban is speaking falsely, measuring civilized spirituality in
terms of his own anarchic brutality, but his emphasis on
the books, and on his master's comparative helplessness
without them, indicates that he understands and fears the
sources of Prospero's power. His realization adds to the
vehemence of his proposals. Against the spiritual domination of Prospero his own instincts arise in a revulsion ultimately inspired in the flesh, the physical. The true motive
of his craving for liberty is expressed more directly in the
same speech, and in others like it:

. . . that most deeply to consider is
The beauty of his daughter.
. . . She will become thy bed, I warrant,
And bring thee forth brave brood.

The use of the word 'brood' to describe the progeny of this
imagined union brings out well the animal spirit in which
it is conceived, the revolt of passion against reason, of 'blood'
against moral control, which it implies. This is the spirit
which has led Caliban, seeking an illusory freedom, to 'lick
the boots' of the coarsest, lowest kind of human being.
That he is still superior to Stephano and Trinculo is shown
by the survival of his poetic instincts ('Be not afeard, the
isle is full of noises') and by his capacity to respond, at
times and after his fashion, to the music which pervades the
isle as an exhalation of harmony; but his subjection is in
essence complete, and springs inevitably from his conception
of liberty. We are reminded of Shakespeare's treatment of
the same problem in *Measure for Measure*. In that play, so
dissimilar from *The Tempest* in so many respects, Claudio,
as he is being taken to prison, freely confesses that the cause

of the predicament in which he finds himself is 'liberty, too much liberty'.[1] Freedom from restraint, unchecked by adherence to any spiritual loyalty freely accepted, can lead man through his instincts only to moral dissolution and chaos. This in turn is the lowest form of slavery. Caliban is bound by his nature to service, but this service, which might have been that acceptable to Prospero when he first took him into his cell and tried to teach him the civilized graces, turns to a mixture of the lowest animal brutality and sheer folly.

IV

In contrast to Caliban as spirit to body, liberty to servitude, 'grace' to nature, stands the figure of Ariel. Prospero's rule on the island has consisted, since his arrival there, very largely in establishing a balance between them. Both are in his service, though Ariel's is given in return for liberation from servitude and is to end in complete freedom, whereas Caliban's is grudgingly, resentfully conceded to a superior power. Once strangers from the outer world have been admitted to the island, this balance is upset and the relation between his original servants undergoes a decisive change. Whereas Ariel, in a series of transformations, becomes increasingly identified with the purposes of his master, Caliban—originally, through Sycorax, a power on the island —is progressively isolated from the main development, the growing unity of vision which leads to the final reconciliation.

The earliest utterances of Ariel in the play lay stress on the elemental quality which makes him capable, as it were, of refining the natural properties of the island until only their essential, intangible distillation remains as the expression of his being. His first response to Prospero's call is charged with this elemental condition:

1. *Measure for Measure*, I. ii.

> I come
> To answer thy best pleasure; be't to fly,
> To swim, to dive into the fire, to ride
> On the curl'd clouds, to thy strong bidding task
> Ariel and all his quality.

'To fly', 'to swim', 'to dive into the fire': the combination of air, water, and flame are at once derived by Ariel from the island and make him, in turn, its emanation, its presiding spirit. Almost immediately, this same spirit is projected into a fiery form—

> I *flamed* amazement . . .
> . . . on the topmast,
> The yards and bowsprit, would I *flame* distinctly,
> Then meet and join—

to be united, now mingled with air and water, to the perturbation of the elements:

> Jove's lightnings, the precursors
> Of the dread thunder-claps, more momentary
> And sight-outrunning were not: the fire and cracks
> Of sulphurous roaring the most mighty Neptune
> Seemed to besiege, and make his bold waves tremble,
> Yea, his dread trident shake.

The marriage thus consummated, poetically speaking, between the lightness of Ariel's imaginative substance and the manifestations of natural power which he controls for the ends proposed by Prospero is true to the main conception. It will be confirmed, in due course, in the great speech of judgement which Ariel himself is to utter and towards which the whole action tends for its illumination. In this way, the continuity of conception which binds together the complete development is foreshadowed from its opening episode.

These final derivations of Ariel's description of the storm are not, however, yet apparent. At this stage, it is enough

238

to note that his action produces, in the more material
beings submitted to it, a suspension of sanity which will be
maintained in their later behaviour and is, in effect, their
response to the elemental commotion in which they are
involved:

> Not a soul
> But felt a fever of the mad, and play'd
> Some tricks of desperation.

This alienation of sanity, like the tempest which brought it
into being, is part of Prospero's purpose. His former enemies
have to lose their sanity (or what they conceive as such)
before they can hope to find it again. In a moral sense,
indeed, they have lost it already in different degrees by their
behaviour in the world, and their only way to recover it
will be to achieve, under new conditions, some measure of
the self-knowledge they have so conspicuously lacked. The
action of the storm thus corresponds, not simply to an
external device willed by Prospero, but to a stage in the
symbolic conception which it is Ariel's function to guide to
its full development.

The tempest, its end once achieved, is followed by the
restoration, also willed by Prospero and carried out by his
ministering spirit, of calm. As his enemies reach dry land,
they are abstracted from their normal selves, enter into a
state of temporary isolation in which their surface qualities
are laid to sleep and the true being which, for the most part
unknown to themselves, has inspired their behaviour comes
to the surface. Their state is that which has descended upon
ship and crew as a result of the spell laid upon them:

> Safely in harbour
> Is the king's ship; in the deep nook, where once
> Thou call'st me up at midnight to fetch dew
> From the still-vex'd Bermoothes, there she's hid;
> The mariners all under hatches stow'd;
> Who, with a charm join'd to their suffer'd labour,
> I have left asleep.

To think of this as mere poetic decoration is certainly mistaken. Once more, as Ariel's poetry describes the course of events, it charges them with symbolic meaning, assimilates them to the dream in which their true nature will gradually become apparent. The king's ship lies 'safely in harbour', where the action of the storm no longer presses upon it and where the crew, their 'suffer'd labour' rounded off by subjection to his magic power, are safely 'under hatches stow'd', suspended from their normal waking selves in sleep. The calm of the island has taken the ship to itself, created the conditions for a dream which, by a profound paradox, will become an awakening, an abstraction from reality which is the prelude to return, on a more fully conscious level, to the world.

The beauty of Ariel's description of storm and following calm becomes, thus considered, the reflection of a deliberate purpose, creating through poetic means a balancing of contraries essential to the main conception. It leads, immediately and naturally, to the incorporation, also through Ariel, of a distinctively human emotion. The sorrow of Ferdinand, romantically conceived, is ready from the first for assimilation to the prevailing mood:

> The king's son have I landed by himself:
> Whom I left cooling of the air with sighs
> In an odd angle of the isle, and sitting,
> His arms in this sad knot.

The detachment, gently ironic, implied in 'cooling of the air', combines with the sentimental evocation of solitude and 'sighs', the 'sad knot' of the prince's arms in dejection, to establish the effect of remoteness which the main conception requires at this stage. Personal sorrow, though real, is not intended to have an isolated existence in this play. It will have, in due course, to be taken up into a prevailing harmony associated with the isle as a refuge from tempest, a harmony which will expand, as Prospero's devices impose themselves, to include the full range of human experience, but which is here in the preliminary stage of subjection to the prevailing dream. The spirit of Ferdinand's grief, thus muted, abstracted from personal immediacy, is prepared for assimilation into the complete conception, to which it will contribute, gradually and harmoniously, its own development.

It is at this stage that the poetry of Ariel, responding to the growth of Prospero's harmonizing purpose, finds expression in music. This music, a distillation of the spiritual presences which haunt the isle, falls upon Ferdinand's ear as a deepening of his romantic feeling, as at once an echo of grief and an anticipation of future harmony:

Where should this music be? i' th'air or i' th'earth?
It sounds no more; and, sure, it waits upon
Some god o' the island. Sitting on a bank,
Weeping again the king my father's wreck,
This music crept by me upon the waters,
Allaying both their fury and my passion
With its sweet air; thence I have follow'd it,
Or it hath drawn me rather.

The music, as it acquires in Ferdinand's mind a note of supernatural remoteness as the manifestation of 'some god o' the island', mutes the personal immediacy of his grief, assimilates to its quality, intangible, distilled from common experience, the romantic sentiment which has been present in him since, having escaped the action of the storm, he became aware of his loss. 'Sitting on a bank', wrapt in his still self-conscious grief, the music 'crept' by him on the surface of the waters, smoothing the past fury of the tempest in his memory and 'allaying' the 'passion' which persists in him as he contemplates his father's supposed death. The 'sweet air' works upon Ferdinand as he listens, drawing him towards a new state of mind, less superficially self-aware and more imaginative, ultimately more spiritual. The 'quality' of the island, Prospero's creation through his attendant spirits, begins from this moment to transform past experi-

ence, assuming death and loss into a harmony which anticipates the coming reconciliation.

Ariel's second song, indeed, stresses the note of transformation. By transmuting 'bones' into 'coral' and 'dead eyes'
into the richness of 'pearls', it recalls the burial at sea of
Marina in *Pericles*,[1] her recovery and final restoration.
Beneath the deliberate remoteness from immediate experience which characterizes this passage, a highly individual
emotion, at once tenuous and intense, abstracted and charged
with spiritual meaning, is transforming the symbolic content
of the whole episode. It is essentially the same 'sea-change'
that formerly wrought transformation in *Pericles* that is
being evoked, the passage of storm into following calm and
of tragic experience into the intuition of value by which
mortality, poetically muted, is assumed, with an intensity
itself deliberately remote, isolated from common fact, into
'something rich and strange'. In this way, the peculiar
spirit which has from the first pervaded the island through
Ariel's refinement of the material, imposes itself upon the
human action, transforming grief and loss into the conditions of anticipated harmony.

With Ferdinand thus abstracted, and his tragic memories
subjected to the dream-like quality of island experience, he
is ready to meet Miranda. This meeting, which we have
already considered from the point of view of her awakening
conscience,[2] now falls naturally into the developing symbolic structure. Ariel's 'ditty', though it reminds Ferdinand
once more of his drowned father (it is no part of the play's
intention that human feeling should be lost, only that it
should be taken up, absorbed into an expanding range of
experience), nevertheless confers upon his situation, upon
memories and recent emotions alike, something like an
explicit sense of immortality:

> This is no mortal business, nor no sound
> That the earth owes.

1. See above, p. 28.
2. See p. 207.

Against the background thus variously and carefully indicated, the first meeting between the two young lovers is naturally conceived in terms that transcend any merely personal conception of their relationship. Prospero's awakening of Miranda confirms, in its deliberate elaboration, that this is no mere meeting of two young people on the plane of common reality or romantic sentiment. Besides stressing that his daughter is at a peculiarly decisive moment in her development, it contributes, through the deliberate poetic emphasis of 'The fringed curtains of thine eyes advance', to the sense of removal from common experience that is being sought. That Miranda should see her lover as a 'brave' vision, a thing 'divine', is entirely in keeping with this intention. It confirms that she is passing through a type of experience, transfiguring in quality, already familiar in *Pericles*. Its relation to the complete conception, considerably more complex than in the earlier play, will only be clear at its conclusion, but the final effect, thus related to the pervading spiritual presence of Ariel as harmony, reconciliation, is already in process of creation. The fusion of the resources of poetry and drama to produce an experience that transcends the normal limits of both to aim at the expression of a spiritual state as intense as it is remote is already, at this early stage, foreshadowed.

By the end of the scene, and after Prospero's sharp change to a mood of distrust (the meaning of which we have already indicated), the sensation of dream, of a suspension of the normal human faculties, pervades the action. Ferdinand is as much subject to it as Prospero's various enemies. His nerves, controlled by Miranda's father in spite of his attempted reaction—

> are in their infancy again,
> And have no vigour in them;[1]

---

1. Compare, in a more material sense, but with something of the same rhythm and feeling, Ariel's—

> Your swords are now too massy for your strengths,
> And will not be uplifted. (III. iii.)

and, as he admits, in replying to this assertion of power:

> My spirits, as in a dream, are all bound up.
> My father's loss, the weakness which I feel,
> The wreck of all my friends, nor this man's threats,
> To whom I am subdued, are but light to me,
> Might I but through my prison once a day
> Behold this maid.

The secret of this lies less in the romantic assertion of devotion to Miranda than in the circumstances which accompany it. The 'dream' in which Ferdinand's spirits are bound up is at once related to his past and a prelude to awakening. To arrive at the threshold of this new experience, he has had to undergo the 'loss' of his father, the 'weakness' induced in him by long exposure to the tempest, and the 'wreck' of all the friends who accompanied him on his fatal voyage. Loss, weakness, and grief are all part of that weaning from past emotions, past happiness, which has to take place before the new life, the fresh vision of 'grace', can come to him in its full splendour. His state on the island will, accepting this 'loss', transform it through dream into harmony, become a prelude to awakening; and when the awakening finally comes it will involve, not Ferdinand alone, but also those around him, in a return to the civilized world and its full, living experiences.

The appearances of Ariel in the scenes immediately following are relatively slight in content. The main interest shifts to the analysis of the motives of the principal human actors on the island stage, and his next important entry (III. iii) takes place when this is substantially complete. The two plots—that against Alonso and that against Prospero—have been fully launched and the original seclusion of the island has been most effectively shattered by the entry of human passion and evil impulse. Yet Prospero, in spite of all, has the threads in his hands, and it is precisely at this moment that he chooses to indicate, through Ariel, the key to the moral resolution at which he aims. With his charac-

teristic harmonies so deepened and transformed that they
are fused with the power of the tempest he was also instrumental in raising, Ariel at last assumes material form before
Alonso and his companions and, in an utterance which
occupies a central position in the development of the entire
action, formulates his master's decisive enunciation of
judgement.

This appearance is preceded by an intensifying of the
dream-like atmosphere proper to the island, which Ariel
himself has been so instrumental in creating. It affects the
various courtiers in different ways, according to their own
natures. Gonzalo is the first to express a need for rest which
he shares with his fellows—or at least with those of them
who, being spiritually redeemable, are capable of the vision
of sleep:

> . . . here's a maze trod, indeed,
> Through forth-rights and meanders! By your patience,
> I needs must rest me.

Since they have been brought to the island, Gonzalo and
his companions have been subjected to an intensity of
experience which is at once bewildering and the cause of a
craving for rest. Alonso too is weary, even to the 'dulling'
of his spirits. He has 'lost', with his son, the grounds for
hope, is passing through a state of desolation which he cannot
yet see as the prelude, through sleep, of restoration:

> Even here I will put off my hope, and keep it
> No longer for my flatterer: he is drown'd
> Whom thus we stray to find; and the sea mocks
> Our frustrate search on land.

Alonso's hopelessness corresponds to that which, prior to his
vision of Miranda, weighed upon his son. In both the sense
of loss is a preliminary condition of recovery. Beneath his
despair, there exists in Alonso the desire not to be deceived
by the 'flattery' always associated with court life; in the

ability to see his situation as, for the moment, it presents itself lies the key to the transformation which will enable him to see in the action of the sea not, as at present, a 'mockery', but the instrument of redemption which Ariel will shortly indicate. Meanwhile, the pessimism which has, for him, a saving quality is accepted by his enemies, who still resist the invitation to sleep, as a condition which furthers their own purposes—'I am right glad that he's so out of hope'—by offering them an opportunity to recover the initiative so recently (and by Ariel's intervention) missed.

Sleep, however, or the craving for it, leads, not for the first time, to music, and so to a deepening of all the qualities that we have learned to associate with Ariel. This time, however, it is not airy or full of fancy, but—as befits the revelation to come—'solemn and strange'. Alonso hails it, not without meaning, as 'harmony', and it falls on Gonzalo's ear as 'marvellous sweet'. The general effect both confirms the note of illusion which corresponds to the dream-like quality of the island and infuses into it, through the dream itself, the sense of an awakening to reality. Once again, the emotions evoked by Ariel's intervention correspond to the main moral conception. Whereas Alonso's first instinct is to appeal to celestial protection from the terrifying illusion before him—'Give us kind keepers, heavens!'—Sebastian regards it as no more than a 'drollery', related to the travellers' tales put out by the exuberant imagination of the times. To accept the reality of the spiritual, in its symbolic, 'dream'-like presentation, is to show a capacity for redemption.

Each of the castaways, having reacted in accordance with his own nature to Prospero's last and most powerful creation, prepares to accept the viands put before him. Gonzalo, as befits him, associates this ministration with the state of nature which he conceives to exist on the island and contrasts it, characteristically, with a pessimistic estimate of civilized society:

> . . . these are people of the island—
> Who, though they are of monstrous shape, yet, note,
> Their manners are more gentle-kind than of
> Our human generation you shall find
> Many, nay, almost any.

Like the rest of Gonzalo's theories about the state of nature, this is abstractly, theoretically conceived, and Ariel's subsequent action will remove the whole episode to an entirely different level; but 'nature' itself, though not offering the basis for a complete interpretation of life, is part of the picture, will bear assumption into the final integration. Alonso, in turn, reacts as the disillusioned courtier he is, at once expressing appreciation of the 'excellent dumb discourse' acted before him and confirming his mood of fatalistic indifference:

> I will stand to, and feed,
> Although my last: no matter, since I feel
> The best is past;

whilst Sebastian, equally true to his own nature, is cynically concerned with nothing but the material satisfaction of his appetite:

> FRANCISCO: They vanish'd strangely.
> SEBASTIAN: No matter, since
>   They have left their viands behind; for we
>   have stomachs.

All, however, the idealistic courtier, the repentant prince, and the aristocratic cynic, are equally faced by an illusion. Reality, on the moral plane which here concerns us, is affirmed in Prospero's aside commenting on Gonzalo's words of appreciation:

> Honest lord,
> Thou hast said well; for some of you there present
> Are worse than devils.

His judgement is that of one who stands outside the state of dream and illusion, which he is directing to the ends his superior insight has conceived. In accordance with this design the episode itself, though still affecting the remaining actors as a dream, is transported to its true level when the banquet disappears to the sound of 'thunder and lightning', leaving the stage clear for the transition from magic and illusion to the decisive symbolic revelation.

Ariel's great speech addressed to Alonso and his companions before he deprives them of the enchanted banquet is, in fact, nothing less than the keystone upon which the structure of the play rests:

> You are three men of sin, whom Destiny,
> That hath to instrument this lower world,
> And what is in't, the never-surfeited sea
> Hath caus'd to belch up you; and, on this island,
> Where man doth not inhabit, you 'mongst men
> Being most unfit to live . . .
>   But remember,
> For that's my business to you, that you three
> From Milan did supplant good Prospero,
> Expos'd unto the sea (which hath requit it)
> Him and his innocent child; for which foul deed,
> The powers delaying, not forgetting, have
> Incens'd the seas and shores, yea, all the creatures,
> Against your peace. Thee of thy son, Alonso,
> They have bereft; and do pronounce by me
> Lingering perdition (worse than any death
> Can be at once) shall step by step attend
> You and your ways, whose wraths to guard you from,
> Which here, in this most desolate isle, else falls
> Upon your heads, is nothing but heart's sorrow
> And a clear life ensuing. (III. iii.)

Here at last—rather even than in any speech so far spoken by Prospero—is an explicit statement of what *The Tempest* is about. The speech is introduced with a degree of pageantry

248

and circumstance that makes it stand out with great dramatic force from the general action. Ariel—hitherto the 'gentle Ariel' of Prospero's preference—is brought on to the stage in the form of a harpy to the accompaniment of thunder and lightning. He causes the banquet to vanish by a motion of his wings and then, left face to face with those upon whom he has come to utter judgement, he speaks. His words, piercing through dream to reality and recalling each of those who hear him from illusion to their waking selves, have the weighted simplicity that underlines their unique character and seriousness. The effect is obtained by means so direct that they barely call for analysis. Partly by the persistent use of heavy vocalic stresses, partly by the emphatic introduction of pauses in the middle and at the end of lines, partly by the insertion of parenthetic phrases into long unfolding sentences, the speech attains a measured magnificence unsurpassed, in its kind, anywhere in Shakespeare. Unsurpassed because, perhaps for the first time in his work, the voice of Destiny delivers itself directly in judgement. 'I and my fellows', says Ariel, 'are ministers of Fate.' As such he speaks and, by so speaking, brings out the full meaning of the play.

The most important feature of the speech, indeed, is its affirmation of Destiny. This affirmation is, in its unequivocal expression, unique in Shakespeare's work. Much of the symbolism of the later plays—the use, for example, of the associations of 'grace' in relation to fertility—has religious implications; but nowhere, not even in *The Winter's Tale* with its references, still deliberately rather misty, to 'the gods', is Destiny so *personally* conceived, or conceded such direct and absolute power in the working-out of human affairs. Destiny, according to Ariel, 'hath to instrument the lower world'. 'Delaying', but 'not forgetting', it watches over the whole action and brings those concerned in it with infallible foreknowledge to the conclusion willed by absolute justice. All this, however it may have been foreshadowed in earlier plays, is substantially new, but at the same time a natural development. For all Shakespeare's symbolism, with the harmonizing purpose which underlies it, moves towards a presentation of the problems, moral and artistic, involved in this final acceptance of the reality of Destiny. Without that acceptance, the intuition of 'grace' is only an insubstantial dream, a tenuous harmony woven out of elements that have no more validity than that of a personal mood; with it, possibly, the author lays himself open to the charge of going beyond his experience, of introducing an element of discontinuity in what had been so far the harmonious pattern of his work. Whatever we may conclude in this respect, we should do well to begin by recognizing that the problem, and the effort to resolve it, were implicit in the whole Shakespearean experience. Needless to say, it was not part of the artist's purpose to substantiate this objective conception of Destiny by argument; but it was his aim, inevitable and necessary, to place it in the centre of his play, to allow the symbolic structure elaborated through the converging action of images, plot, and character to form around it, to see if it would, in the last analysis, fit.

In the detailed working out of this conception, Shakespeare returns to familiar ground. The symbolic use of storm and its association with new-born forces of harmony is, as we have seen on many occasions, common to all the last plays. Marina in *Pericles* lost her mother, and was herself apparently lost in a storm at sea, but the storm itself threw her up on a friendly shore and eventually she was restored to her father's arms. In *The Winter's Tale*, when Perdita was exposed to the elements by her father's unreasoning folly, she was found by the shepherds and her finding, while the storm was still raging and the younger Clown saw a ship struggling to preserve itself, was really the first step in recovery: 'thou mettest with things dying, I with things new-born'.[1] So it is in *The Tempest*. Only there 'the never-surfeited seas' are explicitly controlled by a 'Destiny' which has 'incensed' them against the 'foul deed' of those who plotted against

1. Act III, Scene iii.

Prospero and made them, in their anger, the instruments of an inexorable justice. The sea, to which Prospero and Miranda were exposed by human selfishness, has—through Prospero's own action—'belch'd up' the criminals, men 'unfit to live', and brought them to a foreseen judgement.

The keynote of the whole play, which Ariel comes to emphasize, is indeed *judgement*. Only when the good and evil in human nature have been understood and separated (for just separation can only follow upon understanding) will the final reconciliation and restoration of harmony take place. This moral judgement is based in *The Tempest* upon an objective sanction which, as we have seen, needs to be proved in operation. For this purpose—and really for this purpose alone—the various actors in the forgotten story of Naples and Milan have been brought together through the providential action of the storm upon 'this most desolate isle', 'where man doth not inhabit'. Desolate surely because the work of purgation which is about to be accomplished needs to be accompanied by abstinence and a certain asceticism; and desolate too, because it is not a place upon which men are to live their full civilized lives—after the final reconciliation it is left by all, except those whose nature debars them from playing a part in the 'brave new world' of beings at once spiritualized and social to which they are now being offered entry—but on which they are to achieve moral understanding and learn to accept the judgement passed upon them. It is upon their acceptance of the tremendous accusation now worded by Ariel, which touches the deepest nature of each of them, that their possibility of salvation will depend. They have been brought to the island to *learn*, and, through learning, to leave a world of shadow and fancy for re-assimilation into a truly civilized order.

In this process of education the fundamental need is, inevitably, for repentance. Repentance is the necessary consequence, on the human side, of accepting judgement. Here again, the conception is not new in Shakespeare. His last plays, not excluding the later tragedies, throw an increasing stress upon the Christian conception of penitence. Lear is restored to his daughter after becoming aware of his own folly, although the restoration, still insufficiently developed to prevail against the tragic spirit that dominates the play, is only temporary and, in one sense at least, illusory; Leontes, after sixteen years of penance for the follies to which his own passion has prompted him, is restored to Hermione and, through the innocence of his daughter, to his broken friendship with Polixenes. Ariel calls for a similar repentance from Alonso and his fellows. Unless their sojourn 'on this most desolate isle' has taught them their own evil and folly, unless it has shown them the need for 'heart's sorrow' and a 'clear life' to follow, their doom is certain. For it is in the nature of unbridled passion, as Shakespeare had already presented it in the great series of tragedies from *Othello* to *Timon of Athens*, to lead its victims to self-destruction; and *The Tempest*, with its insistence upon ideas of penance and amendment that can only follow from acceptance of a personal, spiritual conception of Destiny, is conceived as nothing less than a counterpoise to this tragic process of ruin.

The scene is rounded off, once more, by the distinct reactions of the courtiers to the vision just set before them. Gonzalo, true to his nature, sets against it his evocation of 'something holy', and seeks thereby to recall his master to sanity. Alonso's mind, however, is moving on a new level of self-understanding, relating what he has just heard to the confessed iniquity of the crime in which he formerly shared:

> O, it is monstrous, monstrous!
> Methought the billows spoke, and told me of it;
> The winds did sing it to me; and the thunder,
> That deep and dreadful organ-pipe, pronounced
> The name of Prosper: it did bass my trespass.
> Therefore my son i' the ooze is bedded; and
> I'll seek him deeper than e'er plummet sounded,
> And with him there lie muddied.

The effect of this speech is to connect the dream quality of the episode just witnessed still more closely to the moral pattern of the play. For Alonso, aware of his own past, the voice he has just heard has 'monstrous' echoes. Linked with the action of the storm through the memory it rouses in him of the 'winds' and the 'thunder', it recalls, in terms of music emphasized in 'organ-pipe' and 'bass' and so connected with the prevailing symbol of harmony, the name of the man who has raised it—Prospero—against whom he has 'trespassed'. In the light of this admission of responsibility, the presumed death of Ferdinand is at once accepted and, in the process of acceptance, related to the transforming marine quality that has already, on earlier occasions, been associated with death by drowning. 'My son i' the ooze is bedded':[1] the personal loss, now related by Alonso to his own responsibility, is in the process of undergoing a poetic 'sea-change', whilst the father's desire to lie 'muddied' with his son is at once nostalgic and premonitory of rest. This attitude is, at all events, capable of assimilation to the prevailing symbols of the play; whereas the independent self-reliance of Sebastian and Antonio is, as always, based on blindness, on an obstinate failure of moral understanding. Meanwhile, Gonzalo is the only person present who stands sufficiently apart from the action being developed under his eyes to see it as the 'ecstasy' it is, and to realize that 'All three of them'—Alonso, Sebastian, and Antonio—are, each in his own way, 'desperate', that their 'great guilt'—

Like poison given to work a great time after—

is operating upon each according to his own nature, towards repentance and the confirmation of evil respectively, in accordance with their attitude to their own past. The rest, the return to the waking world which the dream has so

---

1. Compare the use of 'ooze', with a similar overtone of mystery, in *Pericles:*
  . . . nor have I time
  To give thee hallow'd to thy grave, but straight
  Must cast thee, scarcely coffin'd, in the ooze. (IV. i.)

persistently reflected and the first conditions of which have just been established, is in the hands of Prospero.

V

The way is now clear for a true reading of the latter part of *The Tempest*, in which the sublimation of the human state, foreshadowed in Miranda's romantic vision, is assumed as its crown into the full symbolic structure of the play. After the decisive intervention of the transformed Ariel, Prospero's own words reflect an increase of confidence in his own powers which itself indicates that the play is passing into a new stage:—

> my high charms work,
> And these my enemies are all knit up
> In their distraction; they are in my power.　(III. iii.)

The power is, of course, magic, symbolical in quality, and not therefore to be realistically judged. Its justification, the proof that it is more than an abstract imposition upon what has been so far a very close analysis of the roots and consequences of selfishness, will be *poetic*, will depend upon Shakespeare's success in making the symbolic framework live through the vitality conveyed in his web of imagery. Meanwhile, the state of his enemies, now subjected to his power on the island, is one in which their normal, worldly confidence, by which they prevailed over him in Milan, is suspended, reduced to a dream or 'distraction'; the 'fits' in which he now leaves them are at once a reflection of the distorted motives which have brought them to this decisive moment of resolution, and an indication of the twilight state of imperfect moral clarity, balanced between continued illusion and the awakening, painful and partial, to a new understanding, through which they are now groping their way.

The process of drawing the symbolic threads to their

appointed conclusion has several stages. The first is to consummate the union of Miranda and Ferdinand. Upon the union of the children, in *The Tempest* as in *The Winter's Tale*, the reconciliation of the parents and of those who affected their past depends. Prospero has chosen to test their constancy severely, but we have already found (III. i) that they have met the test successfully. Their trials have only cemented, through mutual compassion, their devotion to one another; for, as Ferdinand himself puts it—

> some kinds of baseness
> Are nobly undergone; and most poor matters
> Point to rich ends. (III. i.)

Here again, if we are not to be disappointed, it is necessary to accustom ourselves to the symbolic spirit which pervades the play. The suffering of the two lovers, considered from a purely realistic point of view, may seem abstract and even perfunctory; but once we place the emphasis where it should properly lie, upon the poetic content of the drama to which all Shakespeare's development points, it has its sufficient justification. The poet's use of words, relating this apparent commonplace to elements most essential to the verbal texture of *The Tempest*, brings this home to us. 'Nobly' and 'rich' become associated with the vision, shortly to pervade the action, of a redeemed, ennobled humanity and with the new vitality that springs from the harmonizing of the passions. Once more we are reminded of earlier plays. Antony and Cleopatra were 'noble' in the love which constituted their triumph, even in the face of defeat and in spite of their own admitted and even stressed defects, over the political world dominated by Octavius;[1] and riches, in the hands of Duncan, served to manifest the overflowing generosity of 'grace'. The love of Miranda and Ferdinand,

---

1. Compare, at the beginning of the play, Antony's—
> . . . the *nobleness* of life. (I. i.
> Is to do thus,
and, at the end, Cleopatra's
> '*Noblest* of men, woo't die?' (IV. xv.)

once it has fully unfolded under the tutelage of Prospero, will move upon similar levels.

The effect of imagery of this kind is necessarily cumulative. Its first expression needs to be appreciated in conscious retrospect. When Miranda appears to Ferdinand as he is bearing his logs and speaks to him in the unsuspected presence of Prospero, the same impression of unique nobility begins, almost line by line, to penetrate the verse; as we read, we feel the truth of Ferdinand's remark, made before her entry, that 'The mistress which I serve *quickens* what's dead'. The verb, indeed, by bringing to life the conventional idea of service as the relationship which exists between lover and beloved, is an anticipation of the effect to come. Their emotion, as it expands, brings both the lovers to a new and intenser life, in which feeling responds to feeling in reaching out after a further, more inclusive state. The dialogue between them, which follows at once, gives further weight to this development. Miranda, as she finds Ferdinand bowed over his 'base' task, so poorly related to the nobility which she has instinctively sensed in him, at once transfers her own sentiments to the harsh, inanimate matter to which her father has so incongruously and incomprehensibly bound her new-found lover:

> Pray, set it down, and rest you; when this burns,
> 'Twill weep for having wearied you.

Neither this sensibility in Miranda, nor the fact that love suggests to her the possibility, oddly inconsequential but human, that Prospero may be deceived:

> My father
> Is hard at study; pray you, rest yourself;
> He's safe for these three hours—

are vital to the development of this scene. Its true importance emerges rather in the following exchange between the lovers. Ferdinand, who has already in his solitude referred to the transforming effect upon him of his new-found mistress's inspiration,[1] now confirms it more directly in poetic terms when he replies to her solicitude by saying:

> No, noble mistress; 'tis fresh morning with me
> When you are by at night,

and further develops this into an apostrophe of Miranda as 'the top of admiration', explicitly related to the concept of value by having become, in his eyes—

> worth
> What's dearest to the world.

The conventional expressions of love are here in process of being transformed into something more individual, more germane to the play's symbolic purpose. It is of the essence of love, in Shakespeare's later plays, to produce a trans-forming vision of *value;* from the contemplation of the object of admiration (the keynote is reverence rather than desire, though the force of passion is still present in a muted form) springs a radiance, a transfiguring light which rests on surrounding objects and confers upon them a distinctive quality, at once remote and clearly realized in the expression, of its own.

This becomes clear in the two longer speeches in which Ferdinand and Miranda, after these preparatory exchanges, express the full content of their mutual passion. Ferdinand is the first to speak:

> Full many a lady
> I have eyed with best regard, and many a time
> The harmony of their tongues hath into bondage
> Brought my too diligent ear; for several virtues
> Have I liked several women; never any
> With so full soul, but some defect in her
> Did quarrel with the noblest grace she owed,
> And put it to the foil: but you, O you,
> So perfect and so peerless, are created
> Of every creature's best.

1. See p. 244.

It is no accident that Ferdinand here refers to his past experience in the aristocratic world to which he has up to now belonged and to which he will eventually, duly transformed by his new experiences, return. In this other world, so remote and yet so definitely related to the emotion now moving towards expression, he has seen and admired 'full many a lady'; the feelings they roused in him belonged to the sphere of convention, combining literature and sentiment in the artificiality of their expression, but were at the same time premonitions, anticipations of the fuller emotion now offered him. The phrasing used by Ferdinand confirms the intermediate state in which he finds himself, directing the familiar and the literary almost imperceptibly to a new, more intensely personal conclusion which belongs in turn to the main symbolic conception. The 'harmony' in the 'tongues' of his former courtly mistresses, though still belonging to an effect relatively pale and conventional—the use of the well-worn concept of 'bondage' and the touch of criticism implied in 'my too diligent ear' are in this respect significant—foreshadows the deeper, more inclusive harmony on the threshold of which he now stands. The facile balance of 'several virtues', deliberately indefinite, and 'several women', maintains the same effect of detachment; but it gives way, in the latter part of the speech, to the deeper feeling of 'full soul' and 'noblest grace' which, balanced against the continued presence of 'some defect' which 'put it to the foil' and stands for the prolongation of the original conventional conception, indicates nevertheless the growth towards its full expression of a new experience.

This growth, indeed, belongs to the main symbolic structure of the play, which is at once founded upon courtly artifice and incommensurate with it, directed at the creation of a new sensation of life. To meet the new conception Ferdinand has been abstracted from his former surroundings, brought—like his fellows, each of whom has also his own past in the courtly world—to the island and there set face to face with a perfection that is, within its own incompleteness, its isolation from common reality, flawless: the perfection which, at the end of the speech, emerges into full expression:

> you, O you,
> So *perfect* and so *peerless*, are created
> Of *every creature's best.*

Ferdinand has here found, in the contemplation of Miranda, the perfection which court artifice and sentiment could only dimly foreshadow. All the qualities which he has hitherto experienced, partially and imperfectly, in the society with which he has been familiar, are now offered to him in the form of flawless perfection. It will only remain for him, by marrying the object of his contemplation, to bring her into contact with the world which she is now ready to enter, and so to be the instrument of Prospero's reconciling purpose.

If Ferdinand's apostrophe to Miranda begins by referring to experience elsewhere acquired but only now seen in its true light, her reply starts, not less significantly, by affirming her complete isolation:

> I do not know
> One of my sex; no woman's face remember,
> Save, from my glass, mine own; nor have I seen
> More that I may call men than you, good friend,
> And my dear father: how features are abroad,
> I am skilless of; but, by my modesty,
> The jewel in my dower, I would not wish
> Any companion in the world but you;
> Nor can imagination form a shape,
> Besides yourself, to like of.

Miranda, unlike Ferdinand, has been brought up in the most limited of worlds. Her only knowledge of women has been that afforded by her own glass, her only contact with men, before this new arrival, her relations with her father. In her case too, however, a process of transformation is at work, adapting the theme of romantic innocence to a deeper purpose. Her 'modesty' is a 'jewel', bound up with poetic intimations of value and ready to be offered as a 'dower' now that the consummation to which she has, unknown to herself, been dedicated from the first as a woman and Prospero's daughter is in sight. The concluding lines of the speech, responding to the evocation of perfection just put before her by Ferdinand, unite reality to imagination in a common gesture of dedication. In lines such as these, the exaltation of love first undertaken, against a realistic background and balanced by a detached estimate of character, in *Antony and Cleopatra*, is developed on lines already familiar in *The Winter's Tale*, reaching out, through the transformation of idyll and poetic convention, to its full symbolic consummation.

Moved by such love for one another, Ferdinand and Miranda are ready for Prospero's blessing. He gives it, still invisible, in lines pregnant with fertility and 'grace' which are most splendidly interwoven with those of the lovers:

FERDINAND: I,
    Beyond all limit of what else i' the world,
    Do love, prize, honour you.
MIRANDA: I am a fool
    To weep at what I'm glad of.
PROSPERO: Fair encounter
    Of two most rare affections! Heaven rain
    grace
    On that which breeds between them.
FERDINAND: Wherefore weep you?
MIRANDA: At mine unworthiness, that dare not offer
    What I desire to give; and much less take
    What I shall die to want. But this is trifling,
    And all the more it seeks to hide itself
    The bigger bulk it shows.

Once more the parallels with other Shakespearean utterances are numerous and significant. All the symbolic imagery of the last plays is here; the 'grace' which blesses union and expresses itself in fertility and a grief which is balanced with joy and therefore life-giving. Miranda's love opens to expression, at this moment foreseen by Prospero, like the child growing in the mother's womb. Her grief becomes something rich and infinitely precious, itself of redeeming quality; and her father, who has given Ferdinand 'a third' of his own life, lays by his gift the foundations of reconciliation in the eyes of Destiny, to be confirmed by his own words immediately after the decisive intervention of Ariel:

> here, afore heaven,
> I ratify this my rich gift. (IV. i.)

The rather perfunctory masque, commonplace in spite of its involved stressing of the images of fertility and love, is scarcely necessary after the brief scenes which it is intended to ratify. The best of it, and the most germane to the general purpose, is the song shared between them by the spirits representing Juno and Ceres, where the note of fruitfulness is most directly and least artificially expressed, and where the season of birth and that of autumnal fulfilment are bound together in a manner that reminds us of a similar union in *The Winter's Tale:*

> Spring come to you at the farthest
> In the very end of harvest.

As a whole, however, and in spite of lines which contribute to the central conception, it is hard to deny that this interlude, like its not altogether dissimilar predecessor in *Cymbeline*, belongs more to the structural unity of the play than to its intimate poetic sensibility. As such, we may pass over it to the other issues which await Prospero.

For, in spite of these notes of reconciliation and redeeming love, the presence of passion still has to make itself felt. As in the pastoral scene of *The Winter's Tale* the poetry of love is in a sense premature, needs to be confirmed by a wider range of experience, expanded into something more inclusive of the normal order of human feelings. Just as Perdita and

Florizel were torn apart, at the moment when their union seemed on the point of consummation, by the entry of the aged and angry Polixenes, so is the idyll of Ferdinand and Miranda always present in Prospero's mind side by side with his knowledge of the plot taking shape against his life. Prospero, indeed, never forgets the sombre background of these idyllic scenes. His preoccupation with it has been present from the first in a strange irritability which contrasts strongly at times with his prevailing serenity; and now even as he is bringing Ferdinand and Miranda finally together, it comes out just before the masque in a warning which strikes us at first as almost cryptically out of place. A wintry tone, compatible with Prospero's age if not with the pervading beneficence of his purpose, appears to take possession of his words in a mood closely related to the sense of weariness and disillusionment which the contemplation of human behaviour, on the island and off it, seems simultaneously to awaken in him:

> Look thou be true; do not give dalliance
> Too much the rein: the strongest oaths are straw
> To the fire i' the blood; be more abstemious ... (IV. i.)

The fact is that Prospero has good reason to remember the evil effects of passion. The forces of evil are still at work around him. He has brought them there himself for the final and decisive conflict. As we already know from Ariel's speech, he is called upon to judge as well as to reconcile; and as soon as the marriage 'ceremony' is over his other cares press back on his mind:

> I had forgot that foul conspiracy
> Of the beast Caliban and his confederates
> Against my life.

The thought, as Ferdinand observes, moves Prospero deeply and it is in the shadow of it that he makes his reflections on the insubstantiality of human affairs. The spirit in which these are spoken is manifest in the concluding lines which,

although relatively unfamiliar, are perhaps the key to the
type of feeling which produced the whole:

> Sir, I am vexed;
> Bear with my weakness, my old brain is troubled;
> Be not disturbed with my infirmity;
> If you be pleas'd, retire into my cell,
> And there repose; a turn or two I'll walk,
> To still my beating mind.

It is a mood very akin to pessimism, indeed, that the thought
of Caliban's plot arouses in Prospero. We feel him definitely
steeling himself to meet it, to overcome evil in accordance
with the moral conception of which he is the instrument.
The note of age implied in 'old brain' and 'infirmity', and
that of a certain impotence which, albeit momentarily, it
inspires in Prospero, is the equivalent in this play to the disillusioned resentment of Polixenes in the pastoral scene of
The Winter's Tale. Both are characteristic, within their
limits, of the last plays and to ignore them is to convey
something less than the total impression which they should
properly make.

There is, indeed, a deep sense of tension and impending
conflict in Prospero's greeting, which follows immediately,
to Ariel: 'We must prepare to meet with Caliban'. With
Caliban, be it noted, rather than with his fellow-conspirators.
They, when the time comes, will be easily led from their
purposes by the prospect of trumpery spoils. Caliban is
more formidable, because his evil is rooted in an animal
nature which no amount of civilized attention can change.
He is, in fact, an original inhabitant of the isle as Prospero
has known it; and his is the irreducible element of bestiality
in unredeemed human nature:

> A devil, a born devil, on whose nature
> Nurture can never stick; on whom my pains,
> Humanely taken, all, all lost, quite lost;
> And as with age his body uglier grows,
> So his mind cankers.

The lines are pregnant with the rotting, cankering effect of evil on man's being, driven home by the contrast between 'nature' and 'nurture', between inherent savagery and the civilizing sense implied in 'humanely'. All Prospero's efforts to regenerate Caliban have failed, and when he actually comes in, driven by Ariel with his fellow-conspirators, he alone shows himself obdurate in his purposes. While his companions are carried away, as Prospero has foreseen, by the hope of easy loot, he remains firm in his intention to murder his master: 'Let it alone, thou fool, it is but trash' (IV. i). Stephano and Trinculo have corrupted him indeed in so far as they have added to his original nature a ridiculous deification of the vices of civilization symbolized in the figure of the bottle-bearing god; but the evil was in him before their arrival, since he was—after all—the heir of Sycorax against whom Prospero had struggled to purify the island. The purpose of Caliban, as we have seen, is to achieve liberty, to destroy civilized restraints and live a life of anarchic, passion-directed freedom; the existence of this purpose is not affected, though the possibility of attaining it is, by his willingness to become, in the very hour of his apparent liberation from Prospero, the servant of Stephano:

> Do that good mischief which may make this island
> Thine own for ever, and I, thy Caliban,
> For aye thy foot-licker.

Yet this speech amounts to an admission that the liberty desired by Caliban is unattainable, that his freedom from Prospero's direction can only be bought at the price of slavery to something infinitely lower and more degrading; and, in fact, with the help of Ariel, they are all three— Caliban, Stephano, and Trinculo—easily defeated.

With their defeat the way is clear for a building-up of the final resolution. Ferdinand and Miranda can now be united on an island purged by Prospero of the power of evil; and their union will serve at last to bring their divided parents once more together. The last scene of the play is one of those conclusions, so common in Shakespeare, in which the various strands of the action are brought together and its characters marshalled for the final grouping. The type, of course, is common in the earlier comedies, and there are signs of a development from it—even faintly symbolic—in the *dénouement* of *Measure for Measure;* but it is only in the last plays, as we have had occasion to see, that this technique appears fully adapted to the symbolic themes of reconciliation and regeneration. The scene opens with an announcement by Prospero that the moment of final resolution has come:

> Now does my project gather to a head;
> My charms crack not; my spirits obey, and time
> Goes upright with his carriage   (v. i);

and Ariel confirms that this is 'the sixth hour', at which 'You said our work should cease'.

Having thus anticipated the coming resolution Ariel goes on to paint his master a picture of the state in which he has left Alonso and his companions, a state in which he stresses the deep penitence of those who are capable of regeneration; and Prospero responds to this picture of repentance in the manner typical of the last plays, that is by forgiveness:

> Though with their high wrongs I am struck to the quick,
> Yet with my nobler reason 'gainst my fury
> Do I take part; the rarer action is
> In virtue than in vengeance; they being penitent,
> The sole drift of my purpose doth extend
> Not a frown further.   (v. i.)

The wording of the speech is worth pausing over. The victory of compassion over retribution is now a victory of the 'nobler reason' over passionate fury. Nowhere is the part played by the Christian ethic in shaping this play more clearly stated. Reason and nobility are closely associated through all Shakespeare's tragic period. For Hamlet it is the use of reason that distinguishes man from the beast, makes him the 'paragon of animals'; and it is just because reason does not lead him to realize this ideal of nobility in action that he is plunged into tragedy. Now, in *The Tempest*, the nobility of reason is finally asserted in an act of compassion which transcends the exercise of reasonable justice itself. In Ariel's great speech, as we have already seen, the necessity of retribution is stated. Now, once it has been affirmed and the actual punishment meted out, it gives way to the higher, still more 'reasonable' (because 'nobler') virtue of compassion; and the bond between them, the thing which makes the transition possible, is simply the reasoned admission of guilt on the part of those whom Destiny has punished. To their reason, which has at last ennobled itself by acceptance, only a similar nobility in forgiveness can fitly respond. When it does so, in the words of Prospero, the pattern of the play is to all intents and purposes ready for completion. The illusion which he has been concerned to build up on the island, the state of dream-like suspension from self-awareness in which each offending or meritorious instinct has been released as though in sleep, is now ready to be broken, the sway of magic to give way to the return of conscious reality.

The moment of resolution is, indeed, now at hand. Alonso and the group of courtiers who accompany him are brought in, spell-bound, and Prospero's first action is to restore them to their full reason. The instrument of restoration, in accordance with the prevailing symbolism, is music which imposes harmony upon elements otherwise discordant. To its notes they wake, recover their being, or—more accurately—are transformed into a new life—

> The charm dissolves apace;
> And as the morning steals upon the night,
> Melting the darkness, so their rising senses
> Begin to chase the ignorant fumes that mantle
> Their clearer reason . . .

> Their understanding
> Begins to swell, and the approaching tide
> Will shortly fill the reasonable shore
> That now lies foul and muddy.

Once more the symbolic purpose is clear enough. The restoration to normality of Alonso and his followers is at the same time a triumph of the dawning reason over the night of passion-inspired sensuality. The 'rising senses' are purified of the 'ignorant fumes' that have hitherto clouded them, and become the true instruments of the 'clearer reason'. This does not mean, of course, that the senses are evil in themselves. No one who has read *Antony and Cleopatra*, written not so long before *The Tempest*, can imagine that Shakespeare meant such a thing. It is not the senses in themselves, but the disharmony with reason, control, 'degree' that produces tragedy; and Prospero's whole activity has been an effort to restore the balance, to see reason and the senses working in a harmonious, fruitful co-operation, fertile in its consequences and crowned by 'grace'. This is the moment of his triumph. The 'approaching tide' of life fills the 'reasonable shore' and heralds the arrival of a new, more gracious humanity.

Yet even in the moment of triumph Prospero remembers the claims of judgement. Not all the courtiers before him can be expected to move on the same moral plane. Gonzalo, expressly described in religious terms as 'holy' and 'honourable', is of course capable of entering into the new world of 'grace'; so is Alonso, purified by repentance of his former sinfulness. These two Prospero now embraces with an overflowing richness of affection that has, ever since Duncan, been associated in Shakespeare with the poetry of 'grace':

> I embrace thy body. . . .
> Let me embrace thine age, whose honour cannot
> Be measur'd or confin'd.

But this fullness of emotion, expressing itself in the passionate directness of 'I embrace *thy body*' and in the unlimited exaltation of its object, is an answer to penitence, to Alonso's definite desire to resign his dukedom to its proper owner. In Antonio and Sebastian there is no such repentance, and therefore no corresponding reconciliation. When Prospero rebukes them in an aside their only comment is 'The devil speaks in him'; to which he replies, even in the moment of forgiveness, with an intensity of denunciation that brings home to us the continued existence of evil at this point:

> For you, most wicked sir, whom to call brother
> Would even infect my mouth, I do forgive
> Thy rankest fault—all of them; and require
> My dukedom of thee, which perforce, I know,
> Thou must restore.

Justice, based on the moral condemnation which is felt so strongly behind 'infect' and 'rankest' and in the bitter afterthought 'all of them', needs to be satisfied as well as love; even in the culminating moment of happiness, the reality of sin is alive to the memory. Forgiveness and condemnation are fused into a single gesture, and Antonio and Sebastian are by their own choice excluded from the new world which their presence must in itself destroy.

The time has now come to complete the reconciliation. As we have said, the children are to be responsible for bringing the fathers together. Their love, indeed, has been an essential part of the process which we now know to have been willed by Destiny. Alonso is still suffering, for the loss, which he believes final, of his son: suffering so much that he calls his state 'irreparable' and past the cure of patience. But Prospero too has lost his daughter, in the sense that he has allowed, even inspired her to love the son of his former enemy; and in their common *loss* is the matter for reconciliation. The desire for it now comes most opportunely into Alonso's mind. He wishes that the two children were alive as 'king and queen' in Naples, and that he himself, not forgetful of his past errors, 'were muddied in that oozy bed' where his son lies. With this gesture

Prospero is satisfied. He discovers Ferdinand and Miranda at their game of chess and the stage is set for the final reconciliation in the freshly dawned light of grace. Miranda's words to Ferdinand—

> Yes, for a score of kingdoms you should wrangle,
> And I would call it fair play—

remind us, in the implied comparison between the value of love and that of earthly kingdoms, of the first appearance of Antony and Cleopatra in the earlier tragedy: very different characters but the same boundless emotion of transfiguring love.

The lines which follow are completely typical of Shakespeare's latest manner. Upon their poetic quality depends the success of the symbolic purpose. For, realistically considered, the whole action of these last scenes—Alonso's repentance, Prospero's 'loss' of his daughter to counterbalance the supposed loss of Ferdinand—is thin and inadequate. But the details of the plot at this stage of *The Tempest* have no more importance than that which attaches to them as the necessary thread of incident upon which is based the whole choreography of a great *ballet;* and indeed the whole of the last scene of the play, like the conclusion of *The Winter's Tale*, is really conceived as a kind of formal *ballet* in which words replace visual images as the main artistic medium. This was the dramatic conception towards which Shakespeare was moving in his last plays and which he achieves most fully, after the resolution of *The Winter's Tale*, in this concluding episode of *The Tempest*. It opens with a recognition on the part of Ferdinand of the essential part played throughout this story by the sea as the minister of Destiny:

> Though the seas threaten they are merciful,
> I have curs'd them without cause.

The tragedy and suffering which have been caused by human sinfulness have turned, in other words, into the instruments of reconciliation to a richer and fuller life. The entry into this life is symbolized, as usual, by the mutual act of blessing and forgiveness by which fathers and children are united in reconciliation. Once more the situation, which recalls that of Cordelia and the restored Lear or that of the final scenes of *The Winter's Tale*, has about it more than a touch of what we should now call *ballet* technique; to appreciate the effect fully we need to see the actors significantly grouped for the religious act of benediction. Ferdinand kneels for blessing and is joined to Miranda. In their words to one another the vision of a reconciled, redeemed humanity is at last given clear poetic expression:

> ALONSO: Now all the blessings
> Of a glad father compass thee about!
> MIRANDA: O, wonder!
> How many goodly creatures are there here!
> How beauteous mankind is! O, brave new
>   world,
> That has such people in't!

The vision of a new humanity, already glimpsed by Miranda in her innocent compassion when she first saw Ferdinand, enriched, by his responding love, and now deepened by the trials to which Prospero has put her, here reaches its full expression: and in the lines which follow immediately after Ferdinand recognizes both that his bride has been given him by 'immortal Providence' and that he has received from Prospero nothing less than 'a second life'. In this second life his fellows—those of them who have shown a proper disposition—naturally participate. As the children are finally joined the two fathers are also brought together, Alonso craving pardon and Prospero granting forgiveness, both with the blessing of the divine grace:

> ALONSO: O, how oddly will it sound that I
> Must ask my child forgiveness!

270

PROSPERO: There, sir, stop,
          Let us not burthen our remembrances with
          A heaviness that's gone.
GONZALO: I have inly wept,
          Or should have spoke ere this. Look down, you
              gods,
          And on this couple drop a blessed crown!
          For it is you that have chalked forth the way
          Which brought us hither.

In the light of earlier plays this is not difficult to interpret.
Alonso, like Lear, like Leontes, has come through penitence
to realize his errors and to ask his child forgiveness; and
Prospero replies that the time has come to cast off the
burthen of past memories and to look forward to a harmony
that long and often bitter experience has gained.   And,
apart from them both, the faithful Gonzalo is given for a
moment a dignity that he has not so far reached in the play,
a dignity that makes him at. this stage—rather even than
Prospero—the mouthpiece of Destiny.   In his words the
gods are invoked to 'crown' the new-born vision of humanity
with a symbol of royalty: the gods who have unwound the
whole plot and brought it at last, through the actions of
Prospero, to its harmonious conclusion.   The crown that
they bestow is, in effect, a sign of the 'second', the redeemed
and 'reasonable' life which has been given the protagonists
of the play through their experiences on the island.   As
Gonzalo puts it a few lines further down:

                    In one voyage
          Did Claribel her husband find at Tunis,
          And Ferdinand, her brother, found a wife
          Where he himself was lost; Prospero his dukedom
          In a poor isle; *and all of us ourselves,*
          When no man was his own.

In the light of these lines the whole action of the play—
the loss no less than the finding, the separations no less than

271

the re-unions—is clearly seen to be a closely woven texture of symbolic elements. Recognized as such, it grows vastly into a significance that rounds off our understanding of the whole conception. For it is at this point, if anywhere, that the pattern of *The Tempest*—and with it the whole design initiated in the historical plays and carried through the tragedies to the last symbolic comedies here under consideration—is substantially complete.